Gender Equity in Science and Engineering

Routledge Studies in Management, Organizations, and Society

This series presents innovative work grounded in new realities, addressing issues crucial to an understanding of the contemporary world. This is the world of organised societies, where boundaries between formal and informal, public and private, local and global organizations have been displaced or have vanished, along with other nineteenth century dichotomies and oppositions. Management, apart from becoming a specialized profession for a growing number of people, is an everyday activity for most members of modern societies.

Similarly, at the level of enquiry, culture and technology, and literature and economics, can no longer be conceived as isolated intellectual fields; conventional canons and established mainstreams are contested. Management, Organization and Society addresses these contemporary dynamics of transformation in a manner that transcends disciplinary boundaries, with books that will appeal to researchers, student and practitioners alike.

Gender Equity in Science and Engineering

Advancing Change in Higher Education

Diana Bilimoria and Xiangfen Liang

Routledge
Taylor & Francis Group
NEW YORK   LONDON

First published 2012
by Routledge
711 Third Avenue, New York, NY 10017

Simultaneously published in the UK
by Routledge
2 Park Square, Milton Park, Abingdon, Oxon OX14 4RN

*Routledge is an imprint of the Taylor & Francis Group,
an informa business*

The right of Diana Bilimoria and Xiangfen Liang to be identified as
authors of this work has been asserted by them in accordance with sections
77 and 78 of the Copyright, Designs and Patents Act 1988.

Typeset in Sabon by IBT Global.

Library of Congress Cataloging-in-Publication Data
Bilimoria, Diana, 1960–
    Gender equity in science and engineering : advancing change in higher
education / by Diana Bilimoria and Xiangfen Liang.
        p. cm. — (Routledge studies in management, organizations, and
society ; 15)
    Includes bibliographical references and index.
    1. Women in science.   2. Women in engineering.   3. Feminism
and higher education.   4. Gender identity in education.   I. Liang,
Xiangfen.   II. Title.
    Q130.B55 2011
    507.1—dc23
    2011024460

ISBN13: 978-0-415-88562-1 (hbk)
ISBN13: 978-0-203-14913-3 (ebk)

For
Kimberly, Guan, and Frances

Contents

Figures

Tables

Acknowledgments

This book is a product of a ten-year professional journey during which we have benefited greatly from numerous interactions with colleagues, mentors, scholars, supporters, and friends. Over these years we have been privileged to work with many outstanding colleagues through the Academic Careers in Engineering and Science (ACES) and ACES+ programs at Case Western Reserve University. Lynn Singer has provided us inspiring leadership, tireless championing, and enthusiastic research support throughout. Mary Barkley, Amanda Shaffer, Dorothy Miller, Beth McGee, Don Feke, Hunter Peckham, John Angus, Patricia Higgins, Cyrus Taylor, Nahida Gordon, Eleanor Stoller, and Jean Gubbins offered colleagueship, creativity, encouragement, and assistance that were invaluable to our research and institutional interventions. Provosts John Anderson and Bud Baeslack were personally supportive to us in this work.

Our special thanks to Simy Joy—this study would not have been possible without her earlier contributions as our co-author on the pilot study to this project. Much of the material in this book is revised and extended from Diana Bilimoria, Simy Joy, and Xiangfen Liang's "Breaking Barriers and Creating Inclusiveness: Lessons of Organizational Transformation to Advance Women Faculty in Academic Science and Engineering," published in *Human Resources Management* (2007) 47(3): 423–441.

We thank the National Science Foundation for support of this study in the form of a grant to conduct the research (*Institutional Transformation to Advance Gender Equity: Lessons from a National Program of Change in Higher Education*, HRD-0914839). Any opinions, findings, conclusions or recommendations expressed in this material are ours and do not necessarily reflect the views of the National Science Foundation. We acknowledge the encouragement we received from *ADVANCE* program officers over the years, particularly Alice Hogan, Jessie DeAro, Kelly Mack, and Laura Kramer, who have been tireless advocates of gender equity in academic science and engineering. We thank Erin Seney for her timely support during our data collection phase, and Daniel Foley for providing us with comparison data from the Survey of Doctorate Recipients.

Several faculty, research associates, and graduate and undergraduate students contributed to research, evaluation, and other ACES projects highlighted in this book, including Miggy Hopkins, Deb O'Neil, Greer Jordan, Diane Bergeron, Verena Murphy, Danielle Zandee, Susan Perry, Jeff Turell, Kathy Buse, Alison Baker, Lakisha Miller, and Hillary Conidi. Helen Williams, Miggy Hopkins, Deb O'Neil, Susan Freimark, Kathleen FitzSimmons, Dave Watterson, and Meg Seelbach have been generative academic coaches and agents of institutional transformation at Case Western Reserve University and beyond.

The PIs, Co-PIs, and project team members of our sister institutions from *ADVANCE* Cohorts 1 and 2 were enormously supportive throughout our study. We have greatly enjoyed and benefited from countless interactions with these individuals, as well as with the academic scholars and change agents who constitute the larger *ADVANCE* community. We particularly thank our co-authors and conference co-presenters over the years from this group, including Abby Stewart, Virginia Valian, Kim Buch, Ronda Callister, Mary Frank Fox, Lisa Frehill, and Annemarie Nicols-Grinenko. Our thanks to all the dedicated women and men of *ADVANCE* who continue to inspire and influence our work.

John Szilagyi and Laura Stearns of Routledge's Taylor and Francis group were most encouraging of the creation of this book, and extremely patient throughout our writing process.

Finally and most importantly, our love and gratitude goes to all our families and friends in the U.S., India, and China, for their wholehearted encouragement of our work. This book is the result of their unconditional love and support.

1 Gender Equity and Institutional Transformation in Academic Science and Engineering

Science and engineering play a significant role in everyday life and are critical engines of innovation and economic growth. Sectors such as biochemistry, telecommunications, energy, health science, health technology, environmental science, materials science, and information technology, among others, continually bring improvements to our daily lives as well as offer growth in business and employment opportunities. Cutting-edge science and engineering are systematically applied to discover new opportunities and solve problems, and shape the formation, design, and development of new products and innovative production processes. Much of the United States' economic growth in the last 50 years has been produced by scientific innovation (National Science Foundation 2004; U.S. Department of Labor 2007). An advanced science and technology enterprise offers distinctive societal advantages to compete and win in the fast-paced global business environment. The U.S. has the single largest value-added world share (35% in 2005) of any country in high-technology manufacturing industries, ranked first in three of five high-technology industries (scientific instruments, aerospace, and pharmaceuticals) and second on the other two (communications equipment and office machinery and computers), as well as leads in market-oriented, knowledge-intensive service industries, responsible for about 40% of world revenues on a value-added basis over the past decade (National Science Foundation 2008).

With the increasing importance of science and technology for U.S. economic competitiveness and growth, considerable attention is being paid to these industries as career choices for men and women. Individuals with science, technology, engineering, and mathematics (STEM) backgrounds are highly sought after by high-tech firms as these talents are conducive to an increased capacity for innovation. According to the Science and Engineering Indicators 2010 published by National Science Foundation (2010), the number of workers in STEM occupations grew from about 182,000 in 1950 to 5.5 million in 2007. This represents an average annual growth rate of 6.2%, nearly four times the 1.6% growth rate for the total U.S. workforce older than 18 years during this period (National Science Foundation 2010). From 2004 to 2007, the science and engineering workforce growth averaged 3.2% but was still twice as high as that of the total U.S. workforce. The sustained growth in the U.S. science and engineering workforce has largely been attributed to three factors: increased STEM degree production, immigration of scientists and engineers, and few retirements because of the relative youth of the STEM workforce compared to the total U.S. workforce (National Science Foundation 2010). Yet future national STEM growth is in danger; some have estimated that if current global trends continue, more than 90% of all scientists and engineers will live in Asia (U.S. Chamber of Commerce 2005).

The full participation of women and men in the national STEM workforce is necessary to solidify and grow the global leadership position of the United States in science and engineering in the coming years and decades, yielding long-term benefits to the U.S. economy. As noted in the influential report *Rising above the Gathering Storm: Energizing and Employing America for a Brighter Economic Future,* without a national policy-level response to enhance the science and technology enterprise, the U.S. will lose quality jobs to other nations, jeopardizing its standard of living and other economic benefits (National Academies 2007a). The 2007 report *The STEM Workforce Challenge: the Role of the Public Workforce System in a National Solution for a Competitive Science, Technology, Engineering, and Mathematics (STEM) Workforce* similarly identifies the STEM workforce challenge and calls for "coordinated efforts among public, private, and not-for-profit entities to promote innovation and to prepare an adequate supply of qualified workers for employment in STEM fields" (U.S. Department of Labor 2007, 1).

A central part of the STEM workforce challenge facing the country is the composition of the academic workforce, particularly the faculty in the nation's higher education institutions. Diversifying the academic STEM workforce to increase the participation of women faculty has become a national priority because "women faculty, specifically contribute to the culture and climate of the university and to the development of students' capacities and potential in science and engineering, with potential consequences for future generations of scientists and engineers" (Fox 2008, 73). Recent research has documented the strong positive influence of female professors on female students' performance in math and science courses, their likelihood of taking future math and science courses, and their likelihood of graduating with a math, science, or engineering degree, effects that are largest for female students whose SAT math scores are in the top 5% (Carrell, Page, & West 2010).

Other recent seminal reports identify this critical importance of women STEM faculty and call for urgency in diversifying the academic workforces in U.S. universities and colleges. These reports include the National Academies' (National Academy of Sciences, National Academy of Engineering, and Institute of Medicine) reports *Beyond Bias and Barriers* (2007b) and *Rising above the Gathering Storm* (2007a), the Department of Labor's report *The STEM Workforce Challenge* (2007), and *Gender Differences at Critical Transitions in the Careers of Science, Engineering, and Mathematics Faculty* (2010) by the Committee on Women in Science, Engineering, and Medicine and the Committee on National Statistics. These studies converge on the urgent necessity for U.S. universities and colleges to invest resources in developing and diversifying their faculty workforces as well as transforming their institutional cultures to support gender equity through the full participation and advancement of women faculty in academic science and engineering.

GENDER EQUITY, DIVERSITY, AND INCLUSION IN ACADEMIC SCIENCE AND ENGINEERING

In particular, academic science and engineering (S&E), inclusive of all STEM disciplines as well as the social and behavioral sciences, has emerged as a focal site in the study of gender equity, diversity, and inclusion in higher education not just because of its central role in U.S. long-term economic competitiveness and growth. Social equity issues in access to and rewards for professional participation in S&E also are of concern (Fox 2008). Drawing on Merton (1942/1973), Fox (2008, 74) points out that since a central ethos of science prescribes that scientists should be rewarded for contributions, scientific careers in particular should be "open to talent" and not precluded or disadvantaged by personal characteristics such as gender.

Gender refers to the socially constructed roles of and relations between women and men. Gender differences include characteristics and behaviors that are not only tied to women's and men's biology (sex) but which also originate from culture-specific perception and treatment of what women and men "should" be. Norms regarding gender-specific speech, movement, activities, thoughts, and feelings may vary by place, time, and culture. Gender determines what is expected, socially permitted, and valued about women and men in a particular context.

Gender equity is "a social order in which women and men share the same opportunities and the same constraints on full participation in both the economic and the domestic realm" (Bailyn 2006). It refers to "parity between males and females in the quality of life, academic, and work outcomes valued by our society" (Koch & Irby 2002, 3). The United Nations' Office of the Special Advisor on Gender Issues and Advancement of Women defines equality between women and men as referring to the "equal rights, responsibilities and opportunities of women and men and girls and boys. Equality does not mean that women and men will become the same but that women's and men's rights, responsibilities and opportunities will not depend on whether they are born male or female" (http://www.un.org/womenwatch/osagi/conceptsanddefinitions.htm).

Gender equity is a critical component of human rights and civil rights. Title IX of the U.S. Education Amendments of 1972 prohibits exclusion from participation, denial of benefits, or discrimination on the basis of sex in education programs or activities receiving federal financial assistance. Title VII of the Civil Rights Act of 1964 prohibits discrimination in education on the basis of sex, race, and national origin. The U.S. federal government has prioritized and invested in the field of gender equity in education since the passage of Title IX. The purpose of the field of gender equity is to "develop, implement, and evaluate the success of strategies, programs, and policies designed to promote equal outcomes" (Koch & Irby 2002, 3). Specifically, the Department of Education, the Department of Labor Women's Bureau, the National Science Foundation's program of research on gender in science and engineering, and the National Institutes for Health's Working Group on Women in Biomedical Careers are national agencies that support work in the field of gender equity in higher education while state and local government agencies help implement federal and state civil- and human-rights laws (Klein, Ortman, & Friedman 2002). While considerable progress has been made in the recent decades, gender inequities persist. "Many deep-seated and apparently intractable social inequities, such as gender related discrimination and stereotyping, have only begun to give way in the face of national mandates that they be changed and national mechanisms to support and enforce those changes" (Klein, Ortman, & Friedman 2002, 23).

While gender equity refers to making the playing field level for the workforce participation, performance, and success of all participants (women and men, majority and minority), two other concepts support their positive relations and contributions. *Diversity*, or the spectrum of human differences, refers to the distribution of the workforce composition, or commonly, the participation (representation) of women and underrepresented minority group members within the workforce. When the workforce participation of minority group members in influential positions within a system forms a critical mass (more than 35% minority members), token dynamics on account of skewed composition (less than 15% minority members), or tilted composition (between 15 and 35% minority members), diminish (cf. Kanter 1977; Yoder 1994). Typical token dynamics occurring in conditions of proportional underrepresentation include performance pressures for minority-group members due to extreme visibility and scrutiny, exaggeration of the differences between tokens and dominants, and magnified intergroup boundaries, and assimilation or role entrapment due to stereotyping or generalizing the characteristics of tokens (Kanter 1977).

Inclusion refers to the social processes that influence an individual's or subgroup's efficacy and sense of belonging and value in a work system. Inclusion represents a person's ability to participate in and contribute fully and effectively to an organization, and be recognized and valued as contributing to the organization's success. Organizational theorists have defined inclusion variously, including "the degree to which an employee is accepted and treated as insiders by others in a work system" (Pelled, Ledford, & Mohrman 1999, 1014), "the extent to which employees believe their organizations engage in efforts to involve all employees in the mission and operation of the organization with respect to their individual talents" (Avery, McKay, Wilson, & Volpone 2008, 6), and "the removal of obstacles to the full participation and contribution of employees in organizations" (Roberson 2006, 217). At the most micro level, inclusion refers to an individual's sense of being a part of the formal and informal processes of the organizational system (Mor Barak 2000). An inclusive work environment is one that facilitates "the full utilization of diverse human resources to maximize both the employees' and organization's potential" (Nishii, Rich, & Woods 2007, 1). Indicators of inclusion comprise the extent to which employees have job security, are involved in meaningful groups (in-groups), can access information and resources necessary for effective job performance, and can influence organizational decision-making processes (Mor Barak 2000). Zelechowski and Bilimoria (2003) measured inclusion in terms of the extent to which women were successfully integrated within their workplace groups to enable their effective performance, advancement, and professional development, such that they are not systematically excluded, isolated, marginalized, or derailed.

As described in Chapter 2, particular institution-level problems concerning the lack of gender equity, diversity, and inclusion in academic STEM include the persistent underrepresentation and lack of a critical mass of women faculty at all ranks and in leadership, a leaky pipeline (the systematic loss of women at each academic career transition point from secondary school through scientific leadership), unequal employment opportunities and job segregation (e.g., disproportionate numbers of women in the nontenure track or less valued academic career paths), inequitable treatment and valuing of women employees (e.g., stereotyping, excessive scrutiny, biased evaluations, and unequal access to resources and compensation), and differential effects of conflicts between work and life/family demands for women and men faculty.

INSTITUTIONAL TRANSFORMATION

As increasingly recognized, if academic science and engineering is to truly realize its potential for fostering innovation, competitiveness and growth in the U.S. workforce in the global economy of the 21st century, higher education institutions must pay significant attention to issues of gender equity, diversity, and inclusion, transforming themselves to become workplaces that catalyze innovative research and inspire diverse students by removing barriers to the equal employment, performance, and professional career development of women and men scientists and engineers. In this sense, *gender equity, diversity, and inclusion transformation* refers to the processes by which institutions become more reflexive about their gender practices and transform their social structures and relations to enable equal employment, opportunities, treatment, evaluation, and valuing of women and men so that all employees can fully participate, contribute, and develop in their careers and enable their organizations to achieve their goals of effectiveness.

The issues of gender underrepresentation and inequities in organizations have received much attention from researchers and practitioners alike, and their manifestations and causes have been well studied (Ely & Meyerson 2000a; Meyerson & Kolb 2000). Organizational solutions vary in the underlying assumptions and approach utilized to redress these problems. Supply-side or pipeline initiatives contend that if sufficient women are encouraged to enter the workforce and are well-equipped to perform, gender gaps in occupational participation, advancement, compensation, and retention may disappear (Etzkowitz, Kemelgor, & Uzzi 2000). Initiatives such as affirmative action and antidiscrimination policies focusing primarily on compliance with existing laws, mentoring, training programs, and special job assignments for women may facilitate career advancement. Demand-side initiatives, as for improved work-life balance, such as flextime and child care support, are other popular remedies. Though rarely, some organizations have attempted to build awareness about the tacit mental models driving behavior (e.g., Stuart 1999; McCracken 2000). The outcomes of these efforts are mixed—some initiatives have yielded positive results (e.g., Dreher 2003) while others have not proved sustainable. Women's representation and inclusion, particularly in leadership, remains a widespread problem for organizations.

The lackluster and unsustainable experience of many ad hoc gender equity-related organizational change efforts to date indicates that simplistic, ad hoc, or piecemeal solutions cannot eradicate systematic, historical, and widespread gender underrepresentation and inequities. For example, infusing more women at lower levels is rarely sufficient for increased representation at higher levels. Offering individual mentoring and skill-development opportunities to women can be less than effective for their advancement if other organizational factors are not simultaneously addressed. What is needed is a wider and deeper change in organizations—a transformation of the organizational structures, processes, work practices, and mental models that perpetuate inequity (McCracken 2000; Meyerson & Fletcher 2000). Enabling equity in organizations is the process of changing the character of the workplace that has traditionally been manned (literally and figuratively) by employees of a certain type to accommodate a different type (Thomas & Ely 1996), recasting the institutionalized routines and practices embedded in the social-structural fabric of the organization. Transformation is thus about changing an institution's structures and culture (Eckel & Kezar 2003). Transformation pertains to fundamentally changing how an organization conducts its day-to-day operations (who we are), as well as how the organization views itself in the future (who we want to be).

Some have argued that it is difficult to envision the end state of gender equity since we are ourselves limited by the gender relations in which we are currently embedded; rather, it is the process of continuously identifying, disrupting, and revising oppressively gendered social practices in organizations (Ely & Meyerson 2000b). Others see more definitively the characteristics of inclusive environments that enable organizational equity—for example, a critical mass of women at all ranks and in leadership, work structures and cultural norms that support positive relations between men and women, freedom from stereotyping about women's and men's roles and occupations, work conditions (e.g., job titles, work schedules, policies, physical environment) that are inclusive of both men and women, opportunities for reward and advancement based on performance and talent not gender, and work policies that help support work-life integration (McLean 2003). Whether viewed as an ongoing process or an end state, through gender equity transformation the organization becomes a workplace that is supportive and motivating for *all* its employees, not just women and minority groups (Meyerson & Fletcher 2000), and it is more able to achieve its instrumental goals of effectiveness (Ely & Meyerson 2000b).

To address systematic gender inequality in academic S&E, that is, the overt, subtle, or hidden disparities in workforce opportunities between women and men faculty, and encourage the gender equity transformation of higher education, in recent years leading U.S. federal funding agencies have begun to seed institutional transformation through organizational change programs and research. For example, since 2001 the National Science Foundation (NSF) has established *ADVANCE* awards to increase the participation and advancement of women in academic science and engineering careers. The National Institutes of Health (NIH) created a 2008 opportunity which sought to fund research on the causal factors and interventions that promote and support the careers of women in biomedical and behavioral science and engineering, as well as a 2010 Director's Pathfinder Award to Promote Diversity in the Scientific Workforce, which sought innovative, pathbreaking research to inform policy and practice about the leading causes of and remedies for gender inequity (National Institutes of Health 2008, 2010).

In the present research study, we systematically examine the initiatives and outcomes of the NSF *ADVANCE* program as described below.

NSF *ADVANCE* INSTITUTIONAL TRANSFORMATION

The National Science Foundation (NSF) initiated the *ADVANCE* program in 2001 to increase the participation and contributions of women in the STEM workforce and address structural impediments to women faculty's success in academic STEM (see http://nsf.gov/advance). NSF is an independent U.S. government agency created by the U.S. Congress in 1950 to promote science and engineering through research programs and education projects. As described by Fox (2008), NSF has had a long history of funding initiatives to address the underrepresentation of women, through Career Advancement Awards and Visiting Professorships for Women in the 1980s, to Professional Opportunities for Women in Research and Education (POWRE) Awards in the 1990s; these earlier initiatives focused on awards made to individual women, principally for support of their research programs in science and engineering (Rosser & Lane 2002).

In the 1990s, NSF began to focus on systemic initiatives, creating the Program for Women and Girls. The results of surveys of more than 400 awardees during the four years of the POWRE program drove an emerging awareness of the need to transition to a more institutional, systemic change program, to attempt to solve problems that cannot be addressed solely by supporting research projects of individual female scientists and engineers (Rosser & Lane 2002). As Alice Hogan, the first program officer for *ADVANCE*, described in an interview, "What NSF finally realized was that it wasn't that women in particular needed help accessing research funds, but that the system they were working in was littered with obstacles to their success" (LaVaque-Manty 2007, 22).

In 1999 an internal staff group was convened by Joseph Bordogna, then deputy director of the NSF, and led by Alice Hogan, then senior program manager, NSF's Division of International Programs, to address the issue of the significant underrepresentation of women in academic science and engineering. The committee concluded that to enable women's full participation, particularly at the senior level, it was imperative that the structures and cultures of their work settings be transformed (Sturm 2006; Fox 2008).

Stemming from this, the NSF *ADVANCE* program was established in 2001 by the NSF's Office of the Director as an NSF-wide program, with Alice Hogan as the founding program director, to catalyze the transformation of academic work environments in U.S. higher education institutions in ways that enhance the participation and advancement of women in science and engineering. Representatives from the participating NSF directorates and offices serve on the *ADVANCE* Implementation Committee (AIC), which works with the *ADVANCE* program office to manage and implement the program. Over the years since its founding, subsequent *ADVANCE* program officers (including some on rotation from their universities) included Fahmida Chowdhury (2006), Laura Kramer (2007–08), Jessie DeAro (2007–09), Kelly Mack (2008 to present) and Amy Rogers (2010 to present), assisted by Patricia Simms, integrative activities specialist, and others, including two American Association for the Advancement of Science (AAAS) Scholars, Anne Fischer and Erin Seney. Currently, NSF *ADVANCE* has three program components:[1] Institutional Transformation (IT), IT-Catalyst, and Partnerships for Adaptation, Implementation, and Dissemination (PAID).

The IT component has been in all program solicitations since 2001, and consists of five-year projects, funded in the range of $2 million to $5 million in total. These are comprehensive, institution-wide projects to transform the institutional practices, policies, climate, and culture of the university or college. *ADVANCE* IT projects are large-scale organizational development interventions composed of a diverse range of transformational initiatives, harnessing the synergies of partnering across multiple units within an institution. As illustrated in Figure 1.1, between 2001 and 2008, four cohorts of *ADVANCE* IT grants were awarded to 37 higher-education institutions (hereafter *ADVANCE* universities or institutions) across the country.

IT-Catalyst (previously IT-Start) awards were piloted in a 2007 solicitation as two-year projects, in the $100,000–200,000 range. Generally these are awarded for planning and assessment activities to prepare for transformational activities. Examples of project activities include climate surveys to establish baseline data, planning meetings with stakeholders, data collection and analysis, and research on potential strategies to eradicate gender bias. The third program component, PAID, consists of one- to five-year projects within or across institutions, with funding depending on the scope of the project. Some projects adapt, implement, and/or diffuse exemplary *ADVANCE* IT strategies to increase the participation of women in STEM academics, while others are social-science research proposals related to gender in STEM faculty and academic leadership positions. Other examples of projects include training and leadership development programs aimed at accomplishing *ADVANCE* goals.

During the period 2001–2009, 111 different institutions of higher education have been funded through the NSF *ADVANCE* program. Of these,

Source: NSF *ADVANCE*.

Figure 1.1 NSF *ADVANCE* institutional transformation (IT) grantees 2001–2008.

84 are public institutions and 27 are private. Several are minority-serving institutions, including seven Hispanic-serving institutions, six historically black colleges and universities (HBCUs), including one women's college, one Alaskan Native–serving institution, and one institution primarily serving persons with disabilities. Three institutions are women's colleges (including one HBCU). Nine professional and nonprofit STEM-related organizations have also been funded. The leaders of these *ADVANCE* projects have formed a unique and active community for the sharing of best practices, problem solving, and learning about gender equity and institutional transformation in higher education.

In sum, over the last decade NSF's *ADVANCE* program has become an increasingly widespread and influential national resource for systemic gender equity-related transformation of academic science and engineering across U.S. universities and colleges. By focusing on the organizational level rather than the individual level of change, NSF *ADVANCE* encourages and disseminates comprehensive, innovative, and systemic initiatives to stimulate gender equity, diversity, and inclusion in academic STEM.

PURPOSES OF THE STUDY

Recently, researchers have begun to explicate the various approaches that academic institutions have implemented through the NSF *ADVANCE* program to improve gender equity, diversity, and inclusion in academic STEM (e.g., Stewart, Malley, & LaVaque-Manty 2007; Bilimoria, Joy, & Liang 2008; Fox 2008, 2010; Pribbenow et al. 2010). Descriptive and anecdotal evidence suggest that some initiatives have yielded positive results while others have not proved sustainable. Missing is a systematic review and empirical analysis of the gender equity, diversity and inclusion initiatives and outcomes of the complex institutional transformation efforts underway. Yet to be answered is whether NSF *ADVANCE* IT projects have yielded the kinds of gender equity, diversity, and inclusion improvements originally envisioned. Most importantly, what still needs to be developed are generalizable conclusions about effective gender equity transformation, across institutions and within disciplines, that may inform gender equity-related institutional transformation elsewhere.

In the study reported in this book, we address these shortfalls by empirically examining the gender equity, diversity and inclusion initiatives, institutionalization actions, and outcomes of the first two cohorts (19 university and college awardees) of the NSF *ADVANCE* IT program. We chose this sample because at the time of undertaking this study, only the first two cohorts (19 *ADVANCE IT* recipients) had completed or were close to completing their projects. Awards in the range of $2,998,953 to $3,950,000 over a five-year period were made to these institutions.

Our study goals are to assess the program effectiveness of NSF *ADVANCE* IT and develop a generalized framework for how institutions of higher education (and other organizations) can enable greater gender equity, diversity, and inclusion.

The specific research questions of the study are:
1. What innovative and "best practice" initiatives have been employed to enhance gender equity, diversity and inclusion in *ADVANCE* IT projects at the 19 higher-education institutions studied?
2. How have gender equity changes been made permanent (i.e., institutionalized by embedding within the structures and cultures) at these institutions?
3. Has *ADVANCE* IT improved the workforce participation of women faculty at all ranks in academic STEM, particularly in senior positions and in leadership at these institutions?
4. Have equity and inclusion of women faculty in academic STEM improved at these institutions?
5. Has the workforce participation of women faculty at all ranks improved in specific science and engineering disciplines (engineering, natural sciences, and social and behavioral sciences) at these institutions?
6. What general insights about gender equity and institutional transformation emerge from the various projects at *ADVANCE* institutions? What guidance can be offered to leaders of other organizations interested in improving gender equity, diversity, and inclusion?

To answer these questions, we report on the results of a study of recent organizational change projects undertaken at 19 first- and second-round university recipients of NSF's *ADVANCE* IT program. Specifically, we analyze the results of change projects across these 19 universities and within specific disciplines (engineering, natural sciences, and social and behavioral sciences). Extending an earlier article (Bilimoria, Joy, & Liang 2008), this book offers a framework for institutional transformation in higher education, serving as a comprehensive, stand-alone description of successful approaches to increase the participation and contributions of women in academic STEM. While we provide specific insights and recommendations for university administrators and higher education policy, leaders in business and other nonprofit organizations engaged in promoting organizational change related to equity, diversity, and inclusion likely will benefit also from the experiences of and insights emerging from NSF *ADVANCE* IT efforts.

Outline of Chapters

The study is reported in the book's chapters as follows.

Chapter 1. Gender Equity and Institutional Transformation in Academic Science and Engineering.

Drawing on arguments based on the U.S.'s future global competitiveness and technological innovativeness, we develop the rationale for improvements in gender equity, diversity, and inclusion in academic science, technology, engineering, and mathematics (STEM) at the nation's colleges and universities. We introduce the National Science Foundation's *ADVANCE* Institutional Transformation (IT) program and describe the purpose and research questions of our study of 19 *ADVANCE* IT Cohort 1 and Cohort 2 institutions. In particular we seek to assess the gender diversity (workforce participation), equity, and inclusion outcomes engendered and develop a framework for gender equity transformation that can guide similar interventions in higher education and beyond.

Chapter 2. State of Knowledge about the Workforce Participation, Equity, and Inclusion of Women in Academic Science and Engineering.

In this chapter, we highlight recent statistics and literature about the workforce participation, resource equity, and inclusion of women in science and engineering. We draw on the metaphor of the leaky pipeline to describe institutional level (cultural and structural) impediments to women's participation and advancement in academic S&E careers, and provide evidence of problems, barriers, and resource inequities faced by women at each key transition point in the academic career pipeline. Building on prevailing images of science, the ideal scientist, and the scientific workplace as exclusionary to women, we discuss extant quantitative and qualitative research describing the oftentimes negative workplace experiences reported by women science and engineering faculty. Finally, we review the literature on the institutional transformation actions and processes recommended by organizational change theorists as well as gender equity experts to repair the leaky pipeline and stem the steady attrition of women scientists and engineers from the academic workplace.

Chapter 3. Study Sample and Methods.

In this chapter we provide a description of the study's methods, including detailed descriptions of the sample of 19 universities, definitions of the science and engineering disciplines included in the study, data collection methods, and data analysis procedures.

Chapter 4. Factors Facilitating Institutional Transformation.

In this chapter, we analyze the internal, external, and assessment factors that facilitated *ADVANCE* institutional change. *Internal facilitators* included senior administrative support and involvement, a transformation champion, collaborative leadership, widespread and synergistic participation, and visibility of actions and outcomes. *External facilitators* included a network of change agents in peer organizations for the sharing of learnings and best practices, and support and legitimacy from an external institutional authority. *Assessment, evaluation, and research in support of transformation* included tracking key indicators of diversity, equity, and inclusion, undertaking workplace climate assessments, conducting other research and evaluation in support of change, and improving institutional data-collection and analysis systems. We also discuss two *inhibitors* of institutional transformation at the *ADVANCE* institutions—faculty resistance and environmental/resource uncertainties and constraints—and describe actions taken by *ADVANCE* universities to overcome these challenges.

Chapter 5. Institutional Transformational Initiatives.

In this chapter, we summarize the institutional transformation initiatives undertaken at the 19 universities to remedy gender inequities and enhance inclusiveness in academic science and engineering. We develop a two-pronged framework of transformational initiatives employed by *ADVANCE* institutions. First, we describe transformational initiatives to enhance the individual career trajectories of women in the academic STEM pipeline, including initiatives to increase the inflow of women into the pipeline, initiatives to better equip women to successfully progress in the pipeline, and initiatives to improve institutional structures and processes related to key career transition points in the academic pipeline. Second, we describe transformational initiatives to enhance micro (department-level) and macro (university level) gender equity climate.

Chapter 6. Institutionalization of Transformation.

In this chapter, we discuss the meaning of institutionalization of transformation and describe how it occurred at the 19 universities studied. We describe how the institutionalization of initiatives to improve gender equity, diversity and inclusion occurred in four ways: generation of new permanent positions, offices and structures, implementation of new or modified policies, creation of new and improved practices and processes, and development of new supports for effective programs.

Chapter 7. Gender Diversity Outcomes: Changes in the Academic Workforce Participation of Women Faculty in STEM.

In this chapter, we examine the gender equity outcomes brought about by the systematic efforts to transform at the 19 universities. To accomplish this, we examine the composition of tenure-track women faculty at all ranks in STEM, including women in endowed chair and administrative leadership positions, over a five-year period. We specifically examine changes in STEM faculty composition by gender and rank over *ADVANCE* award durations, the number of institutions (out of 19) reporting percentage changes in STEM women faculty, and the average annual proportion of women faculty in STEM at *ADVANCE* universities in comparison with national reference groups. From the findings presented in this chapter, we conclude that overall, the *ADVANCE* universities have significantly increased the number of women faculty in STEM at all ranks over the duration of their institutional transformation projects while lesser or no growth occurred in their numbers of men STEM faculty during the same periods. *ADVANCE* universities were particularly successful in increasing the representation of women assistant and full professors in STEM areas. Comparisons with all other research universities from a national database suggest that *ADVANCE* universities generally led the pace in increasing the workforce participation of women STEM faculty over the same time periods. Despite these advances, the data indicate the continued underrepresentation of women faculty particularly as the associate professor and professor ranks in the academic STEM workforce in the nation's research universities.

Chapter 8. Equity and Inclusion Outcomes for Women Faculty in Science and Engineering.

In this chapter, we examine the gender equity and inclusion outcomes brought about through *ADVANCE* institutional transformation interventions in three areas: (a) resource equity assessment and improvement, (b) the inclusion of women in faculty leadership and administrative positions, and (c) faculty climate assessment and improvement. The results indicate that *ADVANCE* institutional transformation efforts have engendered significant equity and inclusion improvements at the universities studied. The most prominent improvements were observed in the areas of (a) increased systematic attention to salary distributions and resource equity between men and women faculty, (b) increases in the inclusion of women in senior leadership positions, and (c) improvements in specific facets of the academic workplace culture and climate such as increased campus-wide awareness of gender issues, improved work-life integration, providing increased voice to women faculty, and improved recognition of and attention to the factors leading to faculty success and retention. However, certain challenges remain on these campuses regarding gender equity and inclusion outcomes, particularly the challenge of workplace climates and university reward systems that are still perceived overall to be highly gendered.

Chapter 9. Gender Diversity (Workforce Participation) Outcomes by Discipline.

In this chapter we examine the gender diversity (academic workforce participation) outcomes of *ADVANCE* institutional transformation within three specific disciplines—engineering, natural sciences, and social and behavioral sciences at the 19 universities. The findings of our analyses indicate that targeted interventions through *ADVANCE* to increase the academic workforce participation of women faculty in all three S&E disciplines have been generally successful. Overall, however, national sample comparisons confirm the continued severe underrepresentation of women faculty in engineering and the ongoing low workforce participation of women faculty in natural sciences.

Chapter 10. Conclusions.

In this chapter we recap the goals of the study and summarize the main findings. We develop a generalizable framework of institutional transformation to enhance gender equity, diversity, and inclusion. This model can be employed by higher education institutions as well as corporate and non-profit organizations seeking gender equity, diversity, and inclusion transformation. Drawing on these findings, we develop the main conclusions that emerged from our study. We develop the implications of these conclusions and suggest recommendations relevant for higher education institutions as well as other organizations. Study limitations are addressed as well as directions for further research on institutional transformation to increase the workforce participation, equity, and inclusion of women faculty in academic S&E.

2 State of Knowledge about the Workforce Participation, Equity, and Inclusion of Women in Academic Science and Engineering

For purposes of this review we include science, technology, engineering, and mathematics (STEM) fields as well as the social and behavioral sciences (SBS), under the overall rubric of science and engineering (S&E). As described in Chapter 1, the inclusion of women in S&E is directly connected to the future composition of the nation's S&E workforce and to the continued development of a globally competitive marketplace for talent.

THE PARTICIPATION OF WOMEN IN THE SCIENCE AND ENGINEERING WORKFORCE

In the past 20 years, the proportion of women and minorities in S&E occupations has increased considerably. As indicated in Figure 2.1, college-educated women constituted 27% of S&E occupation holders in 2007, up from 22% in 1990 (Science and Engineering Indicators 2010, Figure 3.27, pp. 3–32). The proportion of women with doctoral degrees in S&E occupations was 34% in 2007, up from 23% in 1990. Among workers whose highest degree is S&E bachelor's, the share of women has risen to above 60% in social sciences and life sciences in the recent cohort 2002–2005 (National Science Foundation 2010, Figure 3.29). Similarly, among workers whose highest degree is S&E doctorate, women also remained a higher percentage in the recent cohort (2002–2005), especially in social sciences (about 60%) and life sciences (about 45%) (National Science Foundation 2010, Figure 3.30).

In the STEM professional workforce, women were 19% of all managers and 15% of top-level managers in business or industry compared with 34% of all scientists and engineers in business or industry in 2006 (National Science Foundation 2009). They constituted 8% of engineering managers and 11% of natural sciences managers. Only in medical and health services were women more than half of managers (National Science Foundation 2009).

The workforce participation of women in the STEM professions is considerably larger at lower rungs in the corporate hierarchy–41% of qualified scientists, engineers, and technologists are women–yet, over time, 52% of these women quit their jobs, not in a steady trickle, but during their mid to late thirties (Hewlett, Luce, Servon, et al. 2008). These authors provide

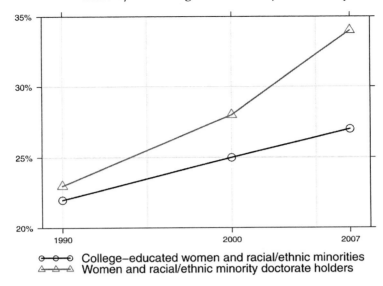

Figure 2.1 Women and racial/ethnic minorities with college or doctorate degrees in science and engineering occupations: 1990, 2000, 2007.
Source: Adapted from Figures 3–27 and 3–28, Science and Engineering Indicators 2010 (p.33), National Science Foundation.

a fivefold explanation of this massive brain drain: hostile macho cultures, isolation from being the lone woman on a team or site, systems of reward that emphasize risk-taking, extreme work pressures, and lack of clarity about career paths (Hewlett, Luce, Servon et al. 2008).

THE PARTICIPATION OF WOMEN STUDENTS IN S&E FIELDS

Women also made considerable progress in obtaining S&E degrees over the years. Figure 2.2 presents the representation of women by earned degree from 1993 to 2007. In 2007, 485,772 students earned bachelor's degrees in the United States, and half of them (244,075) were women, up from 45% (165,720 out of 366,035) in 1993. Since 2000, half of the S&E bachelor degree's recipients have been women. At the graduate-school level, women students constituted 46% (54,925 out of 120, 278) of S&E master degree's recipients in 2007, up from 36% (30,971 out of 86,425) in 1993. The percentage of female students who earned S&E doctoral degrees also increased, up from 32% in 1993 to 47% in 2007.

According to Science and Engineering Indicators 2010 (National Science Foundation 2010), women earned 58% of all bachelor's degrees since 2002 and about half of all S&E bachelor's degrees since 2000, but major variations persist among fields. In 2007, men earned a majority of bachelor's degrees awarded in engineering, computer sciences, and physics (81%, 81%, and

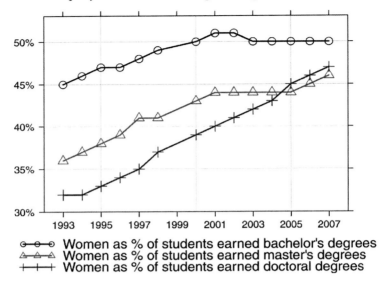

Figure 2.2 Women as a percentage of students by earned degree in S&E: 1993–2007.
Source: Data drawn from Appendix Tables 2–12, 2–26, 2–28, Science and Engineering Indicators 2010, National Science Foundation (www.nsf.gov.statistics/seind10).

79%, respectively) while women earned half or more of bachelor's degrees in psychology (77%), biological sciences (60%), social sciences (54%), agricultural sciences (50%), and chemistry (50%). Fields with marked increases in the proportion of bachelor's degrees awarded to women from 1993 to 2007 are earth, atmospheric, and ocean sciences (from 30% to 41%); agricultural sciences (from 37% to 50%); and chemistry (from 41% to 50%). However, women's share of bachelor's degrees in computer sciences, mathematics, and engineering has declined in recent years.

Women's participation in graduate S&E fields has also increased. Women made up 42% of S&E graduate students in 1993 and 50% in 2006, although large variations among fields persist. In 2006, women constituted the majority of graduate students in psychology (76%), medical/other life sciences (78%), biological sciences (56%), and social sciences (54%). They constituted close to half of graduate students in earth, atmospheric, and ocean sciences (47%) and agricultural sciences (48%) and more than one-third of graduate students in mathematics (37%), chemistry (40%), and astronomy (34%). Their percentages in computer sciences (25%), engineering (23%), and physics (20%) were low in 2006, although higher than in 1993 (23%, 15%, and 14%, respectively) (National Science Foundation 2010).

In 2009 women's share of engineering degrees hovered around 20% at all degree levels—17.8% of bachelor's degrees, 23% of master's degrees, and 21.2% of doctoral degrees. The percentage of women awarded doctoral degrees in engineering increased from 15.9% in 2000 to 21.2% in

2009 (Gibbons 2009). However, there is large variance by field: women's percentage of doctoral degrees varied from 12.6% in nuclear engineering to 37.7% in biomedical engineering (Gibbons 2009).

In brief, the number of female students and PhD recipients in S&E fields has been increasing in recent years. However, as the numbers presented in the next section show, these increases do not reflect corresponding increases in the number of female faculty in STEM areas, particularly at higher ranks, prompting many to refer to this phenomenon as a 'leaky pipeline' of faculty in these fields.

THE PARTICIPATION OF WOMEN FACULTY IN ACADEMIC S&E FIELDS

The job market of academic S&E disciplines has changed substantially in the past few decades. Full-time faculty positions have been declining, and postdoctoral and other full-time nonfaculty positions (e.g., research associates, adjunct appointments, and lecturers) have been increasing since the early 1970s (National Science Foundation 2010). The full-time faculty share of all academic employment was 72% in 2006, down from 88% in the early 1970s; the full-time nonfaculty share rose from 6% in 1973 to 13% in 2006; and postdocorates rose from 4% in 1973 to 9% of all academically employed S&E doctorate holders in 2006 (Science and Engineering Indicators 2010, Table 5.6, pp. 5–20). Along with these movements, women have gained an increasing share of the academic workforce composition. In 2006, 33% of all S&E doctorate holders employed in academia were women, up from 9% in 1973 (Science and Engineering Indicators 2010, Table 5.9, pp. 5–22). Women doctorate holders constituted more than half of part-time positions in academic S&E during 1993 and 2006.

In academic S&E fields, women hold a larger share of junior faculty positions than senior positions. In 2006, women constituted 25% of full-time senior faculty (full and associate professors) and 42% of full-time junior faculty (assistant professors and lecturers). Despite these gains, women are significantly more likely to hold nontenure-track positions (30% of full-time women faculty compared to 18% of men), are appointed to tenure track positions in most fields in far lower proportions than their representation in the candidate pool of doctoral degrees granted in the last decade, and are less likely to be tenured faculty than men, especially in doctoral institutions where "full-time women faculty are only half as likely as men to have tenure" (West & Curtis 2006, 10). Importantly, the percentage of women with S&E doctorates (including social and behavioral sciences) who are full-time full professors increased from 14% in 1999 to 20.6% in 2008; however, the percentage of underrepresented minority S&E doctorate holders in full professor positions remained relatively flat, from 4.5% in 1999 to 5.7% in 2008 (National Science Foundation 2011).

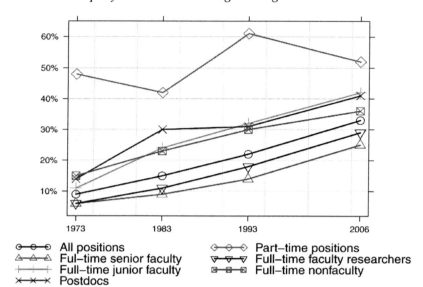

Figure 2.3 Women as a percentage of S&E doctorate holders by position in academic employment: selected years, 1973–2006.

Source: Drawn from Tables 5–9, p. 5–22, Science and Engineering Indicators 2010, National Science Foundation.

Notes: Academic employment limited to U.S. doctorate holders employed at 2- or 4-year collegs or universities. Senior faculty includes professors and associate professors. Junior faculty includes assistant professors and instructors. Full-time non-faculty includes positions such as research associates, adjunct positions, lecturers, and administrative positions. Part-time employment excludes those employed part-time because they are students or retired.

Figure 2.3 shows the relative status of women doctorate holders by academic positions held. Overall, women doctorate holders have made encouraging progress in occupying academic positions but they are under-represented at senior faculty positions, and moderately represented at the junior faculty positions.

Analyses of the workforce participation of women faculty reveal under-representation in several STEM fields. Leboy (2008) noted that since close to half of the top ten National Institutes of Health–funded academic health centers in 2006 had no women among their junior tenure-track faculty in their biochemistry and cell biology departments, a young woman might get the impression that her shot at a faculty position in these schools would be difficult, if not out of reach. In schools of engineering, women constituted 12.7% of the tenured or tenure-track faculty in 2009 (up from 10.4% in 2004)—21.6% of assistant professors (17.9% in 2004), 14.5% of associate professors (12.4% in 2004), and 7.7% of full professors (5.8% in 2004) (Gibbons 2009). By field, the percentage of women tenured or tenure-track faculty in 2009 varied from 6% in mining engineering to 22.1% in environmental engineering (Gibbons 2009).

Academic chemistry exhibits very similar patterns of the underrepresentation of women, even though relatively more women complete doctoral degrees in chemistry. In 2003–2004, women held only 12% of all tenure-track faculty positions and only 21% of assistant professor positions at the top 50 chemistry departments (Nolan, Buckner, Kuck, & Marzabadi 2004). The American Chemical Society reported that the percentages of full-time, female, doctorate faculty members at PhD-granting universities, master's granting institutions, baccalaureate institutions, and two-year colleges were 13%, 20%, 26%, and 32%, respectively (Nolan et al. 2004).

The estimated total number of full-time faculty in mathematical sciences for 2004–2005 was 20,224, of which 5,302 (26%) were females (Kirkman, Maxwell, & Rose 2005). The number of females as a percentage of full-time faculty varied considerably among the groups in 2004, from 12% for doctoral-granting departments in private institutions to 32% for master's-granting departments. In fall 2004, the percentage of women in mathematical sciences was generally higher in statistics (26%) than in the doctoral mathematics groups (18%). Similarly, the percentage of tenured faculty who are women was highest in departments granting either a master's or a baccalaureate degree only (21%), and lowest in doctoral-granting departments (9%). Women in mathematical sciences accounted for 52% of non-doctoral full-time faculty, and 4% of the part-time faculty in 2004. The percentage of tenured/tenure-track women faculty in mathematical sciences over the period 1998–2004 remained relatively stable (Kirkman et al. 2005).

Among S&E doctorate holders with academic faculty positions in four-year colleges and universities, females are less likely than males to be found in the full professor positions and more likely to be assistant professors (National Science Foundation 2011). This is consistent with findings from Nelson (2007), who examined the percentage of male and female tenured and tenure-track faculty in several disciplines, including S&E, at the top 50 U.S. educational institutions, based on research expenditures: few female full professors in S&E with the percentage of women among full professors ranging from 3% to 15% in different fields. Nelson (2007) also noted that in all but computer science, the rank of assistant professor has the highest percentage of female faculty. In converse, the rank which has highest percentage of male faculty is typically that of full professor, and that is the rank held by the majority of male faculty as well. Fewer differences in rank exist between male and female faculty in early-career stages in S&E, but greater differences tend to appear between 15 and 20 years after receipt of the doctorate.

Research also indicates that women are underrepresented in senior academic ranks and faculty leadership positions such as presidents, chancellors, provosts, deans, and chairs (Hollenshead 2003). This may be related to the difficulties women faculty in STEM face in academic career advancement (e.g., due to gender stereotyping and lack of mentoring) and the fact that they may not obtain the same levels of professional recognition for their scholarly work as do their male colleagues. In a comprehensive study of almost 60,000 faculty members at 403 academic institutions, Astin and Cress (2003) reported that male faculty attained tenure in a shorter amount of time than female faculty in all fields, with the exception of engineering. Other research has shown that women are less likely than men to receive tenure or promotion in STEM fields (Rosser & Daniels 2004). It has also been pointed out that the gender gap in compensation may be due in part to gender differences in rank, field (Astin and Cress 2003), and promotions (National Science Foundation 2003). As Astin and Cress (2003, 58) note, "At research universities, 25% of men are in the more highly paid fields of physical science, mathematics/statistics, and engineering combined, compared to 6% of women. Likewise, more than twice as many women (33%) as men (16%) are in the less financially lucrative fields of education, health science and humanities combined."

EDUCATIONAL ATTAINMENT AND WORKFORCE PARTICIPATION OF MINORITIES IN ACADEMIC S&E

Underrepresented minorities (blacks, Hispanics, and American Indians/ Alaska Natives as a group) and Asians/Pacific Islanders earned 17.4% and 8.7% of S&E bachelor's degrees in 2008, up from 15.9% and 8.2% in 2000 (National Science Foundation 2011). Underrepresented minorities (URMs) earned 7.2% of S&E doctorates to U.S. citizens and permanent residents in 2008, up from 6% in 2000, while Asians/Pacific Islanders earned 5.8% of S&E doctorates in 2009, down from 6.2% in 2000. URM and Asian shares of S&E bachelor's and doctoral degrees have risen slightly or flattened over the last decade; more importantly, they remain a small proportion of the total (National Science Foundation 2011). Underrepresented minorities constituted 10% of all scientists and engineers in business or industry in 2006, 7% of top-level managers, and 6%–13% of managers in most S&E fields (National Science Foundation 2009).

The data regarding URM faculty in S&E are also disturbingly low. The 2010 report *A National Analysis of Minorities in Science and Engineering Faculties at Research Universities*, a comprehensive demographic analysis of tenured and tenure track faculty in the top 100 departments of science and engineering disciplines, shows that minorities are significantly underrepresented in the academic S&E pipeline (Nelson & Brammer 2010). The report concludes, "Our data reveal that URMs among our science and engineering faculty are shockingly underrepresented despite increased general growth in their representation among B.S. and Ph.D. recipients. As expected, compared to their share of the U.S. population, URMs are underrepresented at almost every point in the academic pipeline. In most disciplines, there is a drop in representation at each point measured, with a gradual decrease up to the rank of 'full' professor, where the lowest representation is found; this reflects an increase in recent hiring in those disciplines. However, in some disciplines, the representation of Blacks, Hispanics, or Native Americans, among assistant professors (the most recently hired rank) is lowest and occasionally zero" (Nelson & Brammer 2010, 18). These data provide evidence that the academic pipeline is leaky for racial/ethnic minority faculty as well.

The case of Asian Americans in academic S&E careers is a particular problem of underrepresentation (Chen & Farr 2007). While Asian Americans are a population minority (about 5%) in the United States, they are overrepresented among students and professionals in S&E, holding more than 15% of all S&E doctoral degrees (National Science Foundation 2003). As faculty at many research universities, Asian Americans are not considered to be underrepresented; rather, they constitute minorities who are not underrepresented. The *glass ceiling* is a concept reflecting the workplace barriers to workforce participation and advancement facing specific minority groups. Chen and Farr (2007) delineate four criteria for a glass ceiling: (a) the inequality represents a demographic difference (e.g., gender or race/ethnicity) that is not explained by other job-relevant characteristics of an employee (e.g., education, training, discipline, location), (b) the inequality is greater at higher levels, (c) the inequality is one of opportunity and not merely an inequality in proportions of people at high levels, and (d) the inequality increases over the trajectory of a career. These authors analyzed data over the period 1993–1999 and found the existence of a glass-ceiling effect for Asian Americans (both men and women) at all stages of their S&E careers, and confirmed the effect for all women (regardless of race) in S&E (Chen & Farr 2007). Xie and Shauman (2003) found that women immigrant scientists are more severely disadvantaged than native-born women scientists in employment and advancement, unlike male immigrant scientists in comparison with their native-born counterparts; this gender difference was attributed to differences in the migration paths taken by men and women—men scientists more likely to be primary immigrants and women scientists more likely to be secondary immigrants.

In summary, multiple sources and historical data reveal the long-standing and consistent underrepresentation of women in S&E fields. Most problematic is the low proportion of women faculty at higher levels in the academic hierarchy.

UNDERREPRESENTATION AND INDIVIDUAL DIFFERENCE EXPLANATIONS

The concept of *underrepresentation* is itself subject to multiple interpretations (Stewart, Malley, & LaVaque-Manty 2007). Underrepresentation may mean that women should participate in every activity in society in rough proportion to their numbers in the population (about half), or it may mean that women should be expected to participate on university faculties in rough proportion to their attainment of doctoral-level degrees. Underrepresentation may occur in terms of many dimensions such as tenure status, rank or position, and leadership opportunities (Stewart et al. 2007).

Two concepts illustrate various dynamics of underrepresentation: token or solo status, and critical mass. The literature on *tokens or solos*—individuals who are the sole representatives of their group (e.g., by race, gender, rank, or tenure status)—suggests that they are perceived and treated differently than others in a work setting (Kanter 1977; Yoder & Sinnett 1985; Yoder 1991; Niemann & Dovidio 1998). Solos are more likely to be subject to stereotyping, scrutiny, and negative judgment (Thompson & Sekaquaptewa 2002), and experience greater internal stress (Bilimoria & Stewart 2009). When individuals constitute a "significant minority" and not tokens, they begin to be viewed through more individualistic and less stereotyped lenses. The phenomenon of solo and minority women faculty in academic STEM departments is widespread, especially in top research universities.

A second related concept is that of *critical mass*. The theory of critical mass suggests that a meaningful representation of women in a group facilitates their individual differentiation (thereby helping them evade token treatments, reduce performance pressures, and escape role entrapment) and increases the possibility of their forming alliances and coalitions to alter the prevailing culture (Kanter 1977). Critical mass is linked to positive educational and career outcomes. For example, Latinos/Latinas student success was found to be higher at community colleges in which they constitute more than half of students and more than a third of the faculty (Hagedorn, Chi, Cepeda, & McLain 2007). Defining critical mass departments as those with more than 15% women faculty and departments with token status as having less than 15% women faculty, Etzkowitz, Kemelgor and Uzzi (2000) found that women faculty in critical mass departments reported relationships with significantly higher levels of social support and identity enhancement, more network contacts, and more reciprocation from network contacts as compared with women faculty in departments with token status.

Similar to the definition of a critical mass of students as defined by the American Educational Research Association, Elam, Stratton, Hafferty, and Haidet (2009) suggested that a critical mass of faculty may be defined as a contextual benchmark that allows an institution to exceed token numbers within its faculty body and to promote the robust exchange of ideas and views that is central to an institution's mission. Etzkowitz, Kemelgor, Neuschatz, Uzzi, and Alonzo (1994) identified a strong minority of at least 15% as necessary fulcrum to move toward critical mass. While the specific operational definition and the contextual benchmark of a critical mass of women faculty in academic S&E is yet to be specified (Elam et al. 2009), in the field of corporate governance it has been empirically determined that while a lone woman can and often does make substantial contributions and two women are generally more powerful than one, in a small-group setting such as a corporate board it takes three or more women to achieve a critical mass that can cause a fundamental change in deliberation processes and enhance corporate governance (Kramer, Konrad, & Erkut 2006; see also Erkut, Kramer, & Konrad 2008). This study found that having a critical mass of women directors is good for corporate governance in at least three ways: different views and perspectives of multiple stakeholders are likely to be considered, difficult issues and problems are considerably less likely to be ignored or brushed aside, and discussions are more open and collaborative.

Varied explanations have been offered for the continued underrepresentation of women and girls in science and engineering fields, constituting a "culture-to-biology spectrum" (Ceci & Williams 2007, 20). At the biological-differences end of the spectrum is the proposition that girls have lower cognitive skills (specifically, certain mathematical and spatial rotation abilities) than do boys—and that these nuanced deficiencies ultimately lower women's chances of success at ensuing stages of their academic S&E careers. While specific sex-based cognitive skill differences have been cited by some to explain the low proportions of women and girls in scientific and engineering research careers (see Ceci, Williams, & Barnett 2009), it is beyond the scope of the current study and the present review to deeply delve into some of the highly nuanced merits of such arguments; we focus instead on the institutional level cultural and structural causes of women's underrepresentation and the institutional remedies that more readily yield possibilities of improvement in women's workforce participation, equity, and inclusion. Nevertheless, we acknowledge here, then Harvard University president Lawrence Summer's 2005 citation of possible innate gender differences at the extreme right end of the distribution of mathematical and spatial cognition abilities (coupled with a dismissal of rival socialization, stereotyping and unconscious bias, and institutional-barriers explanations) as sparking considerable interest and debate over the biological causes of women's underrepresentation in science.

Many have strongly refuted cognitive-difference explanations for the dearth of women in S&E on the following grounds. First, girls' scores in mathematics achievements in other countries refute arguments about the possible innate nature of observable differences in the U.S.—girls in Japan and Singapore outperform boys in the U.S. on math tests, to the extent that "The cross-national differences dwarf the sex differences" (Valian 2007, 29). Second, U.S. girls have considerably improved their scores on mathematics measures as well as their performance in undergraduate and graduate STEM fields over the past decades, indicating that the gap is not immobile (e.g., Xie & Shauman 2003). The American Association of University Women's 2010 report *Why So Few? Women in Science, Technology, Engineering and Mathematics* provides a summary of evidence that recent gains in girls' mathematical achievement demonstrate the importance of culture and learning environments in the cultivation of abilities and interests (Hill, Corbett, & St. Rose 2010). As this report states, "Thirty years ago there were 13 boys for every girl who scored above 700 on the SAT math exam at age 13; today that ratio has shrunk to about 3:1. This increase in the number of girls identified as 'mathematically gifted' suggests that education can and does make a difference at the highest levels of mathematical achievement" (Hill, Corbett, & St. Rose 2010, xiv). Third, it appears that specific kinds of spatial cognition training can elevate girls' (and boys') spatial skills (Newcombe 2007), and both test scores and career choices can be positively influenced by removal of internalized stereotypes and biases. Believing in the potential for intellectual growth, in and of itself, improves test scores and intentions to pursue STEM careers; internalized negative stereotypes about girls' and women's STEM abilities can be overcome by improving the classroom environment and individual training (Steele & Aronson 1995; Spencer, Steele, & Quinn 1999; Nguyen & Ryan 2008; see also Dweck 2007, 2008).

Other individual level differences may contribute to women's employment decisions and success, particularly their demonstration of psychosocial abilities such as self-confidence, political skills, and propensity to engage in negotiations, as compared with men's. A recent study of more than 1,300 intramural postdoctoral researchers at the National Institutes of Health documents a self-confidence gap (in the expectations of success) between women and men postdoctoral researchers (Martinez et al. 2007). This survey found that women are more likely to quit at the postdoctoral researcher to principal investigator (PI) transition on account of two reasons: (a) family responsibilities—spending time with family, plans to have children, affordable child care, travel, and proximity to spouse's workplace were some of the considerations that were weighed more heavily by women, whereas salary was more important to men, and (b) self-confidence—although men and women rated themselves equally when it came to professional skill, men were significantly more confident that they could obtain a PI position and become tenured than were women (Martinez et al. 2007). The causes of women's less optimistic outlook about their future success as PIs were not examined in this study. Rather, the investigators urged future research to examine "whether this lower confidence originates from foreseen future challenges that affect women more than men—such as childbearing, child care, and/or a less favorable professional environment—or whether they indicate that women underestimate their professional ability" (Martinez et al. 2007). An interview-based study of 31 women engineers found that "persistent" women engineers (those who stayed in the engineering workforce for an average of 21 years) versus those who opted out (those who left the engineering workforce after an average of 12 years) demonstrated more self-efficacy in dealing with work-related issues, were more other-oriented, were more likely to adapt to the masculine engineering culture, were more engaged in engineering-related learning and professional growth, and perceived themselves as having alignment between their personal and career aspirations (Buse, Perelli, & Bilimoria 2010). In another study of 3,700 women engineering-degree holders, Fouad and Singh (2011) found that women engineers who were more self-confident in their abilities to navigate their organization's political landscape and juggle multiple life roles reported being highly satisfied with their jobs as well as their careers.

Political skills involve an individual's behaviors to gain information regarding formal and informal work relationships and power structures within an organization (Chao, O'Leary-Kelly, Wolf, Klein, & Gardner 1994). They reflect the ability to get things done by understanding and working through others outside of formally prescribed organizational mechanisms (Ferris, Davidson, & Perrewé 2005). Higher levels of political knowledge and influence behaviors are associated with increases in annual salaries (Judge & Bretz 1994) and supervisor ratings of job performance (Ferris et al. 2005). However, women are less likely than men to engage in or use organizational politics, possibly due to a perception of incompetence, lack of confidence, and distaste for political activity, preferring to rely instead on formal mechanisms of influence, sometimes at the cost of career progression (Arroba & James 1988; Mann 1995). Similarly, sex differences in the propensity to negotiate have been employed to explain various career outcomes (e.g., Babcock & Laschever 2003; Babcock, Gelfand, Small, & Stayn 2006). However, while women may be less likely to engage in negotiation behaviors, there may be good reasons for this—recent research has documented that women face social sanctions (such as be disliked or perceived as demanding) and be penalized for initiating negotiations (Bowles, Babcock, & Lai 2007).

INSTITUTIONAL EXPLANATIONS OF WOMEN'S UNDERREPRESENTATION: THE LEAKY PIPELINE

Focusing exclusively on programs to remedy gaps in individual skill differences has had limited success in unlocking S&E educational pathways and improving S&E workforce participation for women; instead, a more systemic approach is needed (National Academies 2003; Rosser 2004; National Academies 2007a). A singular emphasis on individual-level explanations to rectify extant underrepresentation and inequities overlooks powerful workplace dynamics that constrain women's participation and success. For example, in the same study of 3,700 women engineering-degree holders mentioned above (Fouad & Singh 2011), perceptions of the engineering workplace climate were critical in their decisions to not enter or leave the engineering profession. Of those women who chose not to enter the engineering profession after college, a third indicated it was because of their perceptions of engineering as being inflexible or the engineering workplace culture as being nonsupportive of women. Of those women who left engineering, almost half said they left engineering because of working conditions, too much travel, lack of advancement or low salary, and one-third said they left because they did not like the workplace climate, their boss, or the culture (Fouad & Singh 2011).

Individual skill-based differences such as those cited in the section above lend themselves to recommendations for specific training and development to better equip women to more successfully navigate for success in their workplaces and careers. Exclusively relying on such support interventions has been sometimes referred to as *fix the woman* or *women's problems* or *band-aid* approaches, and "have been characterized as efforts that focus on a 'deficit' model, in which it is assumed that these individuals lack something—ability, experience, interest, inspiration, motivation—that they need in order to succeed" (Muller 2003, 122–123). Although these approaches do not systematically address root causes, they support and encourage individual girls and women, and as such have a role to play in a comprehensive institutional strategy for remedying workplace underrepresentation and inequities, and may also catalyze longer-term shifts in institutional culture (Muller 2003).

Going behind the numbers and outcomes of underrepresentation is important (Long 2001). Attention only to aggregate growth trends in workforce participation masks several aspects of the demographics of the S&E workforce (Rosser & Taylor 2009). First, it masks a decrease over recent decades in white U.S. men, the traditional group from which the U.S. has drawn its STEM workforce. Second, the aggregated data also hide the wide variance in women's participation in specific fields. Women earn most of the bachelor's degrees in non-STEM fields and men earn most of the degrees in STEM (e.g., computer sciences, physical sciences, and engineering). Third, aggregated data mask the attrition of women at every phase of the educational and career STEM pipeline. More women than men leave S&E, even though their grades or academic attainments are equivalent.

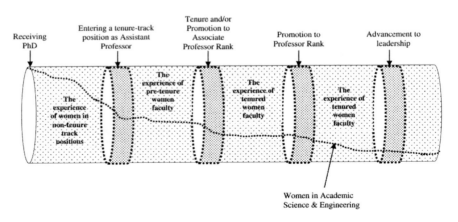

Adapted from Mason, Stacy, Goulden, Hoffman & Frasch, 2005

Figure 2.4 Pictorial representation of the leaky pipeline for women in academic Science and Engineering.

The leaky pipeline has been used to describe this steady attrition of girls and women along the educational and academic career pathway. Academic career development can be conceptualized as a pipeline which carries women students from secondary school through higher education and on to a faculty job and beyond. At each transition point in the academic pipeline, however, a lower proportion of women advance to the next milestone than their male colleagues, compelling many to refer to this pathway as a 'leaky pipeline' since it loses women at every step. As illustrated in Figure 2.4, the leaky pipeline is metaphorically used to describe the loss of women faculty at each transition point. This figure illustrates the steady attrition of women at successive stages in the educational and career pipeline.

Of course the metaphor of the leaky pipeline is not without criticism. For example, Herzig (2004) notes that the pipeline metaphor poses students as passive participants in their education, whose progress through their education is affected only by market forces. Further, a leaky pipeline does not adequately address why students of some demographic groups stay in STEM while others leave in greater proportions, and it fails to model important features of postsecondary STEM education that may contribute to attrition, such as its competitive and individualistic nature (Herzig 2004). Some, such as Mattis (2007, 336), propose a pathway rather than a pipeline since the former "connotes flexibility and freedom of movement, whereas pipeline brings to mind a mechanical and constrained course of action." Xie and Shauman (2003, 209) propose a life-course perspective, providing evidence that "in contrast to the rigid 'leaking only' career path dictated by the pipeline metaphor, career processes are fluid and dynamic, with exit, entry, and reentry all being real possibilities at any point in a career." Despite these and other critiques, the pipeline continues to be the prevailing reality in academic careers, and the leaky pipeline persists as a widespread and powerful symbolic representation of the problematic issues surrounding the workforce participation of women in academic STEM.

Below we describe relevant systemic—cultural and structural—challenges and barriers facing women S&E faculty as they progress through each major career stage in the academic pipeline. For each transition point, we describe the main causes of the leakages (challenges and barriers) as well as the experiences of women while they are at that stage.

Pipeline Leaks Prior to the Tenure Track

Barriers to Entering the Tenure Track Facing Women PhD Holders

Sufficient numbers of female doctoral graduates are generally present in the disciplinary recruitment pools for S&E faculty (Trower & Chait 2002), but qualified female doctoral applicants may be invisible to search committees. Search committees often lack gender diversity themselves, and their search activities often do not include systematic identification of the candidate pool, gender-blind screening of applications, and an equitable campus visit and interview process (Stewart, LaVaque-Manty, & Malley 2004). Conventional recruitment practices contribute to the homogenous replication of the faculty body; such practices are passive, time-limited, noninclusive and nondiverse, and search-committee members lack expertise in basic recruiting and hiring practices and are bias-prone (Bilimoria & Buch 2010).

Prior research has found that women and members of underrepresented minority groups are judged more fairly when they are at least 30% of the applicant pool (Heilman 1980; Sackett, DuBois & Noe 1991), yet this level of representation is difficult to achieve in academic STEM disciplines, where women represent, on average, less than 20% of qualified applicants. The increase in women PhD graduates holding postdoctoral positions in S&E is symptomatic of the barriers women face in entry to tenure track positions. According to the National Postdoctoral Association, a postdoctoral scholar ("postdoc") is an individual holding a doctoral degree who is engaged in a temporary period of mentored research and/or scholarly training for the purpose of acquiring the professional skills needed to pursue a career path of his or her choosing. A postdoctoral position is a critical transition stage in the academic pipeline, beyond which the number of women scientists and engineers continues to decline. As shown earlier in Figure 2.3, the proportion of women S&E doctorate holders who are in postdoctoral positions was 41% in 2006, increasing from 14% in 1973 through 31% in 2003.

Other research has shown that female applicants for academic positions tend to be evaluated less favorably than male applicants with identical qualifications, by both men and women. In one study of identical curricula vitae of a hypothetical male or female candidate for a faculty position, both men and women evaluators preferred male job applicants (Steinpreis, Anders, & Ritzke 1999). Another study found that female postdoctoral fellowship applicants had to be significantly more productive than male applicants to receive the same peer review score (Wenneras & Wold 1997).

Isaac, Lee, and Carnes (2009) performed searches for randomized controlled studies since 1973 of interventions that affect gender differences in the evaluation of job applicants. Their systematic review reaffirmed a negative bias against women being evaluated for positions traditionally or predominantly held by men. They also found that although interventions that provided raters with clear evidence of job-relevant competencies were effective, clearly competent women were rated lower than equivalent men for male sex-typed jobs unless evidence of communal qualities was also provided. They also noted that a commitment to the value of credentials before review of applicants and women's presence at or above 25% of the applicant pool eliminated bias against women. They concluded that "when ambiguity exists in an individual's qualifications or competence, evaluators will fill the void with assumptions drawn from gendered stereotypes" (Isaac, Lee, & Carnes 2009, 1444).

Analyses of S&E searches undertaken over multiple years at two research universities yielded the following findings: a statistically significant linear relationship existed between the percent of female and underrepresented minority (URM) applicants in the candidate pool and their inclusion on the short list; the level of representation of female and URM applicants on the short list was associated with the likelihood of hiring a female or URM candidate; and the majority of Native American, black, and "race-unknown" candidates were hired when there were more females on the short list (Bilimoria & Buch 2010). These findings highlight that the applicant pool and search committee practices to diversify this pool are critical elements in increasing faculty diversity.

Differences in the content of recommendation letters written for women and men candidates have been suggested as possible explanations for the difficulties women face in entering the academic pipeline. Trix and Psenka (2003) found systematic differences in letters of recommendation for medical school faculty positions for female and male applicants: their study documented that recommendation letters written for female applicants were shorter than those of men, lacked key information from their CVs, and were more likely to refer to their compassion, teaching, and effort while letters written for male applicants highlighted their achievements, research, and ability. Double the letters written for women applicants (almost 25%) raised doubts (e.g., by hedges, qualifiers, and faint praise) as those written for men applicants in this study (Trix & Psenka 2003). Another recent analysis of letters of recommendation for faculty applicants of a psychology department in a research university found other differences in the descriptions of women and men applicants (Madera, Hebl, & Martin 2009): after controlling for years in graduate school, number of publications, honors, number of postdoctoral years, number of courses taught, and type of position, the number of words per letter for women applicants in comparison to men applicants was significantly more likely to be communal adjectives (e.g., affectionate, helpful, kind, sympathetic, sensitive, nurturing, agreeable, tactful, interpersonal, warm, caring, and tactful) and social-communal orientation descriptors (e.g., husband, wife, kids, babies, brothers, children, colleagues, dad, family, they, him, and her), and less likely to be agentic adjectives (e.g., assertive, confident, aggressive, ambitious, dominant, forceful, independent, daring, outspoken, and intellectual). A second study conducted by these same authors provided evidence that that communal characteristics have a negative relationship with hiring decisions in academia that are based on letters of recommendation (Madera, Hebl, & Martin 2009).

The family situations of women and men are cited as relevant differences in academic STEM career entry and advancement (Mason & Goulden 2002, 2004). For example, while 70% of male tenured STEM faculty had children living in their home 12 to 14 years after earning a doctorate, only 50% of female faculty did (Mason & Goulden 2002). In this same study,

77% of the male faculty but only 53% of the female faculty who had babies within the first five years after receiving a doctorate had achieved tenure 12 to 14 years after earning a doctorate. Ginther and Kahn (2006) found that women are less likely to take tenure-track positions in science, but the gender gap is entirely explained by choices around fertility.

Significant in explaining the barriers to tenure-track entry is the *penalty for motherhood*. Examining the tenure-track positions at the University of California, Berkeley, Mason, Stacy, Goulden, Hoffman, and Frasch (2005) found that qualified female PhDs make up less than a third of the applicant pools. These same researchers observed that married women with and without young children are the least likely of all PhD recipients to secure tenure-track faculty positions (Mason et al. 2005). Correll, Benard, and Paik (2007) documented the existence of powerful schemas about parenthood in both laboratory and field studies. In the laboratory study, when evaluating identical applications, mothers were less likely to be recommended for hire, promotion, and management, and were offered lower starting salaries than nonmothers; evaluators rated mothers as less competent and committed to paid work than nonmothers; and fathers were seen as more committed to paid work and offered higher starting salaries than nonfathers. In the field study, prospective employers called mothers back about half as often as nonmothers, while fathers were not similarly disadvantaged in the hiring process (Correll, Benard, and Paik 2007).

Based on survival analyses of the Survey of Doctorate Recipients (a national biennial longitudinal dataset funded by the National Science Foundation and others 1981–2003) in S&E, and after accounting for a variety of control variables such as discipline, age, ethnicity, time to PhD, and PhD program ranking, married women with young children had 35% lower odds than married men with young children to get a tenure-track position, 28% lower odds than married women without young children, and 33% lower odds than single women without young children (Goulden, Frasch, & Mason 2009).

Related to these dynamics, women faculty members are particularly prone to *bias avoidance* with regard to their family lives. Drago (2007) documents that women faculty marry at lower rates than men faculty, are childless at higher rates, report having fewer children than they would like, and are less likely to utilize family-friendly policies (such as tenure clock extensions for the birth or adoption of young children) for fear that they may be penalized in future evaluations for using them.

Dual-career couples face a unique problem in higher education—obtaining tenure-track positions at the same institution, especially if they are in the same field. This issue is particularly salient for women S&E doctorate holders because 83% of them have academic partners who are scientists compared with 54% of their male peers (Schiebinger, Henderson, & Gilmartin 2008).

Women's Experience in Off-Track Positions

As noted earlier and in many other studies, women are more likely to be employed in nontenure-track positions, such as temporary teaching positions, research positions funded by "soft" or short-term restricted funding, part-time faculty, visiting scholars, adjunct faculty, postdoctoral fellows, and lower-level administrative positions (Harper, Baldwin, Gansneder, & Chronister 2001; Long 2001; National Science Foundation 2010). Individuals in these off-track positions are rarely provided opportunities for professional advancement, may not have their performance regularly reviewed or rewarded, may rarely find their positions converted to full-time or receive priority consideration when they are, and may be shut out of the faculty governance processes by the institutions that appoint them (American Association of University Professors 1993). At the entry point to an academic career, these factors already inhibit women's participation in S&E.

Pipeline Leaks after Entering the Tenure Track

Even after gaining tenure track S&E positions, women faculty face greater barriers in obtaining tenure, promotion, and advancement to leadership, and encounter more negative experiences in their workplaces, than do their male counterparts.

In a recent report entitled *Staying Competitive: Patching America's Leaky Pipeline in the Sciences*, Goulden, Frasch, and Mason (2009) found that family formation—most importantly marriage and childbirth—accounts for the largest leaks in the pipeline between PhD receipt and the acquisition of tenure for women in the sciences. Their findings indicate that women in the sciences who are married with children are 35% less likely to enter a tenure-track position after receiving a PhD than married men with children. Upon entering a tenure-track job, women in the sciences who are married with children are 27% less likely than their male counterparts to achieve tenure. Based on results from interviews, case studies, and statistical research, Rosser and Taylor (2009) concluded that the need to balance career and family and a lack of professional networks are the two primary factors that stand out among the multiple forces pushing women to leave the academic STEM workforce.

Barriers to Advancement to Tenure

Achieving tenure may be the most difficult hurdle of transition in academia. Female faculty are less likely to be tenured than male faculty (Long 2001). In a comprehensive study of almost 60,000 faculty members at 403 academic institutions, Astin and Cress (2003) reported that male faculty attained tenure in a shorter amount of time than female faculty in all fields, with the exception of engineering. Other research has shown that women are less likely than men to receive tenure or promotion in STEM fields (National Science Foundation 2001; Rosser & Daniels 2004).

Croson and McGoldrick (2007) described the lack of clear communication about tenure requirements. In their study of women economics faculty, participants reported that they did not know how many publications would be necessary for tenure, or what the trade-offs were between fewer publications in top journals and more publications in lower-tier journals. Very few women faculty knew how important (or unimportant) it was to get grants, good teaching ratings, or do good service in the tenure evaluation.

Fox, Colatrella, McDowell, and Realff (2007) addressed three sets of conditions to support equitable evaluation, including more complete information on candidates' records and qualifications, clarity of evaluation standards, and open processes. The rationale is that bias in assessment is more likely to result if the criteria and process of evaluation are subjective, loosely defined, and a matter of judgment. "Non-performance-based characteristics, such as gender and race, are more likely to be activated as bases for evaluation when there are few relevant and known criteria on which to judge individual performance" (Fox, Colatrella, McDowell, & Realff 2007, 171). Secret and nonsystematic processes tend to activate "particularistic considerations" in evaluations; when criteria for evaluation are ambiguous, outcomes based upon race, gender, national origin, and other personal and social characteristics are more likely to occur.

The effects of implicit biases have been documented in the first authorships of scientific papers. After the journal *Behavioral Ecology* instituted double-blind reviews (where neither the identities of manuscript authors nor reviewers are revealed) in 2000, the proportion of female first authors increased significantly during 2002–07 as compared with 1995–2000. No such shifts occurred over the same time period in another journal with a similar subject matter and impact factor—*Behavioral Ecology and Sociobiology*—or with four out of five other ecology and evolutionary biology journals, most of which had continued to practice single-blind reviews (Budden, Tregenza, Aarssen, et al. 2008). The editorial team of one of these journals, *Journal of Biogeography*, which appeared to have an increased proportion of male-authored papers in Budden et al., subsequently conducted its own analyses of authorships over the three-year period 2005–2007, making special efforts to ascertain the gender of authors especially in previously unknown cases, and concluded that there was no difference in the acceptance/rejection ratio for papers submitted by male and female corresponding (not first) authors (Whittaker 2008).

Leakage also occurs from the lack of networks and mentoring of women in the S&E educational and career pipeline. Networks and mentors provide information and supports to a faculty member about how to conduct work, improve performance, and understand the political workings of the university system, as well as provide opportunities for collaboration and greater visibility in their discipline. Mentoring and peer support (Kram 1985, 1988) are important for professional connections (de Janasz, Sullivan, & Whiting 2003) as well as psychosocial benefits (Kram 1988). Mentored individuals are more likely to have higher compensation, greater salary growth, and more promotions than nonmentored individuals (Allen, Eby, Poteet, Lentz, & Lima 2004). Who mentors and who is mentored in academic S&E vary according to a number of individual and organizational factors (Fox & Conseca 2006).

Gender differences occur in the structure of mentor relationships in academic S&E as well as the resources obtained from these relationships: women's collaborative networks outside of their institutions are larger, and they matter for grant success—collaboration network size is positively associated with the probability of grant receipt, and women faculty have a lower probability of receiving a grant (Kiopa, Melkers, & Tanyildiz 2009). Previous research has shown that women faculty benefit from mentoring and institutional supports more than do men faculty (Bilimoria et al. 2006). As reported in the 2010 report *Gender Differences at Critical Transitions in the Careers of Science, Engineering, and Mathematics Faculty*, female assistant professors with no mentors had 68% probability of having grant funding versus 93% of women with mentors; the same was not found to be true for male faculty with and without mentors (National Academies 2010). Yet, access to mentorship is often more difficult for women and underrepresented minority faculty (Smith, Smith, & Markham 2000; Niemeier & Gonzales 2004). Additionally, women S&E faculty have less diverse networks and fewer graduate and postdoctoral students to support their work than men faculty, and receive fewer referrals from their networks to consult in the commercial marketplace, serve on science advisory boards, and interact with industry (Murray & Graham 2007).

Barriers to Promotion to Professor Rank and Faculty/Administrative Leadership

Statistics also indicate that women are underrepresented in senior academic ranks and faculty leadership positions such as presidents, chancellors, provosts, deans, and chairs (Hollenshead 2003). The lowest proportion of women S&E faculty is at the highest professor level of the academic hierarchy. Among S&E doctorates who hold academic faculty positions in four-year colleges and universities, women are less likely than men to be full professors and more likely to be assistant professors (National Science Foundation 2006, Figure H-5). Fewer differences in rank exist between male and female faculty in early-career stages in S&E, but greater differences appear between 15 and 20 years after receipt of the doctorate (National Science Foundation 2001, Figure H-5). In the top 50 U.S. universities, women comprised only 3% to 15% full professors in various fields of S&E (Nelson 2007).

A nationwide study of faculty at four-year colleges and universities showed that women associate professors are 10% less likely than men to attain promotion to full professor even after accounting for productivity, educational background, institution type, race, ethnicity, and nationality (Perna 2001). More recently a focus-group study of the advancement of women and men associate professors at the Massachusetts Institute of Technology found similar results—women are less likely to be promoted to full professor than men and take longer to achieve promotions (Misra, Lundquist, Holmes, & Agiomavritis 2010).

In a comprehensive critique of the appointments of women to professor rank in Dutch universities, van den Brink (2010, 214) has systematically deconstructed the various ways in which gender is practiced in the most senior academic appointments—"supposedly gender-neutral organization processes, such as the implementation of transparency policies, the search for talent and the construction of scientific excellence, have been exposed as being based on hierarchical conceptions of masculinity and femininity." Her findings expose and refute prevalent myths explaining the low numbers of women professors, including the myths that (1) there are too few professorial positions available, (2) there is too little female potential for these positions, (3) professorial appointment practices are transparent and decision makers are held accountable, (4) professorial recruitment is a level playing field, (5) the concept of scientific excellence can be defined and is gender neutral, and (6) gender practices are similar in all academic subfields (van den Brink 2010).

In a related study, van den Brink, Benschop, and Jansen (2010) shed light on how norms of transparency and accountability are implemented in highly gendered ways. They describe numerous subtle practices by which micropolitics—the myriad strategies and tactics of exerting informal and formal influence to further personal interests—surround the implementation of these norms at every stage in the professorial appointment process. For example, although norms of transparency and accountability drive efforts to diversify appointment committees, women committee members are most often doctoral students or human resource specialists whereas men members are professors. While vacancies are advertised in the media, in reality the preferred candidate is already known and any other applicants are part of a purely cosmetic appointment procedure. Often special chairs are created and offered to women candidates in closed recruitment procedures, thereby inflating the number of women in chaired appointments; however, such women's chairs are often temporary and their legitimacy is disputed. Women candidates are only selected when they are "excellent" beyond all doubt, whereas the standards are broader when exercised for men candidates. Based on these and other findings, the authors conclude that "it is often difficult to enhance gender equality because of the existence of multi-faceted gender inequality practices alongside gender equality practices that lack 'teeth', especially in a traditional masculine academic environment with ponderous traditions and 'thick' values. . . . We conclude that gender inequality practices continue to dominate and that they detract from, distort, or even hijack attempts to introduce gender equality practices" (van den Brink, Benschop, & Jansen 2010, 1478–1479). Three policy approaches are offered to address these shortcomings: (a) to deploy the tools of transparency and accountability to their full potential particularly by making the process and decisions more visible for the larger academic society, (b) to enable university boards to monitor compliance to the regulations and put in place the incentives and sanctions that can ensure full implementation, and (c) to utilize multiple perspectives on gender equality in training to make committee members aware of double standards and routine gender inequalities in the appointment process (van den Brink, Benschop, & Jansen 2010).

In addition, a recent study of NIH awards found that more experienced researchers (those who have already received R01 grants) who submitted and received renewal applications were more likely to be male (Pohlhaus, Jiang, Wagner, Schaffer, & Pinn 2011). The study found an inverse correlation between age and the participation/success of women in NIH award programs in three ways: there were fewer women applicants and awardees for awards targeted at higher average ages, more experienced women researchers were less likely to apply and receive R01 grants than first-time women researchers, and investigators with multiple concurrent R01 awards were older and more often male than investigators with one award (Polhaus et al. 2011).

Women are also more likely than their male colleagues to be underrepresented in administrative and leadership positions (e.g., department chairs, deans, and senior administrators). For example, only 10.31% of permanent deans of medical schools (13 out of 126 in 2009, up from12 out of 126 in 2006) were women (Association of American Medical Colleges 2009). Among science and engineering doctorate holders in academia, women were 27% of deans and 30% of presidents of colleges and universities (National Science Foundation 2009).

A common myth about the pipeline is that achieving greater proportions of women in senior academic positions is merely a matter of time—that as the pipeline fills more women will occupy senior positions. However, the popular myth that there are insufficient numbers of women in the pipeline is not supported by the data (Trower & Chait 2002). As pointed out in *Beyond Bias and Barriers*, "For over 30 years, women have made up over 30% of the doctorates in social sciences and behavioral sciences and over 20% in the life sciences. Yet, at the top research institutions, only 15.4% of the full professors in the social and behavioral sciences and 14.8% in the life sciences are women" (National Academies 2007a, 2).

In summary, while considerable progress has been made over the years, women faculty are still less likely to achieve tenure, advance to professor rank, and occupy administrative and faculty leadership positions.

Women's Experience in the Tenure Track

A variety of problems emerge from the lack of a critical mass of women and few women at the top of the academic hierarchy in STEM, particularly resource inequities, barriers, and problems related to differential treatment and evaluation at every level in the institution. The groundbreaking study conducted by the School of Science's Committee on Women Faulty at MIT (Massachusetts Institute of Technology 1999) indicated the marginalization and exclusion of senior women faculty (in particular) as academic colleagues, documenting their receipt of lower space, salary, and other resources, exclusion from informal and formal social gatherings, and exclusion from research and teaching collaborations. Other studies have documented a persistent gender gap in salaries (West & Curtis 2006); female faculty members earn significantly less than male faculty members even after controlling for human capital, scholarly productivity, and personal characteristics (National Science Foundation 2003). Additionally, women have less access to research assistance and funding than men (Creamer 1998; Xie & Shauman 1998), and they enter academic positions with more limited start-up packages, less office and lab space, and less graduate-student and support-staff assistance (Massachusetts Institute of Technology 1999; Park 1996).

Rosser (2004) reported that low numbers of women S&E faculty result in women feeling isolated, having limited access to role models and mentors, and having to work harder to gain credibility and respect from their male colleagues (see also Fox 2010). With constrained access to key academic networks, women junior faculty are left on their own to learn how to navigate the promotion and tenure process in a male-dominated environment. Many women opt out of academic S&E, choosing private-sector positions because they become frustrated with the academic setting (Valian 2004). Noting the clustering of most female professors at the assistant professor level, Nelson (2007) suggests that the number of female faculty who can safely take steps to change their departmental environments is much smaller than it might first appear.

In two waves of early focus groups and interviews about the career experiences of women faculty members at a research university between 2001 and 2004, the researchers found several important themes including: (1) an overall chilly climate and unwelcoming community for women described by participants as exclusionary, unfriendly, marginalizing, tough, isolating, male-dominated, and silencing; (2) a climate where 'everything is negotiable,' manifested in perceptions of side deals and of unequal application of procedures; (3) lack of transparency in university rules, policies, procedures and practices; (4) a pervasive lack of mentoring; (5) disproportionate service and teaching pressures faced by women faculty; and (6) unfair or unequal access to/allocation of resources, including purchase of library materials, assistance from teaching assistants, access to services from support staff, travel money, and protected research time (Case Western Reserve University 2003). Other writings address the multiple dimensions of gender-based resource inequity in academia (Long 1990, 1992; Evetts 1996; Preston 2004; Valian 2004). For example, women faculty receive less office and lab space, have less access to graduate-student assistance, and get fewer services from support staff (Park 1996).

The experiences of women faculty in STEM seem to derive from particular sets of beliefs held by (predominantly male) faculty and administrators. For example, participants in the focus groups mentioned above brought out the notion that leadership seems naturally male, and that masculinity appears to lead to power, manifested in conscious and unconscious ways at the university. Other beliefs regarding academia voiced by participants included that the academic enterprise requires complete dedication at the expense of everything else, especially in early-career years, and that academia is essentially an individual profession, with individualized results and rewards.

These mind-sets contribute directly and indirectly to the treatment and evaluation of women faculty. Similar other belief structures, detrimental to women in academia, have been identified by research from other institutions as well. For instance, Silver et al. (2006) summarize several factors that retarded the achievement of full professional equality at the University of Rhode Island, as mentioned in a December 2000 independent audit team report stemming from a grievance settlement to a claim of sexual harassment in the College of Engineering: "a belief that some male professors and administrators did not view female colleagues as equals but rather as second-class members of the faculty. Adding to the women's discomfort was their perception that individuals who raised complaints about disparate treatment were viewed as 'troublemakers,' a perception that discouraged the seeking of redress for mistreatment" (Silver et al. 2006, 3). These factors included: demeaning and insulting statements and remarks made by the dean and faculty members toward women faculty; "window-dressing" efforts by the dean to support women in engineering programs rather than providing adequate funding for such efforts; public treatment of women faculty in a less respectful manner than male faculty; and commenting to women faculty on the perceived appropriateness of their clothing (Silver et al. 2006).

Prior research has described how the masculine image of academic S&E work translates to the treatment and evaluation of women in the workforce. Van den Brink and Stobbe (2009, 451) note that "the most important factors (re)producing gender inequality at universities relate to the images of science, scientific practice and the ideal scientist." Research careers in S&E, in particular, are perceived to demand a single-minded, full-time focus on a specific topic, exclusive devotion to career, and aggressive self-promotion (Dean & Fleckenstein 2007). A prevalent image is that of a scientist or engineer as a man hard at work in a laboratory during all hours of the night and weekends. The ideal worker concept (Acker 1990, 1992) suggests that "the abstract worker is actually a man, and it is the man's body, its sexuality, minimal responsibility in procreation and conventional control of emotions that pervades work and organizational processes" (Acker 1990, 152). Benschop and Brouns (2003) suggest that the image of the *ideal academic* represents a faculty member fully absorbed in his research program, and Bailyn (2003, 139) describes the *perfect academic* as someone who "gives total priority to work and has no outside interests or responsibilities." These powerful cultural images suggest that academic scientific research is exclusionary of women, contributing greatly to the negative experiences of women.

The chilly climate for STEM students has been described previously (Hall & Sandler 1984; Mills & Ayre 2003). For example, from their study of computer-science women and men undergraduate students at Carnegie Mellon, Margolis and Fisher (2002) found that the overwhelming image of a computer science major is the "geek," which more than two-thirds of the women (and almost one-third of the men) interviewed said did not fit them. "The rub for women in computer science is that the dominant computer science culture does not venerate balance of multiple interests. Instead the singular and obsessive interest in computing that is common among men is assumed to be the road to success in computing. This model shapes the assumptions of who will succeed and who 'belongs' in the discipline" (Margolis & Fisher 2002, 71). As these authors put it, "A critical part of attracting more girls and women in computer science is providing multiple ways to 'be in' computer science" (Margolis & Fisher 2002, 72), not just one linear path. Similar concerns were raised by women engineering students in the UK—interview findings revealed that women students had good experiences (mostly regarding peer and instructor support and relationships, and the opportunity to have an internship experience in industry), bad experiences (mostly regarding structural issues such as teaching and learning methods, and curriculum content and relevance), and ugly experiences (mostly regarding people's attitudes toward women students and everyday negative occurrences) (Powell, Bagilhole, & Dainty 2007).

From interviews with 80 female faculty members at the University of California, Irvine, the authors concluded that "Where power operates behind the scenes, subtly shaping structures of daily life and political beliefs, the assessments of those subject to its oppressive impact are adaptive and their responses challenge it indirectly. Our speakers, for instance, show a keen understanding of where the Academy stands relative to the necessary sacrifices all its participants must make in terms of family life" (Monroe, Ozyurt, Wrigley, & Alexander 2008, 231). For these women faculty "the concept of professional success needs to be redefined so it allows for alternative models, not simply the traditional, linear male model in which the professional is full time and focused on a career, with few family duties" (Monroe, Ozyurt, Wrigley, & Alexander 2008, 231).

Results of various interview and climate studies indicate the everyday experience of women faculty in S&E fields. In a cross-institutional study of 765 faculty conducted in eight research institutions during 2002–2004, Fox (2010) reported that women are less likely than men to report speaking daily about research and more likely than men to report speaking less than weekly. Women also gave significantly lower ratings of access to equipment and lower recognition from faculty colleagues in home units (e.g., departments), and were significantly less likely than men to characterize their home units as (a) informal (compared to formal), (b) exciting (compared to boring), (c) helpful (compared to unhelpful), (d) creative (compared to noncreative), and (e) inclusive (compared to noninclusive). In another climate study conducted at a large public university, in comparison with their male counterparts, STEM women faculty reported significantly lower equality of treatment, perceived the organizational climate as significantly less supportive, perceived lower support for family friendliness, reported more overt discrimination in areas such as salary, promotion, and access to resources, perceived that they undertook greater service involvement, and believed that their departments viewed them as less productive than their departmental averages (Blackwell, Snyder, & Mavriplis 2009).

Results from interviews with women and men faculty members at another research university indicated that female faculty were more likely to report negative interactions with colleagues, negative experiences with the process of evaluation, promotion and tenure, difficulty balancing work and family life, and overwhelming workloads (Hult, Callister, & Sullivan 2005). Several other climate studies conducted by universities indicate that male faculty experience more favorable interpersonal relations than women faculty. Tenure-track women faculty often provide lower ratings than their men counterparts on items measuring institutional support, such as child care, career planning, teaching improvement, tenure-clock adjustments, and accruing resources. In addition, female faculty on the tenure track report lower satisfaction with their academic jobs than do male faculty (Bilimoria et al. 2006; Callister 2006), and they are more likely to opt out of academic S&E (Valian 2004). In a sample of 248 nonmedical faculty members, Bilimoria et al.(2006) found that women's job satisfaction derived more from their perceptions of the relational support provided to them in their departments than the academic resources they received, whereas men's job satisfaction resulted equally from their perceptions of resources and relational supports received. Similarly, Callister (2006) noted that female faculty members are not inherently unsatisfied or unhappy with their jobs, but rather that they greatly value department climate.

A valuable concept from sociology addressing the experience of women faculty in S&E is the *accumulation of advantage*, which is the magnification of initial small differences into later large differences (Merton 1942/1973). Initial small advantages operate over time and may add up to larger advantages over the course of a career (Long 1992). Valian (1999) likens the accumulation of advantage to interest accruing on capital and the accumulation of disadvantage to interest accruing on debt. The impact of accumulative disadvantage on the career outcomes of S&E women is recognized. For example, the 2001 report, *From Scarcity to Visibility: Gender Differences in the Careers of Doctoral Scientists and Engineers*, noted that "while controlling for background differences eliminates much of the gender difference in salary, it does not eliminate it altogether . . . Further, with each progressive stage of the stratification process, it becomes more difficult to distinguish outcomes that are the result of individual differences between women and men from the result of men's cumulative advantage over women in science" (Long 2001, 216–217). A demonstration of the effects of accumulative disadvantage showed that very small differences in how individuals (or groups) are treated can result in very large disparities in career outcomes (Martell, Lane, & Emrich 1996). In this computer simulation of organizational promotion practices, the effects of a small disadvantage for females in promotion through eight hierarchical levels were modeled. The disadvantage accounted for only 1% of the variability in promotion. The researchers ran the simulations with the lowest organizational level equally staffed by males and females. After the eight minutely advantaged moves, the highest level in the hierarchy was staffed by 65% males.

Institutional Transformation to Repair the Leaky Pipeline

A burgeoning literature has begun to emerge around institutional approaches to address the issues described above and repair the leaky pipeline. The participation, status, and advancement of women in academic S&E have been recognized as organizational issues, which are subject to organizational transformation (Rosser & Lane 2002; Fox & Colatrella 2006; National Academies 2007b; Stewart, Malley, & LaVaque-Manty 2007; Fox 2008). Simplistic, ad hoc, and piecemeal solutions, or those that focus only at individual-level, "fix-the-women" type interventions, cannot eradicate systemic, historical, and widespread gender underrepresentation and inequities. Instead, a comprehensive transformation of the organizational systems, structures, processes, policies, practices, and mental models that perpetuate inequity is needed (cf. Thomas & Ely 1996; McCracken 2000; Meyerson & Fletcher 2000; Rosser 2004). Such change calls for the reorganization of the core elements of the institution, including mission and vision, goals, accountability, authority, decision making, policies, and practices (cf. Levy & Merry 1986; Nutt & Backoff 1997; Kezar 2001; Fox

2008). In short, as recommended by Rosser (2004), what is needed for a brighter future is a "change the institution, not the women" approach.

Drawing on earlier writings about change in higher education (e.g., Astin & Associates 2001; Eckel & Kezar 2003), Fox (2008) has described institutional transformation in higher education as change that is systematic, deep, intentional, and cultural. Transformation in higher education is systematic in that it involves alteration in the full range of functioning parts of the institution; transformation is deep to the extent that it affects values and assumptions, as well as structures and processes in higher education; transformation is intentional because it involves deliberate and purposeful decision making about institutional actions and directions; transformation in higher education is cultural because it involves the dominant and prevailing patterns of assumption, ideologies, and beliefs that people have about their organization and that shape their attitudes, priorities, and actions regarding teaching, research, and service (Fox 2008; see also Eckel & Kezar 2003).

An institutional change lens on gender equity, diversity, and inclusion concerns, rather than an individual change approach, has been recommended by a number of reports and studies. For example, the 2007 report *Women, Work, and the Academy* recommended that "Rather than making it a priority to change women and minorities so that they fit academic institutions in their current configuration, adopt strategies for changing these institutions so that they are more inclusive on a number of dimensions. These strategies should include pathways to professional success that do not pose intractable conflicts between work and the rest of life" (Wylie, Jakobsen, & Fosado 2007). Looking at the full system of S&E in the country, the National Academies' (2007a) *Beyond Bias and Barriers* report provided institutional transformation recommendations not only for universities but also for professional societies and higher-education organizations, federal funding agencies and foundations, federal government agencies, and the U.S. Congress.

In an early forerunner, Rosser (1993) proposed that overcoming the pervasive male orientation of science requires recognition of gender bias and creation of gender-equitable science content and teaching. She proposed proceeding systematically through the following six phases of change: (1) the absence of women in science is not noticed, (2) recognition that most scientists are men and thus science may reflect a masculine perspective, (3) identification of barriers that prevent women from entering science, (4) search for women scientists and inclusion of their contributions, (5) recognition that science is done by women, and (6) redefining and reconstructing science to include all (Rosser 1993).

Borrowing from the smoking-cessation literature, another framework to understand the phases of diversity-related institutional transformation was proposed by Carnes, Handelsman, and Sheridan (2005). They posit that institutions seeking transformation go through five stages of change: (1) precontemplation (unawareness that a problem exists), for example, where the institution engages in no dialogue about diversity and engages no resources; (2) contemplation (awareness that a problem exists and thinking about making a behavioral change in the future), for example, where the institution may sponsor workshops, discussions, task forces, and committees around diversity matters; (3) preparation (feeling confident that making a change is possible and planning to make a change in the immediate future), for example, where the institution may offer resources (e.g., for targeted hiring initiatives) or training (e.g., for search committees); (4) action (making a change), for example, where the institution undertakes specific initiatives to accomplish the goals; and (5) maintenance (continuing to engage in the new, desirable behavior and avoiding relapse), for example, where the institution provides rewards and reinforcements for new behaviors, and undertakes data monitoring and policy reviews. According to these authors, transformation is most successful when appropriate interventions target the institution's stage of change.

While focusing on institutional transformation to increase women students, Margolis & Fisher (2002) recommend that departments undergo programmatic changes to improve their cultures and curricula, improve the attitudes and beliefs of male faculty and students through education, and engage in systemic changes in outreach, recruitment, and admissions activities that focus on increasing women students. Proposing a similar focus on creating a more inclusive culture, Whitten et al. (2007) have suggested that in the context of physics, undergraduate education departments think of pathways rather than pipelines to actively recruit and retain women students (see also Whitten et al. 2003).

Drawing on contrasting metaphors of soccer and football to describe the everyday experiences of female and male faculty, Cress and Hart (2009) recommend a fundamental rethinking of the equation between research, teaching, and service in academic reward systems by: (1) challenging search committees and promotion and tenure committees to reward scholarship that is emerging in new areas including interdisciplinary scholarship and support diverse ways of working and time allocation, (2) systematically collecting data about service commitments as well as hidden workloads and responsibilities, (3) better compensating faculty who contribute disproportionately in service and teaching areas, and (4) providing release time and research support for faculty with extraordinary teaching and service responsibilities.

Valian, Rabinowitz, Raps, & Pizer (2004) have made other suggestions for institutions seeking to improve equity, diversity, and inclusion of women in academic science careers, including taking a "fix the institution, not fix the woman" approach, teaching decision makers about how schemas about gender and race disadvantage people in the workplace, performing frequent reviews of hidden and subtle forms of bias, training oneself and other evaluators to correct errors in evaluation and decision procedures, communicating information equally to men and women about the criteria for success at the institution, ensuring equal job responsibilities, participation in public settings and service duties of women and men, implementing consistent policies for recruitment, training, appraisal, mentoring, and development to both men and women, understanding that equity will not be achieved or sustained without special effort, and committing to making and institutionalizing that effort. Focusing specifically on faculty development needs as a change strategy, and proposing a vision of a new type of system based on a holistic, long-term view of faculty careers, Laursen & Rocque (2009) recommend transformational actions that focus on three tiers of faculty development needs: individual career stage-specific needs (early career skills, mid-career skills, and late career exploration), organizational needs across career stages (community/collegiality and department life), and systemic needs (reward system, work-life balance, diversity, and other systemic concerns).

While there have been many recommendations regarding the kinds of changes and approaches to change, to date, however, there has been little systematic study of the outcomes of institutional change in higher education pertaining to the inclusion and advancement of women faculty in S&E. Few longitudinal analyses and sustained research projects are in place, and there are many gaps in our knowledge that need exploration, particularly with regard to the results of change efforts underway (Kezar 2001). Most glaring is the lack of a comprehensive theory of change that underlies successful institutional transformation to engender equity, diversity, and inclusion. The lack of such theory to guide transformational efforts at universities and colleges has been particularly vexing for institutions seeking change. As Laursen (2009) has commented, articulating a theory of change and its underlying assumptions has been a challenge for many institutional-change projects. Particularly for issues such as women's workforce participation, equity and inclusion in STEM higher education, identifying a theory of change is inherently difficult: the desired change is large and difficult, the context is complex, and the root causes are multiple and interconnected (Laursen 2009).

In the following chapter, we describe the methods we undertook to address these gaps in the extant literature—primarily to investigate the outcomes of institutional transformation at 19 *ADVANCE* colleges and universities and to develop a comprehensive theory to guide future institutional transformation efforts to enhance gender equity, diversity, and inclusion.

3   Study Sample and Methods

The specific aims of the study were to: (1) provide a comprehensive, stand-alone source of data on the "best-practice" organizational change initiatives targeting the increased participation and advancement of women faculty in academic STEM undertaken at universities, (2) provide information on how these changes have been made permanent, (3) assess whether the academic workforce participation of women STEM faculty at all ranks and in leadership has improved through *ADVANCE* IT efforts, (4) assess the gender equity and inclusion outcomes generated by *ADVANCE* universities, (5) undertake discipline-specific analyses regarding these outcomes, and (6) propose an empirically derived model of organizational change to serve as a guide to academic and other organizations seeking transformation related to diversity, equity, and inclusion.

SAMPLE

To accomplish the goals stated above, we selected the first two cohorts of NSF *ADVANCE* IT recipients as the study's sample. As of December 2009, these 19 universities had completed or were close to completing their NSF-funded IT projects, thus providing sufficient outcome data to assess overall program effectiveness. Table 3.1 lists the sample of 19 universities used in this study.

The nine first round *ADVANCE* IT recipients (Cohort 1) started their projects either in fall 2001 or spring 2002, and completed their projects between fall 2006 and spring 2009. Although the IT funding period was originally specified as five years' duration, several projects received no-cost funding extensions from NSF beyond their original time periods in order to complete their proposed activities. The ten second round *ADVANCE* IT recipients (Cohort 2) started their *ADVANCE* IT projects in fall 2003, except for one university which started in spring 2004. The completion dates of these projects range from fall 2008 to spring 2011. At the end of 2009, all nine institutions of Cohort 1 and one institution of Cohort 2 had completed their *ADVANCE* IT projects. Eight of the remaining Cohort 2

Table 3.1   The First Two Cohorts of NSF *ADVANCE* Institutional Transformation Award Recipients (19 Universities)

Cohort 1

Georgia Institute of Technology

Hunter College, the City University of New York

New Mexico State University

University of Colorado Boulder

University of California, Irvine

University of Michigan, Ann Arbor

University of Puerto Rico, Humacao

University of Washington

University of Wisconsin, Madison

Cohort 2

Case Western Reserve University

Columbia University

Kansas State University

University of Alabama, Birmingham

University of Maryland, Baltimore County

University of Montana

University of Rhode Island

University of Texas, El Paso

Utah State University

Virginia Tech

institutions planned to complete their projects in 2010 and one institution planned to complete in 2011. For purposes of this study, the *ADVANCE* IT period over which changes were assessed for each university consisted of the total time period during which NSF *ADVANCE* funding was deployed at that university, as of December 2009.

Sample Characteristics

The sample of 19 universities consists of a variety of institutions, as follows.

   Institutional Type: The sample consists of 17 public universities and two private universities (Case Western Reserve University and Columbia University).

   Carnegie Classification: By the Carnegie Classifications scheme (Carnegie Foundation 2011), the sample consists of:

- 11 Research Universities/Very High Research Activity (RU/VH)
- 6 Research Universities/High Research Activity (RU/H)
- 1 Master's Colleges and Universities—Larger Programs
- 1 Baccalaureate Colleges—Diverse Fields.

The 19 *ADVANCE* universities studied included a variety of STEM areas in their projects. Some included all NSF-fundable areas (including social science and management/business science disciplines) and/or basic science (nonclinical) disciplines of schools of medicine, veterinary medicine and pharmacy. Other institutions limited the scope of their *ADVANCE* projects in varied ways, including only the schools/colleges where women faculty were underrepresented or where the *ADVANCE* team had been able to establish positive working relationships.

To calculate the following size characteristics of the sample, we used the classifications of the National Science Foundation that define science and engineering (S&E) as comprising physical, mathematical, computer, environmental, life, engineering, psychological and social/behavioral sciences, and science technology, engineering, and mathematics (STEM) as comprising physical, mathematical, computer, environmental, and life sciences as well as engineering. Following this definition, we exclude arts and humanities in the reporting of faculty composition across our sample.[1] Appendix 1 provides details about the specific STEM disciplines included by each university in its *ADVANCE* project. Appendix 2 provides details of the specific engineering disciplines included by each university in its *ADVANCE* project. Appendix 3 provides details of the specific natural sciences disciplines included by each university in its *ADVANCE* project. Appendix 4 provides details of the specific social and behavioral sciences disciplines included by each university in its *ADVANCE* project.

Size—Number of S&E Departments Included in the ADVANCE Project: In terms of the number of S&E departments involved in their *ADVANCE* IT projects, four institutions (University of Puerto Rico, Humacao, Hunter College, University of Maryland, Baltimore County, and University of Montana) involved 5–14 S&E departments, 14 institutions involved 17–38 S&E departments, and one institution (University of Wisconsin) involved 99 S&E departments/units.

Size—Total Number of S&E Faculty Included in the ADVANCE Project: In terms of the total number of S&E faculty, five institutions (University of Alabama, Birmingham, Hunter College, University of Montana, University of Maryland, Baltimore County, and University of Puerto Rico, Humacao) had less than 202 S&E faculty (including one less than 100); nine institutions (Columbia University, Kansas State University, Virginia Tech, University of Washington, Case Western Reserve University, Utah State University, New Mexico State University, University of Rhode Island and University of Texas, El Paso) had 240–560 S&E faculty; four institutions (University of Michigan, Georgia Tech, University of Colorado,

Irvine, and University of Colorado) had 570–900 S&E faculty; one institution (University of Wisconsin) had more than 900 S&E faculty.

Size—Number of Women S&E Faculty Included in the ADVANCE Project: 14 universities had less than 100 women faculty over the course of the *ADVANCE* grant period. Five universities had more than 100 women faculty in S&E in at least one year of the grant period.

Size—Percentage of Women S&E Faculty Included in the ADVANCE Project: Six universities reported 11–19% women faculty during the *ADVANCE* grant period; eleven universities reported 16–26% women faculty during the same period; and only two universities reported 34–38% women faculty at the same time period.

Institutional S&E faculty size characteristics of the sample are summarized in Table 3.2.

Since the workforce composition of science, technology, engineering, and mathematics (STEM) disciplines are of particular interest for this study, below we provide also the characteristics of the sample in terms of STEM disciplines only. STEM disciplines, defined by the NSF STEM Classification of Instructional Programs (CIP), comprise the following areas: agricultural sciences, chemistry, computer science, engineering, environmental science, geosciences, life/biological sciences, mathematics, and physics/astronomy. STEM fields are thus a subset of S&E; S&E also includes the social and behavioral sciences (SBS) (including psychology, sociology, anthropology, and political science).

In our sample, five universities (University of Michigan, University of Washington, Utah State University, University of Maryland, Baltimore County, and Kansas State University) did not report any SBS faculty data in their *ADVANCE* annual and final reports. SBS departments were not a focus of their *ADVANCE* IT projects. The other fourteen institutions included varied numbers of SBS departments in their change projects. Sample characteristics based on STEM disciplines only follow.

Size—Number of STEM Departments Included in the ADVANCE Project: The number of STEM departments involved in their *ADVANCE* IT projects varied by institution, ranging from four to 70 STEM departments or units.

Size—Total Number of STEM Faculty Included in the ADVANCE Project: The total number of STEM faculty involved varied by institution, ranging from 75 to 1,234 STEM faculty. During the *ADVANCE* grant period, two institutions had less than 100 STEM faculty (75–79), six institutions had 106–251 STEM faculty, eight institutions had 293–497 STEM faculty, two institutions had 498–890 STEM faculty, and one institution involved more than 1,200 STEM faculty.

Size—Number of Women STEM Faculty Included in the ADVANCE Project: Two institutions (University of Wisconsin and University of Michigan) had more than 100 women STEM faculty (between 129 and 245) and 17 institutions had less than 100 women STEM faculty (between nine and

Table 3.2   S&E Faculty Size Ranges of the 19 Universities over *ADVANCE* Award Periods

ADVANCE IT Institution	Percentage of Women Faculty in S&E*	Number of Women Faculty in S&E*	Total Number of Faculty in S&E*	Size Classification by Total Number of Faculty in S&E*
University of Wisconsin[1]	22–26%	405–475	1807–1831	More than 900
University of Michigan[1]	16–19%	129–170	821–890	570–900
Georgia Tech[1]	11–13%	68–91	610–696	
University of California, Irvine[1]	21–26%	118–178	572–696	
University of Colorado Boulder[1]	21–25%	128–165	617–660	
Columbia University[2]	17–21%	84–117	491–554	240–560
Kansas State University[2]	13–16%	67–89	498–540	
Virginia Tech[2]	12–15%	55–76	472–516	
University of Washington[1]	13–17%	60–77	457–467	
Case Western Reserve University[2]	18–21%	72–82	371–411	
Utah State University[2]	13–16%	41–52	307–330	
New Mexico State University[1]	22–25%	62–76	283–300	

University of Rhode Island[2]	19–23%	54–67	261–293	
University of Texas, El Paso[2]	16–24%	39–69	240–291	
University of Alabama, Birmingham[2]	17–21%	30–42	174–201	201 or Less
Hunter College, CUNY[1]	34–36%	59–68	172–188	
University of Montana[2]	17–26%	28–45	167–180	
University of Maryland, Baltimore County[2]	17–25%	29–42	166–173	
University of Puerto Rico, Humacao[2]	36–38%	31–35	87–91	Less than 100

Notes: [1]Cohort 1 institution; [2]Cohort 2 institution.

*Faculty members at the assistant, associate, and full professor positions are reported here for all 19 institutions. Tenure line faculty are reported for 15 institutions. Reported data are unclear regarding faculty tenure status in four institutions (Georgia Tech, University of Wisconsin, University of Montana, and University of Puerto Rico, Humacao). Except for one institution (University of Wisconsin) that reported faculty numbers by appointment count (or full-time equivalents), we adopted head counts in the reporting of faculty composition for the other 18 institutions.

S&E includes science technology, engineering and mathematics (STEM) fields and social and behavioral science (SBS) fields. The specific fields within STEM at each institution included in this table are provided in Appendix 1. The specific fields within SBS at each institution included in this table are provided in Appendix 4.

Data for only four years were available for University of Puerto Rico, Humacao.

Table 3.3   STEM Faculty Size Ranges of the 19 Universities over the Duration of the *ADVANCE IT* Projects

ADVANCE IT Institution	Percentage of Women Faculty in STEM*	Number of Women Faculty in STEM*	Total Number of Faculty in STEM*	Size Classification by Total Number of Faculty in STEM*
University of Wisconsin[1]	16–20%	199–245	1208–1234	More than 1200
University of Michigan[1]	16–19%	129–170	821–890	498–890
Georgia Tech[1]	11–13%	68–91	610–696	
Kansas State University[2]	13–16%	67–89	448–497	293–497
Virginia Tech[2]	10–14%	44–70	457–465	
University of Washington[1]	13–17%	60–77	415–454	
University of Colorado Boulder[1]	14–19%	58–85	370–450	
University of California, Irvine[1]	14–19%	53–86	307–330	
Utah State University[2]	13–16%	41–52	321–355	
Columbia University[2]	12–15%	38–52	371–411	
Case Western Reserve University[2]	15–17%	43–54	293–320	
University of Rhode Island[2]	16–20%	37–49	222–251	106–251
New Mexico State University[1]	18–21%	41–52	232–247	
University of Texas, El Paso[2]	14–20%	21–37	141–182	
University of Maryland, Baltimore County[2]	19–25%	29–42	130–173	
University of Montana[2]	14–21%	20–29	133–139	
University of Alabama, Birmingham[2]	8–11%	9–13	106–118	

University of Puerto Rico, Humacao[1]	35–38%	27–29	76–79	Less than 100
Hunter College, CUNY[1]	27–29%	21–23	75–79	

Notes: [1]Cohort 1 institution; [2]Cohort 2 institution.

*Tenure line faculty are reported for 15 institutions. Reported data are unclear regarding faculty tenure status in four institutions (Georgia Tech, University of Wisconsin, University of Montana, and University of Puerto Rico, Humacao). Except for one institution (University of Wisconsin) that reported faculty numbers by appointment count (or full-time equivalents), we adopted head counts in the reporting of faculty composition for the other 18 institutions.

The specific fields within STEM at each institution included in this table are provided in Appendix 1.

Other notes:

(1) Data for only four years were available for University of Puerto Rico, Humacao.

(2) For Georgia Tech, faculty at the assistant, associate, full, and regents professor levels are reported here. Data from the psychology department were included, because they could not be separated from available school- level data.

(3) For Virginia Tech, Psychology was excluded from STEM.

(4) For University of California at Irvine, Schools of Business, Social Ecology, and Social Sciences were not included in STEM. STEM fields included biological sciences, engineering, information and computer sciences, physical, and school of medicine–basic sciences. The distribution of STEM faculty by rank over the years was summed by school based on the available Web data.

(5) For the University of Maryland, Baltimore County, data from the geography department were not included since these data were not consistently available over all years.

(6) For the University of Rhode Island, only faculty data between 2004 and 2007 were available.

(7) For University of Alabama, Birmingham, faculty data between 2005 and 2007 only were available from the annual reports. The department of Finance, Economics and Quantitative Methods in the School of Business (included in the 2007 annual report) has been excluded.

91). In particular, four institutions (University of Montana, University of Puerto Rico, Humacao, Hunter College, and University of Alabama, Birmingham) had less than 30 women STEM faculty (between nine and 29) included in their projects.

Size—Percentage of Women STEM Faculty Included in the ADVANCE Project: The majority of universities (16 out of 19) had no more than 21% women faculty over the course of their *ADVANCE* IT grant periods.

Institutional STEM faculty size characteristics of the sample are summarized in Table 3.3.

Sample Characteristics by Discipline: Natural Sciences, Engineering, and Social and Behavioral Sciences

Our data analyses also examine the changes from *ADVANCE* IT efforts in the workforce participation of women faculty in the disciplines of natural sciences, engineering, and social and behavioral sciences (SBS) within the 19 universities. The fields and subfields of these disciplines vary by institution. In our analyses, natural sciences generally included astronomy, biology, chemistry, physics, mathematics, statistics, and other related areas. Medicine-related departments, such as school of medicine basic science departments (SOMBS) and departments in a school of veterinary medicine or school of pharmacy were not counted in natural sciences. Four out of 19 universities provided valid faculty data from the basic sciences departments of their schools of medicine. Given the small number of universities involved, for consistency purposes we excluded medicine disciplines from counts in natural sciences. Engineering included multiple areas such as biomedical engineering, chemical engineering, civil engineering, electrical engineering, materials science, mechanical engineering, and other related areas. Social and behavioral sciences generally include anthropology, economics, political science, sociology, psychology, and other related areas. Business- or management-school departments were not counted in SBS, given the small number of universities that involved these departments in their *ADVANCE* projects. Four out of 19 universities included selected departments in their schools of business or management in their *ADVANCE* projects. Details of the specific disciplines defined for each *ADVANCE* university are provided in Appendices 2, 3, and 4.

Size—The Number of Departments within Discipline: The number of departments within disciplines in at least one year of the *ADVANCE* IT period at the 19 universities is summarized in Table 3.4.

Size—The Number of S&E Faculty within Discipline: The total number of S&E faculty within the disciplines in at least one year of the *ADVANCE* IT period at the 19 universities is summarized in Table 3.5.

Size—The Number of Women Faculty within Discipline: The number of women faculty within disciplines in at least one year of the *ADVANCE* IT period at the 19 universities are summarized in Table 3.6.

Table 3.4 Number of Departments within Disciplines over the Duration of the *ADVANCE* IT Projects

Disciplines (# of *ADVANCE* universities with valid data)	1–5 Depts.	6–11 Depts.	12 Depts. or more
Natural sciences (n = 19)	4	10	5
Engineering (n = 16)	5	10	1
Social and behavioral sciences (n = 13)	6	4	3

Table 3.5 Number of Faculty within Disciplines over the Duration of the *ADVANCE* IT Projects

Disciplines (# of *ADVANCE* universities with valid data)	Less than 100 faculty members	100–210 faculty members	211–600 faculty members
Natural sciences (n = 19)	5	6	8
Engineering (n = 16)	7	6	3
Social and behavioral sciences (n = 13)	8	4	1

Table 3.6 Number of Women Faculty within Disciplines over the Duration of the *ADVANCE* IT Projects

Disciplines (# of *ADVANCE* universities with valid data)	30 women faculty or less	31–50 women faculty	51–80 women faculty
Natural sciences (n = 19)	7	9	3
Engineering (n = 16)	12	3	1
Social and behavioral sciences (n = 13)*	8	1	3

Note: *One university, whose *ADVANCE* project included more than 200 women SBS faculty, was not included in this table.

Table 3.7 Percentage of Women Faculty within Disciplines over the Duration of the *ADVANCE* IT Projects

Disciplines (# of *ADVANCE* universities with valid data)	15%	16–30%	30–46%
Natural sciences (n = 19)	3	15	1
Engineering (n = 16)	13	3	0
Social and behavioral sciences (n = 13)	0	0	13

Size—The Percentage of Women Faculty within Discipline: The percentage of women faculty within disciplines in at least one year of the *ADVANCE* IT period at the 19 universities is summarized in Table 3.7.

In brief, women faculty in SBS represented the highest percentage of women faculty, followed by women faculty in natural sciences. Women faculty in engineering represented the lowest percentage. In four universities (University of Maryland, Baltimore County, University of Washington, University of Michigan, Georgia Tech), the percentage of women faculty in engineering was at a comparable level with the percentage of women faculty in natural sciences. Overall, the sample data confirm that women faculty are particularly underrepresented in the disciplines of engineering and natural sciences, as compared to SBS fields.

Data Sources

As most *ADVANCE* IT institutions from the first two cohorts had completed or were close to completing their projects at the time of our data collection, a wide range of documents pertaining to these projects have accumulated over the years and are accessible to the general public on their Web sites. For purposes of this study, we analyzed the annual reports, final reports, research publications, evaluation reports, and Web sites of the sample of 19 universities. Most of these data were drawn from documents and materials available at each *ADVANCE* IT project's Web site and through the NSF *ADVANCE* web portal at www.portal.advance.vt.edu/. In some instances, we made direct requests for information to the principal investigators (PIs) of institutions whose data were not available online, and received their reports and permission to use the data.

Data on the workforce participation of S&E faculty by gender, rank, and department (i.e., *ADVANCE* indicator data) for each institution were obtained from the following primary sources:

- Georgia Tech data were retrieved on December 15, 2009, from http://www.advance.gatech.edu/archive/files/FinalGTReport.pdf.
- Hunter College data were drawn from Benchmark Data reports retrieved on December 15, 2009, from http://www.hunter.cuny.edu/genderequity/benchmarks.html.
- New Mexico State University's tenure-line faculty data were drawn from "Table 4: Distribution within Sex and Field of Rank and Tenure Status of NMSU Faculty," in their annual reports, retrieved on December 15, 2009, from http://www.advance.nmsu.edu/Resources/Data_Reports/index.html.
- University of California, Irvine data were drawn from data and reports retrieved on December 15, 2009, from http://advance.uci.edu/.
- University of Colorado Boulder data were drawn from annual reports provided to us by their project PIs and used with permission.

- University of Michigan data were drawn from annual reports retrieved on December 15, 2009, from http://sitemaker.umich.edu/advance/institutional_indicator_reports.
- University of Puerto Rico, Humacao data were drawn from Table 9, 2004–05 annual report, retrieved on December 15, 2009, from http://advance.uprh.edu/Baseline_Data2005.pdf. Only the first four years of project data were provided in 2004–05 annual report.
- University of Washington data were retrieved on December 15, 2009, from WISELI annual reports at http://www.engr.washington.edu/advance/resources/ADV%20Final%20report-2001–2007-FINAL%20with%20APPENDIX.pdf.
- University of Wisconsin, Madison data were retrieved on December 15, 2009, from http://wiseli.engr.wisc.edu/docs/AnnReport_IT_2007FINAL.pdf.
- Case Western Reserve University data were drawn from annual reports retrieved on December 15, 2009, from http://www.case.edu/admin/aces/final.htm.
- Columbia University data were drawn from the table "Full-time Faculty Distribution by Gender and Tenure Status," retrieved on December 15, 2009, from www.columbia.edu/cu/opir/abstract/faculty_staff.html.
- Kansas State University data were drawn from summaries of the NSF indicator tables of their annual reports, retrieved on October 15, 2010, from http://advance.ksu.edu/publications/ and annual reports sent to us by their project PIs and used with permission.
- University of Alabama, Birmingham data were drawn from annual reports retrieved on October 15, 2010, from http://main.uab.edu/Sites/ADVANCE/progress/reports/.
- University of Maryland, Baltimore County data were drawn from annual reports provided to us by their project PIs and used with permission.
- University of Montana data were drawn from annual reports provided to us by their project PIs and used with permission.
- University of Rhode Island data were drawn from annual reports retrieved on December 15, 2009, from http://www.uri.edu/advance/measuring_progress/NSF_reports.html.
- University of Texas, El Paso data were drawn from annual reports retrieved on December 15, 2009, from http://academics.utep.edu/Default.aspx?tabid=40133 and from appendices provided to us by their project PIs and used with permission.
- Utah State University data were drawn from annual reports retrieved on December 15, 2009, from http://advance.usu.edu/reports.aspx.
- Virginia Tech data were drawn from annual reports retrieved on December 15, 2009, from http://www.advance.vt.edu/Measuring_Progress/Measuring_Progress.html.

Although the workforce participation data were collected primarily in fall 2009, in some cases *ADVANCE* projects may have continued beyond this date through no-cost extensions permitted by NSF. Thus, the data may not reflect the actual final year of the *ADVANCE* project for some institutions.

Additionally, our analyses drew on interviews with 54 principal investigators, co-principal investigators, university administrators, team leaders, and senior faculty at these 19 *ADVANCE* IT projects about the nature and outcomes of their efforts. Results of these interviews were presented at the 2006 NSF *ADVANCE* PI Meeting in Washington, DC (Bilimoria & Valian 2006).

Data Analyses

We conducted the following types of data analyses as follows.

(1) Descriptive analyses of institutional transformation initiatives, particularly descriptions of *pipeline and career trajectory initiatives* (individual and organizational), and descriptions of *initiatives related to institutional climate.*

(2) Descriptive analyses of institutionalization outcomes obtained through *ADVANCE* IT at the 19 universities studied, including examples of the creation of
a. New *positions*, offices, and structures
b. New and modified *policies*
c. New *practices*, resources and supports, and
d. New and continued *programs.*

(3) Statistical analyses of the workforce participation of STEM faculty by gender, rank, and discipline through the following methods:
a. Differences in women and men faculty composition over *ADVANCE* IT award durations.
b. Analyses of the numbers of institutions (out of 19) reporting positive, negative, or no change in the composition of women and men faculty over *ADVANCE* IT award durations.
c. Trend analyses of the proportions of women faculty in comparison with national reference groups.
d. Analyses of changes in women and men faculty workforce participation by discipline (natural sciences, engineering, and social and behavioral sciences).
e. Differences in women's participation in leadership (numbers and percentages of women department chairs, senior university administrators, and holders of endowed chairs) over *ADVANCE* IT award durations.

(4) Descriptions of various efforts to better include women scientists and engineers within the academic workplace, particularly through analysis of climate surveys and interview or focus-group studies.

Analyses of Institutional Transformation Initiatives and Institutionalization Outcomes

Expanding the pilot research reported in Bilimoria, Joy, and Liang (2008), we aimed at providing in this book more details about "best practice" organizational change initiatives utilized, and institutionalization outcomes employed, to engender institutional transformation in academic S&E. Primarily, we reviewed the various initiatives listed on the Web sites, NSF-mandated annual and quarterly reports, publications, and research and evaluation reports of the 19 universities in our sample.

Through the reviewing process, we paid special attention to factors that impede or facilitate institutional transformation as described by the *ADVANCE* institutions in their annual reports, such as the successes, difficulties, challenges, barriers, and lessons reported. We also drew on insights learned from our own experience as *ADVANCE* IT project leaders at our own institution, as well as interviews of 54 *ADVANCE* IT project PIs, team leaders, and senior faculty at *ADVANCE* universities about the nature and outcomes of their institutionalization efforts (Bilimoria & Valian 2006). These facilitating and constraining factors are described in Chapter 4.

We specifically reviewed the many initiatives undertaken across the *ADVANCE* institutions and classified them into two groups according to their purpose and intended targets: individual career-related (microlevel) and institutional system, procedures, and climate-related (macrolevel) initiatives. In Chapter 5, we describe the "best practice" initiatives that have been frequently used across the 19 *ADVANCE* institutions, highlighting key initiatives from each institution and, where possible, describing follow-up evaluations and assessments of their effectiveness.

In Chapter 6, we summarize how these change initiatives have been made permanent in the 19 institutions. We describe these institutionalization activities employed in four ways: the creation of new positions, new policies, new practices, and new programs.

Changes in Women and Men STEM Faculty Composition over *ADVANCE* IT Award Durations

Results of the statistical analyses of *ADVANCE* institutional transformation outcomes are provided in Chapter 7. As described above and detailed in Appendix 1, STEM was defined as comprising the natural sciences, technology, engineering, and mathematics disciplines only.

For the analyses of *overall faculty* in STEM, we obtained multiple years' data for all the 19 *ADVANCE* participating institutions. In the analysis of faculty composition *by academic rank*, we obtained data from all institutions except one (Columbia University).[2] Analyses were conducted for the number of faculty by gender at each rank, and the percentage of women faculty within rank.

To identify changes in the workforce participation of women faculty through *ADVANCE* IT, comparisons were made between the baseline year and the final year of each NSF award. A baseline year in general refers to the first NSF-funded year of an *ADVANCE* IT project. In some cases where data from the first funded year of the project were not available, we used the second funded year as the baseline year. Similarly, a final year generally refers to the last NSF-funded year of an *ADVANCE* program, including any no-cost extension years. Year 5 is a typical final year for most of the 19 *ADVANCE* institutions in our sample. In a few cases where faculty data were reported during a no-cost extension period, we used Year 6 or Year 7 as a final year, depending on the availability of the data. For two institutions (University of Puerto Rico, Humacao and University of Rhode Island), Year 4 was used as a final year for the purposes of this study and this was the most recent year for which outcome data were available at the time of the study.

Since our overall sample size was small (n = 19), we conducted a nonparametric test for two related samples—the Wilcoxon signed-ranks test—to test differences between paired scores. The Wilcoxon signed-rank test considers information about both the sign of the differences and the magnitude of the differences between pairs. It tests the null hypothesis that two related medians are the same. We used the Wilcoxon signed-ranks test to compare the number of women (or men faculty) at each academic rank, as well as the percentage of women faculty at each rank, between the baseline year and the final year of each *ADVANCE* IT project.

Analyses of the Numbers of Institutions (out of 19) Reporting Positive, Negative or No Change in the Workforce participation of Women and Men Faculty over the *ADVANCE* IT Award Durations

We counted the number of institutions out of 19 reporting increases, decreases, or no change in the representation of women and men faculty over the *ADVANCE* IT award durations. By providing a comparison over the same time period between changes in the numbers of women and men faculty at each institution, we sought to be able to identify whether targeted efforts to increase the workforce participation of women faculty through *ADVANCE* IT have been effective.

Trend Analyses of the Growth in the Workforce participation of Women Faculty in Comparison with National Reference Groups

In the trend analyses, we provide appropriate biannual comparisons with national reference groups using NSF's Survey of Doctorate Recipients (SDR). The Survey of Doctorate Recipients gathers information from individuals who have obtained a doctoral degree in a science, engineering, or health field. The survey is conducted every two years and is a longitudinal survey that follows recipients of research doctorates from U.S. institutions until age 76 (www.nsf.gov/statistics/srvydoctoratework/). Data from SDR are published biennially in detailed statistical tables in the series "Characteristics of Doctoral Scientists and Engineers in the United States" (www. nsf.gov/statistics/doctoratework/).

SDR data on faculty composition were provided to us in September 2010 by Daniel J. Foley, project officer, Human Resources Statistics Program, National Science Foundation. We obtained data about the composition of faculty at samples of four-year colleges and universities, as well as at very high and high research universities (RU/VH and RU/H) only, by field, sex, and rank in 2001, 2003, and 2006, respectively. Therefore, in our trend analyses, data drawn from SDR serve as national reference groups of STEM faculty at each rank and each discipline. We discuss trends in women's workforce participation at *ADVANCE* IT institutions relative to these national reference groups of samples of women faculty at four-year colleges and universities as well as at RU/VH and RU/H only, in STEM, engineering, natural sciences, and SBS disciplines, respectively.

At the time of our data analysis, SDR data were available for three years (2001, 2003, and 2006). 2008 SDR data while collected were not available for public use. Data were drawn from http://sestat.nsf.gov/docs/tally06/nsdrmem.html and http://sestat.nsf.gov/docs/tally03/nsdrmem.html. Data were selected for SDR respondents (1) whose principal employer was an educational institution, (2) who worked at four-year college or university, other than a medical school, (3) whose faculty rank was assistant, or associate, or full professors, and (4) whose field of study for first U.S. S&E or health PhD (major group) was in one of the following areas: (a) biological, agricultural, and environmental life sciences; (b) computer and information sciences; (c) mathematics and statistics; (d) physical sciences; (e) engineering; (f) psychology; and (g) social sciences.

Analyses of Changes in Women and Men Faculty's Workforce Participation by Discipline

The analyses used in this section were identical to those conducted to assess the changes in the workforce participation of women and men faculty in S&E over the duration of the *ADVANCE* IT awards. Separate analyses were conducted for each discipline (engineering, natural sciences, and social and behavioral sciences) to assess the nature of changes in the workforce participation of women over *ADVANCE* IT periods in these disciplines.

Differences in Women's Participation in Leadership (Numbers and Percentages of Women Department Chairs, Senior University Administrators, and Holders of Endowed Chairs) over *ADVANCE* IT Award Durations

Similar to analyses of the changes in faculty workforce participation by rank, analyses were conducted for changes in women's participation in academic leadership. Three indicators of academic leadership were used to assess whether changes occurred over *ADVANCE* IT periods: women department chairs, women in senior university administration, and women holding endowed chairs or named professorships.

4 Factors Facilitating Institutional Transformation

In this chapter, we describe the internal, external, and research/assessment factors that facilitated *ADVANCE* institutional change, as well as discuss two *inhibitors* of institutional transformation and their solutions at the *ADVANCE* institutions: faculty resistance and institutional uncertainties and constraints.

INTERNAL FACILITATORS OF INSTITUTIONAL TRANSFORMATION

Building on Eckel and Kezar (2003), who describe the core strategies common to transforming higher-education institutions, other higher-education change researchers (e.g., Burnes 1996; Rajagopalan & Spreitzer 1996; Kezar 2001; Fox 2008), and our own interviews with *ADVANCE* IT team members from the first 19 universities (Bilimoria & Valian 2006), below we identify five themes—senior administrative support and involvement, a transformation champion, collaborative leadership, widespread and synergistic participation across units, and visible actions—as the internal factors that facilitated *ADVANCE* institutional transformation.

Senior Administrative Support and Involvement

Engagement of and championing by top leaders are prerequisites for successful organizational change (Garvin 2000; Eckel & Kezar 2003). In many *ADVANCE* institutions, senior university administrators (e.g., presidents, provosts, deans and their staffs) as well as senior faculty leaders (e.g., faculty senate officers) were proactive in communicating the importance of the overall project to varied constituencies, providing resources, guiding or supporting the change process, authorizing policy changes, holding units accountable for progress on goals, and creating new administrative structures to support the transformational efforts. As reported by *ADVANCE* PIs and Co-PIs, this direct or indirect access to and support from the highest levels in university administration has been critical in bringing about changes in institutional policies, infrastructure, and climate to address the recruitment, advancement, and retention of women and minority faculty, as well as to creating new positions and offices for the implementation of future changes (Bilimoria & Valian 2006; Plummer 2006).

A Champion of Institutional Transformation

Critical to the success of an *ADVANCE* project has been the significant role played by an institutional transformation champion.[1] This champion, usually a respected senior faculty member or senior administrative leader, often served as the PI of the *ADVANCE* project. Familiar with the reality of their campus culture, informed about the factors responsible for the underrepresentation of women and minority male faculty in academic S&E, and committed to transforming the institutional culture on their campuses, these champions have served to create, relay, and relentlessly pursue an urgent transformational vision, bring university leadership on board with change initiatives, garner new resources, engender creative opportunities to deploy change initiatives, energize and collaborate with diverse others to drive changes in structures, policies and practices, lead a multidisciplinary team, monitor progress and adapt to changing circumstances, and sustain their projects beyond initial funding.

Such champions have been referenced in previous writings related to organizational change and institutionalization, primarily as *tempered radicals*—boundary spanners who undertake incremental but transformative change tactics to improve their systems (Meyerson & Scully 1995; Meyerson 2003); *institutional entrepreneurs*—internal actors who take deliberate actions to achieve specific interests (DiMaggio 1988); *organizational catalysts*—change agents who are unusually adept at leveraging various sources of credibility, power, and support to mobilize change (Sturm 2006); and *lead change agents*—actors embedded in multiple institutions and fluent in multiple institutional languages, whose personal institutional legitimacy enables them to be effective in engendering change (Meyerson & Tompkins 2007). One such institutional transformation champion, Dr. Abigail Stewart, the PI of the University of Michigan's *ADVANCE* award, was described as "effective, in part, because she was embedded in multiple institutional environments. This embeddedness allowed her to leverage her connection to university elites, sustain her legitimacy as both a scholar and activist, and maintain her critical consciousness and connection to distributed allies and leaders throughout the university" (Meyerson & Tompkins 2007, 304).

Our interviews with the *ADVANCE* leadership teams of the 19 institutions indicated the presence of such an institutional transformation champion at many universities. In most cases, this person was the principal investigator (PI) of their *ADVANCE* project. To better understand the functioning of the institutional transformation champion, we looked into the backgrounds and institutional positions of the PIs listed in *ADVANCE*

IT proposals in greater detail. Out of the 19 projects studied, one institution had appointed its president as the *ADVANCE* PI, five institutions had PIs whose primary appointments were in the offices of university Provosts, and three institutions had PIs who were deans or associate deans of schools/colleges. The remaining ten PIs were typically faculty members primarily from S&E disciplines (e.g., physics, geology, biological sciences, psychology, sociology, women's health research, earth sciences) but also from other disciplines (e.g., English, women's and gender studies), with scholarly reputations that enabled them to gain attention and support from senior university administrators on the basis of their institutional credibility. Of the ten faculty members who were PIs of the 19 *ADVANCE* projects, four were associate professors at the start of their *ADVANCE* projects and one was a senior research scientist; subsequently, three of these associate professors were promoted to the professor rank. At the start of these 19 *ADVANCE* projects, three PIs held endowed chairs; subsequently, eight of these persons were appointed to endowed positions. Over the course of their *ADVANCE* projects and beyond, several PIs and Co-PIs received other promotions and administrative job opportunities to expand their responsibilities within their own or at other universities, including promotions to positions such as university president, provost, associate provost, vice chancellor for research, dean, associate dean, and professor.

Collaborative Leadership

Leadership plays a critical role in institutional transformation because it shapes organizational vision, sends institutional messages and signals, and has the authority to implement change (Fox 2008). Establishing a clear vision of the end state is considered most crucial by organizational change theorists (Jick 1991; Kotter 1995; Galpin 1996; Garvin 2000). The leadership teams of *ADVANCE* institutions have established clear visions, goals, and intermittent milestones for their projects. In our review of the institutional transformation goals and approaches employed by the 19 *ADVANCE* universities studied, we determined that their goals and processes mirrored models established in the literature on organizational change, especially gender equity-related change. These *ADVANCE* IT projects relied on a *dual outcome focus* (Meyerson & Fletcher 2000), which suggests that the likelihood of successful change increases when both gender equity and work effectiveness are highlighted as critical goals of the change effort. They were grounded in a *small wins change strategy* (Weick 1984) which encourages a focus on small, finite, doable projects that result in quick, concrete, and visible results and the building of momentum from these results to create cascading, organization-wide effects of change. Goals targeted in these projects drew on four key *gender equity frames* (Kolb et al. 1998): equip women (Frame 1), create equal opportunity (Frame 2), value difference (Frame 3), and re-vision the work culture (Frame 4). Following the eight *phases of strategic change* identified by Kotter (1996), *ADVANCE* change leadership teams at these universities established a sense of urgency, created a guiding coalition, developed a change vision and strategy, communicated the vision to stakeholders, empowered broad-based action, generated short-term wins, consolidated gains to produce more change, and anchored new approaches in their university cultures.

As described by Shaffer (2010), the *ADVANCE* IT leadership team at Case Western Reserve University (CWRU) met weekly over the duration of their *ADVANCE* IT award in a 60–90 minute standing meeting consisting of the PI, co-principal investigators (Co-PIs), coordinator, primary collaborators, and the evaluation team, when available. The purposes of these meetings were to report on activities and initiatives, facilitate planning and problem solving, enhance collaboration and synergy across efforts, and allow for guests (such as deans and department chairs) to be regularly scheduled in. Outcomes reported as occurring from these meetings included coordination of efforts, information sharing, rapid-response problem solving, and a feeling of mutual support and teamwork.

To foster sustainability and wide-scale impact, the composition of *ADVANCE* IT leadership teams was deliberately cross-functional as encouraged by NSF, drawing from different STEM disciplines and units across the universities, and bringing in social-science knowledge to inform the interventions and innovations. In fact, based on the experience of these 19 universities, subsequent *ADVANCE* IT proposals sought by NSF have required the inclusion of social-science experts in the leadership team in order to bring in research-based knowledge and evidence-based best practices about gender equity institutional change.

Widespread and Synergistic Participation across Campus

Organizational change models stress the importance of having change agents spread across ranks and functions in an organization for the message of change to spread, creative ideas to emerge, and grassroots change to take place (Kotter 1995; Garvin 2000; Eckel & Kezar 2003). The 19 *ADVANCE* IT projects we studied encouraged widespread and synergistic participation across units within each institution. These projects utilized a distributed leadership/key change agent model of faculty leadership that seeks to educate and empower faculty leaders to be nonpositional, generate and direct energy toward institutional transformation, become accountable for outcomes, base action on data and evidence, create networks for sharing of best practices, build toward agreement, be emergent and flexible, shape discourse, and be willing to take risks (cf. Faculty Leadership Model, Indiana University, http://www.pkal.org/documents/IndianaUniversityFacultyLeadership.cfm).

Highlighting the importance of engagement and participation across campus for successful transformation, these 19 *ADVANCE* IT projects sought to make the constituencies affected by change become the agents of change (cf. Armenakis & Bedeian 1999). These projects engaged and involved academic administrators (deans and chairs) as well as male and female faculty at all ranks in the various activities and dissemination of the change efforts (cf. Mento, Jones, & Dirndorfer 2002). The roles these stakeholders played include involvement in designing and implementing activities of transformation (Fox 2008), and participation as a critical mass of faculty members in policy and decision making (cf. Etzkowitz et al. 1994) or as organizational catalysts who are in a position to enlist others to act as change agents (Sturm 2006, 2007a, 2007b). This latter role of organizational catalysts describes influential senior faculty who are situated at points of intersection within the university and who carry organizational legitimacy and informal power from their distinguished record of scholarship and from a track record of advancing women and minority faculty in the academy. For example, the University of Michigan's Committee on Strategies and Tactics for Recruiting to Improve Diversity and Excellence (STRIDE) consisted of respected senior faculty members trained in issues of gender equity bias who provide information and advice to administrators and search committees about best practices in recruitment and retention of diverse faculty members. Similarly, equity advisors (respected senior faculty) were appointed at the University of California, Irvine to monitor recruitment activities, coordinate advising for career advancement, and counsel faculty regarding equity issues, including salary.

As noted in several final or annual reports, the combination of high-level administrative attention to *ADVANCE* issues and widespread participation across campuses in *ADVANCE* activities enabled the deployment and institutionalization of creative initiatives to respond to campus-wide concerns about gender equity, diversity, and inclusion. For example, at Case Western Reserve University, several faculty and student committees and groups were directly involved in their *ADVANCE* IT project, including their Center for Women, faculty senate executive committee and standing committees on women and minority faculty, the president's campus-wide advisory councils on women and minority affairs, women students in STEM, and women faculty in academic medicine groups. At the University of California, Irvine, the offices of Equal Opportunity and Diversity, Academic Personnel, and Institutional Research were key partners with their *ADVANCE* project leadership team throughout their five-year award period. At New Mexico State University, the ongoing involvement of faculty and administrators from across campus was considered essential in changing the institution and for garnering support for the continuation of *ADVANCE* programs after the end of the award period.

Visible Actions and Outcomes

A final internal facilitating factor at the *ADVANCE* institutions was giving visibility to project actions and outcomes. Armenakis and Bedeian (1999) recommend the use of multiple strategies for communication of organizational transformation efforts, and *ADVANCE* institutions have accordingly attracted internal and external attention through myriad ways. Each *ADVANCE* IT project created its own Web site, as well as several brochures, newsletters, event advertisements, press releases, resource guides, and tool kits. Internal and external advisory boards were constituted and meetings convened to inform and educate members about *ADVANCE*-related issues and activities. Throughout their *ADVANCE* award periods, leadership teams have made numerous presentations to formal and informal faculty and administrative groups, including departments, schools/colleges, faculty councils, faculty senates, deans' councils, department chairs' councils, and boards of trustees. They have held update meetings, town hall meetings, and community-building meetings.

Another way that *ADVANCE* institutions have drawn attention to issues of gender equity and inclusion in STEM is through widespread Web publicity about external awards received by women scientists and engineers (e.g., the University of Wisconsin, Madison, the University of Washington) as well as the creation of new internal awards and events that celebrate the achievements of women in S&E. For example, at Case Western Reserve University women faculty, nominated by their deans for excellence in scholarship, are recognized as Women of Achievement at an annual luncheon. *ADVANCE* projects have also instituted faculty mentoring awards at some of the 19 universities studied, including the University of Rhode Island and the University of Wisconsin, Madison. Other *ADVANCE* projects have utilized their funding in part to award named professorships for limited terms to prominent women scientists (e.g., the *ADVANCE* Professorships at Georgia Institute of Technology) and research fellowships (e.g., the *ADVANCE* VT Fellowships at Virginia Tech).

Overall, the importance of these internal factors in facilitating organizational transformation cannot be overstated. In one university where the overall number of women S&E faculty had declined at the time of its *ADVANCE* mid-project evaluation, several of these internal factors were missing. Its evaluation report pointed out that awareness about change initiatives was generally low throughout the university, activities were limited only to selected women (male faculty and students were not included in interventions), the project's collaboration with other university offices occurred only to a small degree, and focused professional development programs such as mentoring and coaching were absent.

EXTERNAL FACILITATORS OF INSTITUTIONAL TRANSFORMATION

Certain external environmental factors also played a significant role in facilitating organizational change in our sample. Two external factors, in particular, enabled the exchange of information, resources, ideas, best practices, and solutions among the *ADVANCE* institutions.

A Network of Peer Institutions

Our review identified that the network of peer institutions undergoing transformation greatly enhanced each institution's innovations by sharing resources, ideas and best practices, and by having collective training and discussion sessions (cf. Astin & Associates 2001; Fox 2008). Organizations oftentimes undertake change initiatives inspired by the examples of other organizations that have benefited from similar projects, seeking to model after the best practices (Barnett & Carroll 1995). In the case of the 19 *ADVANCE* institutions, the involvement of peer institutions went much further than simply serving as passive role models for change. The network became an active resource exchange and support forum for effecting change within each cohort of institutions. Through formal connections (annual PI meetings, research presentations at conferences, and an electronic list) the 19 *ADVANCE* institutions shared learnings and best practices, accumulated a substantive knowledge base on organizational change and gender equity, created and shared tool kits and resources, and undertook collaborative research projects and consulting services to further their overall objectives of institutional transformation.

The multiplicative effects of the network on gender equity transformation have been reported by many *ADVANCE* IT institutions in their annual reports as well as by their PIs in informal discussions with us. For example, the idea for school/college liaisons implemented at Virginia Tech was borrowed from the University of California, Irvine project's equity advisor positions, but the role of the liaison at Virginia Tech was designed to be less formal than at its original institution. The faculty flux chart developed by the Gender Equity Project at Hunter College, CUNY was implemented by many other institutions, such as Case Western Reserve University, Kansas State University, and University of Maryland, Baltimore County. Similarly, innovative practices in peer mentoring (e.g., University of Texas, El Paso) and speed mentoring (e.g., Case Western Reserve University) were quickly tried in other institutions. Professional individual academic coaching of deans, chairs, and women faculty in S&E, pioneered at Case Western Reserve University, was modified and implemented at the University of Michigan, Virginia Tech, and Columbia University, and later at Louisiana Tech. Leadership development workshops offered by the University of Washington were attended by several PIs, Co-PIs, and department chairs from other *ADVANCE* universities. Best practices around external evaluation and external advisory boards were rapidly shared among network organizations.

External Legitimizing and Convening Authority

A second external factor facilitating transformation was the role of an external institutional authority that supports, convenes, and legitimizes institutional change. Many organizational change theories posit that external factors (such as governmental regulations, economic or trade conditions, competition, and technology) influence an organization's decision to change by threatening its very existence (cf. Barnett & Carroll 1995; Armenakis & Bedeian 1999). Our review found that an external institution (in this case, NSF) may alternatively serve as a partner and facilitator, taking an active, catalytic role and benevolent interest in organizational change.

Legitimacy is a generalized perception and assumption that the actions of an entity are desirable, proper, or appropriate within some socially constructed system of norms, values, beliefs, and definitions (Suchman 1995). Institutional theorists posit that compliance with the directives of external agencies such as the government, legal system, and funding agencies increases an organization's legitimacy (Meyer & Rowan 1977; DiMaggio & Powell 1983). For the 19 *ADVANCE* institutions, NSF served not just as the agency that provided and monitored funding. Rather, NSF was seen as the leader of positive institutional change: adopting a developmental role, convening interaction among institutions, and providing continuous, constructive, and collaborative guidance for change-project implementation. Our interviews with the PIs and key leaders of the first two *ADVANCE* institution cohorts (Bilimoria & Valian 2006) revealed that such backing from NSF was crucial in the success of program initiatives among university administrators and male scientists in particular, by giving both moral legitimacy to the objective of transformation and procedural legitimacy to the specific change initiatives (cf. Suchman 1995).

Uniquely, the institutional transformation awards granted through *ADVANCE* were shaped as cooperative agreements between NSF and the awardee institution. These are distinctive forms of partnership between NSF and each awardee university, specifying the elements of the organizational change interventions to be undertaken and the outcomes to be measured. These cooperative agreements required contracts to be signed by senior institutional leaders facilitating not just their buy-in but their ownership of the changes to come. Such contracts also allowed the continuation of *ADVANCE* project activities in the face of turnover in senior leadership at these institutions. Regular reporting to NSF (on a quarterly, annual, and final project basis), a mid-project site visit by an NSF *ADVANCE* panel of reviewers, and mid-project and final project reportings of contracted external evaluations allowed NSF to take not just an active oversight role over the change activities instituted but also a supportive role of information sharing and developmental advice.

The annual *ADVANCE* PI meetings convened by NSF were instrumental in advancing the transformational work being undertaken within the network of institutions. Attendees at these meetings consisted of PIs and key personnel not only of institutional transformation awardees, but of PAID and IT-CATALYST awardees. Most recently, professional societies and nonprofit organizations have been included in the group of institutions receiving NSF support, in addition to institutions of higher education; these groups have been gradually integrated within the cohorts attending the *ADVANCE* PI annual meetings. As the NSF *ADVANCE* program has expanded, offshoots of cohort and regional groups have begun to coalesce, complementary to the larger annual meeting of *ADVANCE* institutions. For example, in June 2010, a Midwest Regional *ADVANCE* group was formed and a two-day meeting convened at Purdue University (an *ADVANCE* IT Cohort 4 institution), bringing together several grantee institutions from the Midwest.

In addition to the annual meetings, NSF also supported the creation and maintenance of a clearinghouse for information on *ADVANCE* and gender equity, diversity and inclusion issues—an *ADVANCE* Web portal at http://www.portal.advance.vt.edu/. This Web site, developed and operated by Virginia Tech, one of the Cohort 2 institutions in our sample, serves as a stand-alone, comprehensive source to provide direct information and links relevant to gender equity-related institutional transformation.

NSF's legitimizing and convening role as an external institutional authority encouraging enhanced equity, diversity, and inclusion in the U.S. STEM workforce was referenced by Alice Hogan, *ADVANCE*'s founding program officer, in a recent interview: "NSF may be unique among the federal agencies that deal with science, because its original mandate not only gave it the responsibility to fund research, but also tasked it explicitly with ensuring the national supply of scientists and engineers" (LaVaque-Manty 2007, 23). More recently, there have been calls to encourage programmatic gender equity initiatives through other federal funding agencies such as the National Institutes of Health, the Defense Advanced Research Projects Agency, and the Department of Energy (e.g., Rosser & Taylor 2009).

ASSESSMENT, EVALUATION, AND RESEARCH IN SUPPORT OF INSTITUTIONAL TRANSFORMATION

Our study identified a third facilitator of institutional transformation—assessment, evaluation, and research—as crucial elements of the organizational change efforts undertaken at the 19 *ADVANCE* institutions we studied. In most organizational change projects, the role of research is, at best, to monitor progress. Some change theorists, however, do acknowledge the need to diagnose and analyze the current situation to generate recommendations and to conduct pilot tests in addition to measuring outcomes (e.g., Galpin 1996).

We observed that a key building block of *ADVANCE* institutional transformation efforts was systematic assessment, research, and evaluation on which to base interventions, track effectiveness, and provide evidence of progress (see Frehill 2006). We found that *ADVANCE* institutions undertook four types of transformation-facilitating activities in this regard— systematically tracking key indicators of gender equity, diversity, and inclusion, undertaking workplace climate assessments, conducting other research and evaluation in support of change, and improving institutional data-collection and analysis systems.

Systematically Tracking Key Indicators of Gender Equity, Diversity, and Inclusion

The measurement of transformational outcomes was primarily achieved through annual tracking of several key indicators required by NSF, such as faculty composition by rank and gender; tenure, promotion, and attrition rates; years in rank and time at institution; and compensation, resources, and space allocation. These indicators were developed by program officers and PIs at the first meeting of *ADVANCE* institutional transformation awardees, and subsequently clarified and standardized as a tool kit for broader use by an *ADVANCE* Institutional Transformation Indicators Working Group (Frehill & Doeller 2005). Table 4.1 describes the NSF indicators required to be furnished annually or periodically by IT funding recipients, as well as additional indicators frequently adopted by *ADVANCE* institutions to track progress in gender equity, diversity, and inclusion.

Similar to these *ADVANCE* gender equity indicators, in 2006 the American Association of University Professors (AAUP) released a report highlighting four gender equity indicators for higher-education institutions, and comparing these indicators for each college and university against national norms for women's: (1) employment status, (2) tenure status, (3) full professor rank, and (4) average salary. The report concluded that "At most colleges and universities there remains significant room for improvement in fully integrating women into the faculty (West & Curtis 2006, 16).

Supplementing the tracked indicator data, several *ADVANCE* institutions made use of a number of additional monitoring tools such as salary-equity studies, cohort analyses, and flux charts. For example, the University of California, Irvine undertook an annual pay equity study which applied the model recommended by the American Association of University Professors to identify women and minority faculty members who appear to be underpaid (see http://www.ap.uci.edu/Equity/studies/index.html). The University of Michigan undertook a cohort analysis in which specific male and female faculty members who joined at a particular period were tracked periodically to keep abreast of their career transitions—award of tenure, promotions, and separations (see http://sitemaker.umich.edu/advance/files/tenurecohortreport-final-050509.pdf). Hunter College, CUNY developed a flux chart to graphically represent the number of male and female faculty in each rank in each year and the movements (new hires, promotions, tenure, separations) between years (see http://www.hunter.cuny.edu/genderequity/benchmarks.html). Following the lead of these innovative initiatives, other *ADVANCE* institutions subsequently implemented these data analytic tools, helping to diagnose trends in gender representation in the S&E pipeline and identify areas characterized by the lack of gender equity and inclusion.

Table 4.1 NSF *ADVANCE* Indicators of Gender Equity, Diversity, and Inclusion

NSF ADVANCE Indicator	Indicates . . .
1. Total number and percentage of women faculty in S&E by rank and department 2. Number and percentage of women faculty in tenure-line positions by rank and department	. . . the workforce participation of women at different stages in the academic S&E career pipeline, and in different S&E fields
3. Tenure and promotion outcomes by gender 4. Years in rank by gender	. . . if advancement is free from bias
5a. Time at institution 5b. Attrition by gender	. . . when leaks in the academic pipeline occur
6. Number of women in S&E who are in non-tenure-track positions (teaching and research)	. . . the workforce participation of women in off-track positions in S&E
7. Number and percentage of women S&E faculty in administrative positions 8. Number of women S&E faculty in endowed/named chairs 9. Number and percentage of women S&E faculty on promotion and tenure committees, and school/college executive committees	. . . the inclusion of women in S&E administrative leadership and other positions of faculty influence
10. Salary of S&E faculty by gender (controlling for department, rank, years in rank) 11. Space allocation of S&E faculty by gender (with additional controls such as department, etc.) 12. Start-up packages of newly hired S&E faculty by gender (with additional controls such as field, department, rank, etc.)	. . . the equity of resource allocations in S&E

Other indicators of gender equity, diversity, and inclusion in S&E include:
   • Workplace climate
   • Work-life and family-friendly policies
	. . . the inclusion of women faculty in S&E

Source: Modified from "Original Indicators, ADVANCE PI Meeting, April 2002" (Frehill, 2009)

Workplace Climate Assessments

The most common assessment undertaken at the 19 *ADVANCE* institutions was the assessment of the workplace climate for faculty. Each of these universities undertook studies to assess their internal climate including by interview and focus group studies of faculty and administrators, climate surveys assessing the macro (university) climate and the micro (departmental) climate, new faculty interviews and surveys, and faculty exit interviews and surveys. Many of the 19 institutions we studied conducted two comprehensive climate survey assessments during their *ADVANCE* award periods; others conducted only one. Some of these universities (particularly from *ADVANCE* Cohort 1) designed their own survey instruments to address gender equity climate; others drew on surveys implemented by earlier cohort institutions or implemented standardized (but customizable) surveys from higher-education associations such as the Association of American Universities Data Exchange *(AAUDE)*. Several institutions additionally assessed climate for specific faculty groups such as pretenured (tenure-track) faculty through externally administered surveys from the Collaborative on Academic Careers in Higher Education *(COACHE)*. An advantage of these externally designed and administered surveys was the availability of comparative climate data from peer institutions, which could be used for benchmarking purposes.

In addition to university-wide surveys, some *ADVANCE* institutions also studied the climate-related experiences of specific faculty groups—for example, the experiences of underrepresented minority faculty (University of Michigan), associate professors (University of Michigan), lesbian, gay, bisexual, and transgender faculty in science and engineering (jointly studied by Case Western Reserve University and the University of Michigan and reported in Bilimoria and Stewart 2009), and sexual minority doctoral students (University of Michigan). Universities also focused their climate assessments and improvement efforts on selected science and engineering departments and schools (e.g., University of Rhode Island, University of Washington, University of Wisconsin, Madison, and Utah State University).

Overall, climate assessments were useful to the *ADVANCE* universities not only to determine the areas on which to focus when implementing change initiatives but also to help both administration and faculty members understand existing strengths and challenges, and design feasible remedies. The results of our review of these studies to assess workplace climates and improve inclusion are presented in greater detail in Chapter 8.

Other Research and Evaluation on Gender Equity, Diversity, and Inclusion

A variety of other research studies were conducted by the *ADVANCE* universities to examine issues of gender equity, diversity, and inclusion. A sampling of these studies include examinations of the career choice behavior of women PhDs (University of Colorado Boulder), the impact of gender and nationality in faculty-graduate student (advisor-advisee) relationships at (Case Western Reserve University), part-time tenure-track options (University of Washington), gender differences in the constitution of job satisfaction (Case Western Reserve University) and intentions to quit (Utah State University), the child care needs of faculty (Virginia Tech), perceptions of faculty recruitment practices (University of Puerto Rico, Humacao), the composition of faculty search pools (Case Western Reserve University), dual-career issues (Virginia Tech), the impact and feasibility of converting nontenure-track women faculty to tenure track (the University of Wisconsin, Madison), work-life balance issues (Virginia Tech), and the factors leading to diverse and productive academic science departments (Case Western Reserve University). Most of these studies utilized interview or survey protocols; others utilized examination of archival tracked data.

Finally, *ADVANCE* institutions engaged in detailed evaluations of programmatic interventions such as training, mentoring, coaching, faculty development, and networking programs. These evaluation studies were aimed at obtaining feedback on the effectiveness of individual program initiatives, and often involved evaluations of program benefits by participants and pre- and postintervention comparisons. These evaluations were useful in determining which interventions to sustain and which to modify or conclude.

Improving Institutional Collection, Analysis, and Use of Data

A critical role of *ADVANCE* IT projects has been to help their universities upgrade existing institutional research, data collection, and analysis systems with the goal of strengthening the infrastructure for continuous monitoring of transformational outcomes. *ADVANCE* projects have created templates for faculty databases, provided initial resources for database creation and maintenance, created just-in-time training tools for more equitable personnel decision making, and presented analyses and recommendations to senior administrators to assist in promotion and tenure decisions and other human resources functions. Through our review we determined that *ADVANCE* projects have served as catalysts for improving the institutional research capabilities of their universities.

FACTORS INHIBITING INSTITUTIONAL TRANSFORMATION

Of course, institutional transformation in higher education is not easy. The macrostructures of academia remain inhospitable to the full inclusion and advancement of women, especially in S&E (Valian 1999, 2004; Stewart, Malley, & LaVocque-Manty 2007). The National Academies' report, *Beyond Bias and Barriers*, describes how systematic structural constraints and expectations built into academic institutions have impeded the careers of women faculty: "Various institutional practices—especially those related to recruitment, tenure, and promotion—have differential effects on women and men. Such practices can have unintended detrimental effects on people whose circumstances do not fit the traditional assumptions on which these practices were based" (National Academies 2007b, 165).

As discussed earlier in Chapter 2, academic career structures remain facilitative of the career development of the now-outdated prototypical faculty member (the "ideal worker" in academia)—a male, with extra-work support in the form of a wife, who can totally dedicate himself to his career (Williams 2000, 2005). The *Beyond Bias and Barriers* report notes that "the traditional scientific or engineering career presumes the model of an out-of-date male life course. It is predicated on the assumption that the faculty member will have an unlimited commitment to his or her academic career throughout his or her working life. Attention to other serious obligations, such as family, is taken to imply lack of dedication to one's career. Historically, that career model depended on a faculty member having a wife to take care of all other aspects of life, including the household, family, and community. The model still fits some men but is increasingly unsuitable for both men and women who need or want to participate in other activities important to them and their communities" (National Academies 2007, 160).

Additionally, the larger "faculty mindset," or set of beliefs about academia driving everyday behavior, has remained essentially unchanged over decades. As described by Bilimoria and Perry (2005), the following beliefs drive academic decision making, unconsciously perpetuating a chilly climate for anyone other than the "ideal worker": (1) the academic enterprise requires complete dedication at the expense of everything else, especially in early career years, (2) academe is a meritocracy where the best talent succeeds and no incentives and efforts are needed for special groups, (3) academic selection and performance evaluation processes are objective and bias-free, (4) academia is essentially an individual profession with individualized results and rewards, and (5) faculty members can make autonomous choices about their scholarship, time allocations, career mobility, and progression.

Institutional transformation is particularly difficult when past successful behaviors and routines are replicated without mindful attention to changed circumstances and priorities. For example, faculty search and recruitment practices, even in cutting-edge S&E disciplines, continue to be based on conventional methods and outdated practices that include a passive "advertise and they will come" approach, time-limited searches, nondiverse search-committee composition, noninclusive processes, lack of training in basic recruiting and hiring practices, and bias-prone decision making (Bilimoria & Buch 2010). Yet many faculty members continue to believe that their search processes are effective and bias-free.

Within the systemic and structural complexities and constraints described here, two major barriers stood out impeding the transformation process in

ADVANCE institutions: faculty resistance and institutional uncertainties and constraints.

Faculty Resistance

More than a century ago, a young professor in a New England college who had just returned from university study in Germany reportedly said "the progress of this institution . . . will be directly proportional to the death-rate of the faculty" (Foster 1911, 131). Thus, it is not surprising that the *ADVANCE* institutional transformation projects may have generated some skepticism or resistance. As the PIs of the University of Colorado Boulder illustrated, "not everyone in the university agreed with the premise of the project (that some groups are disadvantaged) and therefore oppose(d) the project itself" (Nielsen, Marschke, Sheff, & Rankin 2005, 20). Although such intentional faculty resistance to some initiatives was reported to have occasionally occurred in the early phases of some *ADVANCE* projects, much less of this kind of resistance was reported in later phases of the award periods. Rather, faculty resistance was more likely to occur when changes in the routine behaviors and "ways of being" of faculty were non-compellingly sought by specific initiatives.

For example, the *ADVANCE* leadership team at Case Western Reserve University designed a mentoring initiative in ways that placed women faculty in the driver's seat (i.e., directing the nature and amount of their mentoring) under the supervision of their department chairs. However, many pretenured and even tenured women faculty were unaccustomed to these new expectations, which some perceived to be infeasible in light of existing performance pressures and time constraints. Several women faculty did not recognize the usefulness of a formal mentoring structure, were reluctant to optimally utilize their existing and newly appointed mentors, and failed to take responsibility to proactively drive the process of receiving the mentoring needed. Moreover, department chairs, who were unused to closely monitoring the mentoring arrangements of their faculty members, generally did not follow through on what was now expected of them, resulting in a new breakdown of communication between women faculty and their department chairs. Ultimately, the mentoring initiative at this university was completely overhauled by the *ADVANCE* team with the provision of greater resources and flexibility and more innovative cohort-based methods of mentoring such as peer mentoring, panel sessions, and speed mentoring.

We found a few similar experiences at other institutions as well. For example, getting junior faculty to sign up for a mentoring initiative was difficult at another institution. It was later discovered that attending workshops that targeted success and engagement was seen by junior faculty as signaling their promise and potential, in contrast with mentoring, which was viewed almost as remedial and described as being focused on "helping" junior faculty. This may be a reason why their junior faculty wanted to be associated with one set of programs and resisted being associated with the other. These types of faculty resistance were often solved through efforts of program modification, clarification, and education as described above.

Other resistances sometimes experienced by *ADVANCE* project teams came from perceptions by constituencies that *ADVANCE* activities unfairly advantaged women over men faculty (i.e., perceptions of reverse discrimination) or privileged certain subgroups of women (e.g., new hires or pretenure faculty or STEM faculty) over others (see Plummer 2006). Modifications in response to these challenges included extensive articulation of *ADVANCE* project goals as being beneficial for all faculty, and expanding programming that may have been targeted originally at women faculty in STEM fields to other faculty members including men faculty and non-STEM faculty. The logic employed in these latter cases was that successful programs that work with women faculty can inform subsequent programming and be expanded to serve other faculty groups. In addition, campus-wide initiatives were thought to be easier to institutionalize since all faculty benefit.

Other strategies to reduce faculty resistance to gender equity-related initiatives included the inclusion of men in *ADVANCE* programming from the start of the award. For example, the *ADVANCE* project at the University of Wisconsin, Madison (Women in Science and Engineering Leadership Institute—WISELI) developed "programs that both men and women faculty could embrace, enhancing the opportunity for true institutional transformation to occur" (WISELI 2007, 82). At this university, men faculty were integrated in *ADVANCE* activities throughout the award period: workshops for department chairs and for chairs of hiring committees were attended mostly by men; men constituted 20% of the awardees of Celebrating Women in Science and Engineering grants; and 29% of applicants and 21% of awardees of the Life Cycle Grants/Vilas Life Cycle Professorship program, which had been open to men from the beginning, were men.

Institutional Uncertainties and Constraints

Uncertainties and resource constraints exist in the process of institutional transformation. Over the course of the *ADVANCE* projects studied, several underwent significant changes in the senior administration (presidents, provosts, and deans) of their universities. These changes in university leadership not only posed uncertainties to the *ADVANCE* leadership teams on individual campuses, they required expenditure of additional effort and time on the part of the PIs and Co-PIs to introduce and reintroduce new administrations to their project goals, activities, and accomplishments. In some cases, the *ADVANCE* project provided the institutional umbrella under which organizational change proceeded despite substantial changes in university leadership. For example, at Case Western Reserve University, during their five-year *ADVANCE* award duration (2003–2008), there were more than 25 changes (including interim appointments) in the positions of president, provost, and deans of the four schools/college involved. During this time period, stringent financial constraints and cutbacks were instituted at the university in the face of a large recurring operating budget deficit and a downturn in development attainment (Case Western Reserve University 2008).

Other uncertainties arose from changes within the composition of the *ADVANCE* IT leadership teams during the award period. For example, over the five-year course of the project at Georgia Institute of Technology, different individuals occupied leadership (PIs and Co-PIs) and management positions (program directors, coordinators). Besides the replacement of leadership positions, four individuals served successively as *ADVANCE* program directors and two individuals successively served as program coordinator (Georgia Tech 2007).

Finally, of enormous concern to *ADVANCE* projects was obtaining the resources to institutionalize successful programmatic initiatives beyond the NSF funding period. Organizational change interventions involve programming and administrative costs. As described in Chapter 6, the *ADVANCE* institutions have been innovative and entrepreneurial in obtaining additional funding supports from a variety of different sources to sustain their innovations and continue their transformational efforts. Appropriately, greater emphasis on earlier and intentional planning for project sustainability is now being required by NSF as early as the award proposal stage.

In summary, outdated notions of the ideal academic worker, an intransigent faculty mind-set, past successful behaviors and routines, resistance to change, environmental uncertainties, resource constraints, and other challenges make institutional transformation a difficult task. Transformational change depends on pervasive, deep, and sustainable institutional strategies which can counter competing priorities, resources constraints, and misunderstandings (Rosser & Chameau 2006). In the next chapter we describe the transformational initiatives undertaken at the 19 universities to enhance gender equity, diversity, and inclusion in academic S&E.

5 Institutional Transformation Initiatives

As described in this and the next chapter, institutional change initiatives were employed and institutionalized at the 19 universities at three levels: at the whole system (university) level, at the level of specific STEM units (schools/colleges and departments), and at the individual faculty level. Initiatives ranged from individual skill building to departmental interventions to policy changes affecting the whole university. For example, at the whole system level, new expectations, training, monitoring, and accountabilities for gender equity, diversity, and inclusion outcomes were developed and new structures, positions, policies, and programs were created to address work-life and equity issues for all faculty across the institution. At the school/college and department level, initiatives were conducted to reengineer key practices of academic life and to retrain faculty in their conduct (e.g., search and recruitment procedures and promotion and tenure practices). At the individual level, initiatives were employed to improve the mentoring, training, career development, networking, and equitable access to academic resources of individual faculty members. Figure 5.1 portrays the levels of institutional transformation initiatives developed by the *ADVANCE* project at Case Western Reserve University; while particular to this university, this figure provides a framework for understanding the multiple levels of initiatives undertaken at the other *ADVANCE* institutions as well.

Other descriptions, surveys, and analyses of *ADVANCE* initiatives have been conducted previously. For example, Stewart et al. (2007) described in detail several innovative initiatives and benchmark practices to address gender equity, diversity, and inclusion at the first 19 *ADVANCE* institutions. Fox (2008) determined the percentage of 19 institutions undertaking specific such initiatives, the top few of which were leadership initiatives (84%), recruitment initiatives (79%), faculty-development initiatives (74%), networks of external-supporter initiatives (63%), and initiatives for department and chair development (53%). Plummer (2006) identified three sets of initiatives that contributed to lasting change as perceived by project PIs and Co-PIs in 18 first- and second-cohort *ADVANCE* institutions: institutional policies (dual-career and family-friendly policies), departmental processes (faculty search processes and department climate improvement), and individual initiatives (faculty mentoring and department-head training). Another study of initiatives at *ADVANCE* IT and PAID recipient institutions conducted by the *ADVANCE* program at Auburn University (Sollie 2009) highlighted the "small wins approach"—transforming a workplace through a series of small positive changes used to improve the working environment for those who are disproportionately affected by unsupportive and inconsiderate practices in the workplace (cf. Meyerson & Fletcher 2000). Their survey of 36 institutions yielded information about the perceived cost-benefit of various gender equity initiatives undertaken at these colleges and universities and concluded that (a) mentoring programs represented over half of the most cost-effective and highly beneficial practices employed at universities, especially when they focus on the promotion and tenure process and the culture of department; (b) facilitating women's participation in key academic committees has the greatest benefit, relative to cost; (c) publicizing family-friendly policies is also highly beneficial for faculty; (d) lecture series by senior women from the university have a very low cost relative to perceived benefits; and (e) activities considered highly beneficial relative to cost include grant writing/publication workshops, facilitating the use of family-friendly policies, and providing mentoring programs that focus on understanding teaching (Sollie et al. 2009).

Through our own systematic review, two major clusters of *ADVANCE* initiatives emerged: (a) initiatives to enhance the career trajectories of women and minority faculty employed at every stage of the academic pipeline, and (b) initiatives to improve institutional systems, policies, and climate. Figure 5.2 summarizes the transformational initiatives that the *ADVANCE* universities undertook to enhance gender equity, diversity, and

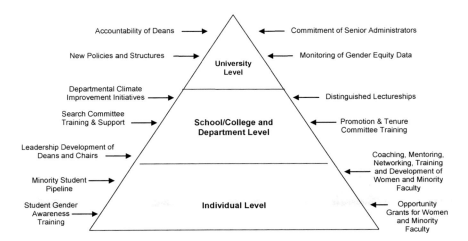

Figure 5.1 Levels of *ADVANCE* institutional transformation initiatives.

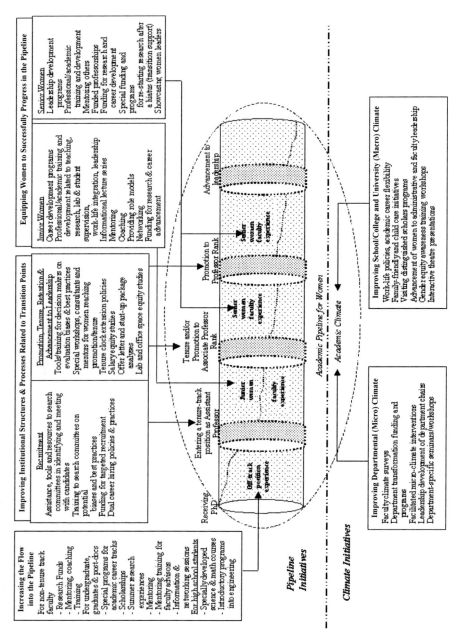

Figure 5.2   ADVANCE institutional transformational initiatives.

inclusion in academic STEM. Below we describe these initiatives, providing examples from the universities in our sample to illustrate each. The examples provided in the text boxes illustrate some of the most distinctive, effective, or pioneering interventions.

While the transformational initiatives described below focused mainly on women faculty (whether majority, underrepresented minority, or international women faculty), in many cases these activities also benefited men faculty from domestic majority and underrepresented minority groups, as well as international groups. Where possible, we highlight initiatives that specifically focused on the career trajectories of underrepresented minority women faculty and international women faculty subsets to illustrate the variety of initiatives employed.

TRANSFORMATIONAL INITIATIVES TO ENHANCE THE CAREER TRAJECTORIES OF WOMEN IN THE ACADEMIC STEM PIPELINE

Three different types of pipeline initiatives addressed improvements in the individual career trajectories of women and minority faculty at the *ADVANCE* institutions: initiatives to increase the inflow of women into the pipeline, initiatives to better equip women to successfully progress in the academic pipeline, and initiatives to improve the institutional structures and processes related to key academic career transition points in the pipeline.

Initiatives to Increase the Inflow of Women into the Academic STEM Pipeline

As described earlier, the flow of women into the academic STEM pipeline is leaky, particularly in some disciplines. To improve this situation, *ADVANCE* universities have employed several initiatives to increase the flow into their STEM pipelines. Focusing on nontenure-track faculty, initiatives such as research funding, conference travel funding, mentoring, coaching, and training were implemented at *ADVANCE* universities to provide women faculty with relevant research and career knowledge, skills, and exposure to enable them to transfer to the tenure track. Focusing on undergraduate, graduate, doctoral, and postdoctoral students, initiatives such as special programs for academic career tracking, scholarships, research and conference travel funding, summer research internship experiences, mentoring, and information sharing and networking sessions were utilized to advance their flow in the pipeline.

The following three *ADVANCE* initiatives that were used most frequently to increase inflow to the academic career pipeline are described below:

- **Small funding for doctoral students and nontenure-track faculty,**

- Workshops targeting graduate students and postdoctoral students, and
- Mentoring women graduate students.

Small funding was provided by many *ADVANCE* IT projects for research or career-relevant activities of women students and nontenure-track faculty. Examples of small funds to sponsor research faculty or nontenure-track faculty included Transition Faculty Awards at the University of Alabama, Birmingham, and awards from the Lydia A. DeWitt Research Fund at the University of Michigan. Examples of small funds to support graduate students and postdoctorates included Graduate Research Assistantship Awards at the University of Texas, El Paso and PhD and postdoctoral fellowships at Virginia Tech. At Virginia Tech, outstanding graduate students and recent PhD recipients preparing for faculty careers were awarded academic-year fellowships to complete their dissertations, teach a course, conduct research, and interact with faculty and the university community in a prefaculty mentoring experience. A mentoring plan with a faculty member was a key part of the application process—this could include presenting research at conferences, teaching a course, submitting grant proposals, or mentoring an undergraduate student (Virginia Tech 2008).

Workshops or seminars for graduate and postdoctoral students on a variety of topics related to careers in academe were implemented by a few *ADVANCE* institutions. For example, the University of Maryland, Baltimore County (UMBC) annually conducted an intensive two-day summer workshop, "Faculty Horizons—A Workshop for Aspiring STEM Faculty," focusing on topics such as securing a faculty position, successful negotiating techniques, getting grants, tenure, promotion, and mentoring in STEM departments, effective teaching strategies, balancing work and family, and handling criticism/rejection in the journal review process. Presentations were given by UMBC faculty and other successful women scientists from industry, government, and academia. In five years (2004–2008), 322 people participated in this program, 94% (302) of whom were women and 44% (142) from underrepresented minority groups. These included 135 senior-level graduate students, 144 postdoctoral fellows, and 26 assistant professors. Evaluation results showed that the Faculty Horizons workshops were very well received and found to be helpful (University of Maryland, Baltimore County 2008, 2009).

Mentoring women graduate students was employed by a few *ADVANCE* projects to encourage them to select academic STEM careers. For example, as described in the text box, the University of Washington's *ADVANCE* project implemented a comprehensive mentoring program for graduate students, managed by their Center for Workforce Development, to which women and individuals of color were strongly encouraged to apply.

Faculty-Graduate Student Mentoring Program at the University of Washington

Goals:

- Provide STEM graduate students with personal and career guidance.
- Encourage students to pursue STEM fields and enhance retention of students pursuing STEM graduate degrees.
- Prepare students with a realistic viewpoint of faculty experiences in STEM fields.
- Utilize faculty expertise for the professional and personal development of STEM graduate students.

Participants:

More than 180 students participated in the program from 2000–01 to 2006–07.

Activities included:

- One-on-one mentoring by a faculty member (graduate students and faculty members are matched based on field of study, interests, and other preferences).
- Career development seminars on making the transition from graduate student to faculty.

Implementation:

Multiple changes were made to the mentoring programs to help them be successful, including

- Revising the mentoring training curriculum.
- Changing the focus from being focused on the job search to being focused on multiple aspects of personal and professional development.
- Increasing levels of contact with participants through e-mail newsletters and regular check-ins.
- Collecting additional data on mentees to better evaluate the program and its effects on mentees.

Source: University of Washington (2008). See also http://www.engr.washington.edu/cwd/CWDMentoringFacGrad.html.

Initiatives to Better Equip Women to Successfully Progress in the Pipeline

In this section, we describe career stage-specific initiatives employed by the *ADVANCE* universities to better equip women and minorities to successfully progress in the academic STEM pipeline. These initiatives drew on extant literature specifying effective practices in mentoring, coaching, networking, education and training, career and professional development, and leadership development (e.g., Kram 1988; Burke 2002; de Janasz, Sullivan, & Whiting 2003; Ehrich, Hansford, & Tennent 2004; Forret & Dougherty 2004; Gibson 2004). Initiatives to better equip junior women faculty included career-development programs, professional/academic education, training and development related to teaching, research, laboratory management and student supervision, work-life integration, leadership development, mentoring, professional coaching, providing role models, networking, funding for research and career advancement, and showcasing women's scholarly achievements. Initiatives for senior women faculty included leadership-development programs, professional/academic training and development, mentoring, funded professorships, funding for research and career development, special funding and programs for restarting research after a hiatus, and showcasing women leaders.

The following five most frequently used *ADVANCE* initiatives to better equip women to succeed in the pipeline are described below.

- Faculty mentoring (including paired, group, panel, peer, and speed mentoring) initiatives.
- Career development workshops for junior faculty and tenured faculty.
- Small funding for research and professional development.
- Leadership development initiatives.
- Networking initiatives.

Mentoring is most beneficial to faculty because it affects both research productivity and the quality of training given to undergraduate students, graduate students, and postdoctoral researchers (Pfund et al. 2006). For universities, mentoring is considered a means to enhance the career success of women faculty (Gibson 2004) as well as a strategy for helping achieve greater parity for women and underrepresented faculty (Chandler 1996; Valian 1999; Hackney & Bock 2000; Wasburn 2007). At the individual level, women faculty members benefit from academic mentoring by having someone who truly cares and acts in their best interest, gaining a strong feeling of connection, being affirmed of their worth, gaining a sense of not being alone in their experiences as faculty, and learning to understand and effectively deal with politics as a part of their academic experience (Gibson 2004).

The following types of mentoring activities were deployed by *ADVANCE* projects, singly or in combination.

(a) *Traditional (formalized) paired mentoring*: Paired mentoring, involving the development of a longer-term, mutually reinforcing relationship between a senior and junior faculty colleague, was the most popular form of mentoring used. The mentor provides advice and advocacy on technical/scientific issues as well as career development, helping the mentees learn the ropes in their chosen field and providing support for upward mobility (cf. Kram 1988). Faculty mentors in *ADVANCE* universities served as senior advisors who transferred technical, disciplinary, professional, and organizational knowledge, wisdom, and sponsorship aimed at providing access to important academic and scientific resources and networks. Selection and administration of the mentoring pairs was often done through a centralized office.

For example, the University of Alabama, Birmingham's (UAB's) formal mentoring program, launched in summer 2007, assigned at least one mentor (and in some cases multiple mentors) to all faculty (women and men) in three schools at the assistant professor level who had less than four years' experience at UAB as well as women faculty at the associate professor level (University of Alabama, Birmingham 2009). The *ADVANCE* Faculty Mentoring Program at New Mexico State University involved once-a-month meetings and regular informal social gatherings of mentors and mentees. Early-career faculty members were paired with established faculty, and senior faculty interested in exploring careers in administration were paired with administrators. Each year over a five-year period (2004–2008) 80 to 120 faculty and administrators, mostly from STEM fields but also from the social sciences, half men and half women, participated in this mentoring program (New Mexico State University 2009). Hunter College's Gender Equity Project employed an innovative contract-based "sponsorship" program requiring faculty participants to meet biweekly with their sponsors, as described in the text box.

The Gender Equity Project's (GEP's) Sponsorship Program at Hunter College, CUNY

Goal:
To advance the professional development and scientific work of women engaged in basic science.

Participants:
The GEP Sponsorship Program benefited 8–12 women scientists (associates) per year, of any age and at any point in their career.

Program Components:
Each GEP associate worked with a sponsor who is a senior and successful member of the associate's field. GEP associates committed themselves via contract to a set of goals and activities, including, but not limited to, submission of grant proposals and journal articles, attendance at colloquia and workshops, and development of skills. Each associate received up to $10,000 to be used for research. They met bi-weekly with their sponsors to review progress, discuss the intellectual content of their work, help set and modify goal deadlines, help strategize about professional development, and make specific and concrete proposals for next steps. Sponsors also signed a contract committing themselves to a set of activities and received up to $5,000 to be used for research. The program also offered a number of workshops and other developmental assistance to associates.

Continued

---

88 Gender Equity in Science and Engineering

Continued

Evaluation:

The program resulted in significantly more external and internal grant proposals and significantly increased submissions of abstracts, posters, and papers to conferences.

Source: http://www.hunter.cuny.edu/genderequity/sponsors.html. See also http://www.advance.gatech.edu/archive/2004conf/5b_rabinowitz.ppt#604,24, Ongoing Challenges with Sponsorship Program

---

(b) *Group mentoring, peer mentoring, and mentor panels*: Group-based mentoring approaches were frequently used in *ADVANCE* projects as they were considered particularly effective for large numbers of faculty needing mentorship. Time investments on the part of faculty participants as well as the costs of administration of these sessions were more limited than for traditional paired programs.

For example, in 2005–2006, the Faculty Mentoring Program for Women at the University of Texas, El Paso used an 18-month group mentoring approach whereby faculty women were placed into "mentoring teams" consisting of up to six other new women faculty from their college and two mentors from their college but not from their own departments (University of Texas, El Paso 2008). At Case Western Reserve University, the Academic Careers in Engineering and Science project employed peer-group mentoring and mentor panels (composed of respected senior faculty and administrators) to discuss career and professional development issues with university-wide and school-specific groups of junior faculty. The Junior Faculty Peer Mentoring initiative was designed as an opportunity for junior faculty to meet, interact, and share career concerns and insights, usually over lunch. Emerging junior faculty leaders were identified in each participating school to coordinate the lunches. Most participants were in their first one to four years of employment, with more senior members near applying for tenure attending irregularly. The lunches were directed at discussions of career development, networking skills, third-year review, mentoring, and tenure package preparation. The lunches alternated between open peer discussions, panels of senior faculty, or brief presentations by administrators on policy or procedure. In one of the schools, a peer group of junior faculty met at roughly monthly intervals and had an average attendance of ten, which represented around 50% of their junior faculty. In another school, a peer group met every month and had an average attendance of six, which represented 14% of their junior faculty. In a third school, the peer group met a total of four times during academic year 2007/2008 and had an average attendance of 20, which represented 50% of their junior faculty (Case Western Reserve University 2008).

(c) *Speed mentoring*: Modeled after speed dating, speed mentoring was innovatively used at some *ADVANCE* institutions. For example, at Case

Western Reserve University, participants interacted personally with several mentors within a 90-minute period about specific professional and career-development concerns they may have had. Participants gained quick and varied insights on career development from volunteer senior faculty mentors in a structured, time-sensitive environment. Each participant spent 15 minutes showing his/her CV to a mentor, discussing academic career-building efforts to date and receiving feedback on progress and development needs, and then moved to a different mentor. Thus each mentee had the chance to personally interact with up to six mentors from a variety of academic disciplines. The event was open to all faculty members, postdoctoral fellows, and graduate students, with women and minorities especially encouraged to attend; 35 mentees attended in 2007, mostly graduate students from STEM fields, and 20 mentees attended in 2008 (Case Western Reserve University 2008).

(d) *Professional academic coaching*: Coaching of women faculty, geared toward their career and leadership development, was conducted at Case Western Reserve University as described in the text box.

Career-development workshops for junior faculty were frequently used by *ADVANCE* projects to share the skills and knowledge necessary for career advancement. Workshop series targeting junior women faculty included the Junior Faculty Workshop at the University of Colorado Boulder, career workshops at the University of Rhode Island, assistant professor workshops at Utah State University, the IMPACT Seminars at the University of Texas, El Paso, Faculty ADVANCEMENT Workshop Series at the University of Maryland, Baltimore County, and Workshop Series for Junior Faculty at Hunter College, CUNY. Workshops focusing on leadership development included leadership seminars open to the entire campus community at Utah State University, leadership-development lunches for faculty members at Virginia Tech, and Running a Great Lab: Workshops for Principal Investigators at the University of Wisconsin, Madison.

These workshops were developed to promote women's careers by encouraging self-efficacy, collaboration, support, and innovation. Workshop topics addressed effective teaching, grant-writing, negotiation and communication, tenure and promotion, conflict management, integrating work and personal life, academic working environment, and dealing with difficult situations. Workshops ranged from one hour to one week, with inputs from one presenter, multiple presenters, or panelists.

For example, the *ADVANCE* project at the University of Washington offered quarterly professional development workshops for all pretenured faculty in *ADVANCE* departments. The program included a welcome lunch and sharing of resources, workshops, and services offered to them, and a forum to discuss the issues faculty are thinking about. Workshops targeted at junior faculty included time management, managing a research lab, mentoring and advising graduate students, navigating the

Career and Leadership Development through Professional Academic Coaching at Case Western Reserve University (CWRU)

Description and Goals:
The academic coaching program implemented by the *ADVANCE* project at CWRU represented an intensive effort to advance the leadership and career development of women faculty members in science and engineering. Academic coaching is targeted, finite, and focused on improving current and long-term academic performance in the following areas: increasing self-awareness, building new skills, encouraging strategic thinking, engaging in purposeful planning, empowering positive change, and enhancing leadership internally and externally. An academic coach is someone who has general academic/organizational experience and who provides performance-related and career-related advice. The coach helps the participant determine their career vision, goals, plans, and actions. They give advice, resources, and feedback on how to best accomplish the vision and goals.

Format of the Coaching Program:
- The coaching program consisted of six 1½-hour one-on-one sessions.
- Bi-monthly coaches cohort meetings, which consist of the Co-PIs and coaches, were held to plan and design the coaching program and debrief the coaching activities.

Participants:
In the five-year period (2004–2008), 88 female and two minority male faculty members (all ranks, tenure-track and non-tenure-track, in science and engineering departments) received individualized coaching.

Coaching Content:

Detailed guides were developed describing the content of the coaching sessions in the program, including career visioning and goal-setting, career planning, leadership and professional development, academic performance issues, issues of work-life integration, professional relationship building, self-assessment instruments, and 360-degree assessment of competencies for senior women. These are available at www.case.edu/admin/aces/coaching.htm.

Evaluations:
By June 2008, 54 women faculty completed the coaching evaluation forms. Feedback from the coaching program evaluation was highly positive. With ratings based on a scale of 1 (poor) to 5 (excellent), evaluations by women faculty of the different measures were at a median of 4.5. Individuals who were skeptical about the coaching program at the outset of their participation highly praised its usefulness at the conclusion.

Source: Case Western Reserve University (2008). See also Bilimoria, Hopkins, O'Neil, and Perry (2007).

tenure track, and balancing research, teaching, and service (University of Washington 2008).

Another example is the Workshop Series for Junior Faculty implemented at Hunter College, CUNY. Their Gender Equity Project (GEP) offered a series of three-day workshops to develop male and female junior faculty engaged in basic science and engineering at the participating CUNY schools (see http://www.hunter.cuny.edu/genderequity/workshopSearch. html). During the three days of each workshop series, the GEP addressed topics that cover the techniques, skills, strategies, and knowledge necessary for professional success.

A unique workshop conducted at Columbia University addressed how intellectual preferences for and professional consequences of interdisciplinary research might be influenced by one's gender, race, and/or ethnicity. The two-day "Women, Minorities, and Interdisciplinarity: Transforming the Research Enterprise" conference occurred in November 2007, addressing issues of women and minorities in cross-disciplinary research from both the institutional and individual perspectives. In this workshop, discussions from participants suggested that (a) institutions interested in increasing their diversity might have a greater chance for success if they value interdisciplinary scholarship and (b) institutions interested in increasing interdisciplinary research may have a greater chance for success if they create environments hospitable for women and minorities (http://advance. ei.columbia.edu/?id=wmi_home).

Workshops for tenured mid-career and late-career women faculty were also conducted by *ADVANCE* institutions. As described in the text box, Kansas State University's Career Advancement Program was aimed at helping tenured women faculty advance into the (full) professor rank and other institutional and disciplinary leadership positions.

Overall, evaluations from career development workshop participants tended to be very positive. For example, the benefits of participating in the IMPACT seminars at the University of Texas, El Paso mentioned by participants included: enhanced interdisciplinary collaboration and colleagueship, offered a sense of connection to others on campus, introduced ways to identify new leadership roles in department, college, and university, explored effective ways to increase productivity through integration of research, teaching and service, and provided support in overcoming barriers to success (University of Texas, El Paso 2005).

Small funding for research and professional development was another frequently used initiative employed by *ADVANCE* projects. These small funds could be used for a variety of purposes, such as release time from teaching to conduct research, summer salary, laboratory equipment or office supplies, research assistance, traveling for academic conferences, and attendance at short courses or conferences that enhance professional development. Examples include research and travel awards for tenure-track women STEM faculty at New Mexico State University, *ADVANCE* Faculty

Career Advancement Program for Tenured Women Faculty at Kansas State University

Description and Goals:
The *ADVANCE* program at Kansas State University (K-State) offered a Career Advance Program (CAP) to assist tenured women faculty advance into senior and leadership positions. Recipients of this award collaborated with a mentor for advice on critical mid-career topics, including promotion to full professorship, assumption of administrative responsibilities, and negotiation of appropriate release time for increased administrative and institutional or professional service duties.

Participants:
As of 2007, 18 awards were made since the beginning of the *ADVANCE* grant period. Of the ten awardees who have completed their projects, eight awardees submitted external grant proposals, with five reporting that their grants were funded. Five submitted journal articles and two individuals reported their articles were published during their year of funding. Seven made presentations at national meetings, two traveled to conduct research on other sites, three reported receiving new research knowledge and learning new skills, one expanded her professional service opportunities, and two received prestigious awards.

Assessment:
A focus group was conducted to discover CAP awardees' overall perspectives of the CAP program. Twelve of the 16 invited CAP awardees attended the focus group. Responses indicated that the most frequently utilized aspects of projects from CAP funds were: a) sustaining or bridging current research, b) hiring of a staff person (e.g., technician, graduate student assistant), c) traveling for professional purposes, d) using seed money to start research projects, e) continuing their research while transitioning to an administrative position, f) developing a new curriculum, g) attending training programs, h) bringing people to K-State, i) covering summer salary, j) developing collaborations.

Source: Montelone and Dyer 2008.

Development Mini-Grants at New Mexico State University, Elizabeth C. Crosby Research Fund at the University of Michigan, research funds at the University of Puerto Rico, Humacao, College of Engineering Research Enhancement Visits Funds at Kansas State University, College of Agriculture Professional Development Program Award at Kansas State University, College of Arts and Sciences Career Enhancement Opportunities (CEO) Funds at Kansas State University, and opportunity grants at Case Western Reserve University.

Some small funding programs specifically targeted supporting the research and professional development activities of junior faculty, such as proposal development grants at the University of Rhode Island, research seed grants at Virginia Tech, career enhancement grants at the University of Rhode Island, and junior faculty research awards at the University of Alabama, Birmingham. Other small-funds programs were targeted to support senior women faculty. For example, Utah State University implemented an associate to full career development program, which offered funding support for associate professors seriously preparing for promotion. The University of Colorado Boulder implemented individual growth (IG) grants targeted at tenured associate and full professors to help them renew or extend their research. The University of Alabama, Birmingham offered senior faculty research awards to senior faculty (both women and men) intended to advance their scholarly pursuits or provide funding for a new research direction. Some other *ADVANCE* institutions employed small-grants programs to encourage cross-disciplinary collaborations among faculty. For example, the faculty collaborative seed grants offered at Utah State University aimed at increasing collaborative research across scientific and engineering disciplines that involves female tenured, tenure-track, and research professors.

Many *ADVANCE* universities utilized institutional matching (cost-share) funds to conduct and subsequently expand and institutionalize their small-grants programs. For example, the *ADVANCE* project at the University of Alabama, Birmingham reported that during the spring of 2007 and the spring of 2008, 18 awardees were given faculty research awards (including junior, senior, and transition faculty research awards) amounting to $178,090, with additional school or department matching of $226,107, for a total of $404,197 (University of Alabama, Birmingham 2009). As a result of these awards, faculty members were successful in securing other funding as well as increasing their publications, presentations at national meetings, and national recognition.

Leadership development initiatives were among the most frequently employed initiatives at *ADVANCE* universities. Particularly for senior women faculty, the topic of equipping themselves for further career development is mostly about leadership development. Leadership development initiatives for senior women faculty comprised a combination of (a) leadership programs, (b) mentoring for academic leadership, and (c) small funds supporting individual faculty leadership development projects.

(a) *Leadership development programs for women faculty*: ADVANCE projects conducted programs to enable women to advance to senior faculty and administrative leadership positions. For example, Virginia Tech employed a series of leadership development lunches. A total of 121 individuals attended one or more of these lunches, and 42 participants responded to the survey (a 35% response rate). Benefits mentioned by the respondents included the importance of networking with other female faculty members, and the ability to hear and ask questions about different perspectives on leadership. Forty-five percent of respondents indicated that they were potentially interested in a leadership position at the university and 57% noted that the lunches were an effective approach to leadership development. (Virginia Tech 2008).

The ADVANCING Leadership program implemented at New Mexico State University included monthly leadership development workshops and a two-day off-campus retreat. The workshops covered a wide array of topics, including in particular the roles, responsibilities, and rewards of being an effective academic leader. As described earlier, Case Western Reserve University provided individualized academic coaching to senior women faculty, focused on their leadership development. Faculty participants were given the option of undergoing a process of 360-degree evaluation and feedback, subsequently developing leadership goals and action plans while working with a professional coach.

(b) *Mentoring senior women faculty for academic leadership*: Mentoring senior women faculty is generally less related to research or academic performance development and more related to developing their leadership skills. *ADVANCE* programs used informal and formal mentoring methods to prepare senior women for academic leadership. As described in the text box, desired outcomes were obtained from Virginia Tech's senior faculty leadership development program.

Another example of women's mentoring was an informal monthly lunchtime mentoring program targeting all STEM women faculty—the Mentoring-for-Leadership lunch series—at the University of Washington in 2003. The purpose was to encourage STEM women faculty to consider academic leadership and to expose them to different career paths. The format was discussion-based and informal. Between May 2003 and September 2007, there were 53 women presenters, 57.4% from the University of Washington and 42.6% from other universities or national organizations. More than 120 women faculty participated in the program during that time. Evaluations of this program were highly favorable, indicating that the luncheons were an effective approach of mentoring for women faculty, helped their professional growth, encouraged them to consider leadership positions, provided different perspectives on leadership, and facilitated cross-unit networking and community building (University of Washington 2008).

(c) *Small funds supporting individual faculty leadership development projects*: At some *ADVANCE* universities, small funding opportunities were designated for women faculty to undertake individualized leadership development projects. For example, the *ADVANCE* project at University of Colorado Boulder created a Leadership Education for Advancement and Promotion (LEAP) associate vice chancellor (AVC) position by funding a one-year fellowship for a senior faculty member to try out the role of academic administrator. AVC fellows were placed in half-time positions in a particular administrative office where they participated in that office's work

---

Leadership Development Program for Senior Women Faculty at Virginia Tech

Goal:
To accelerate the advancement of senior women faculty at Virginia Tech.

Program Participants:
The *AdvanceVT* Leadership Development Program targeted a small cohort of senior women faculty, identified as potential and emerging leaders, from across the campus.

Leadership Assessment and Development:
The program assessed participants' current strengths and areas for development and provided feedback based on that assessment. Working individually with a coach, each woman created a development plan to capitalize on strengths and address development needs. Participants met regularly to discuss leadership issues and inform each other of progress toward goals.

Evaluation:
Of the 17 women faculty members who participated in the Leadership Development program, one of them became a dean, two became department heads, one became an assistant department head, and two were promoted to professor. In follow-up interviews, most participants indicated being satisfied with the program and that they benefited from participating in it.

Source: Virginia Tech (2009).

---

and also worked on an individual project of interest to LEAP and of utility to the university. Six women held this position between 2002 and the end of 2008. Results from interviews of these participants suggest that most of the AVC fellows reported that their experience in this position were beneficial. They gained greater understanding of the structure and functioning of the university as a whole, developed greater appreciation of excellence in areas of the university they had not encountered before, and built broader professional networks (Laursen 2009).

Similarly, the *ADVANCE* project at Virginia Tech initiated leadership fellowships for senior women faculty by encouraging them to carry out an individual leadership development project. One women associate professor chose to work with the university's government relations office as her leadership fellowship project. The benefits she reported included increased internal and external networks, much better understanding about government relations issues as well as the roles and responsibilities of executive administrators at the institution (Virginia Tech 2008).

Networking initiatives were employed to better equip women to succeed in the pipeline. Since many women faculty are solos or tokens (under 15% of the total faculty) in STEM departments, network-expansion activities were used extensively across *ADVANCE* projects. Networking offers multiple benefits. By including faculty in STEM disciplines across campus, networking activities provide women faculty opportunities to meet other faculty members, share research ideas, talk about common issues, learn to navigate the university through informal channels, and develop future plans. New ideas, collaborations, and resources often emerge from network participation, and a sense of community among faculty members builds as well.

Examples of network activities used in *ADVANCE* institutions include the Network to Advance Women Scientists and Engineers at the University of Michigan, Women's lunches at the University of Colorado Boulder, the monthly Lunch and Learn series for women faculty at the University of Alabama, Birmingham, Creating Networking Opportunities: New STEM Women Faculty Luncheon Series at the University of Maryland, Baltimore County, annual Women of Achievement Luncheon at Case Western Reserve University, Topical Lunch Series including both women and men at the University of Rhode Island, and Women in Science Events including informal networking breakfasts and research lunches with invited speakers at the University of Montana. Georgia Tech created a network of termed five-year professorships, one at each college included in their *ADVANCE* project, to mentor women faculty in science and engineering.

In summary, to minimize leaks in the academic pipeline, multiple layers of initiatives have been implemented across *ADVANCE* sites, including a combination of intensive mentoring of women faculty, career development workshops, leadership-development training, research and professional development funds, and regular informal networking events. These initiatives have equipped women and minority faculty with the necessary knowledge, skills, networks, support, and resources to advance successfully in the academic pipeline.

Initiatives to Improve Institutional Structures, Practices, and Processes Related to Key Transition Points in the Academic Career Pipeline

A second set of pipeline initiatives to enhance the career trajectories of women in STEM pertained to improving the institutional structures and processes related to key transition points in the academic career. These initiatives addressed the improvement of institutional structures, practices, and processes involved in the recruitment, advancement, and retention of women faculty in S&E. Across the *ADVANCE* institutions, the most frequently used initiatives to improve career transitions were:

- Recruitment Initiatives
  - Search committee training and support
  - Financial support to diversity faculty recruitment
  - Dual career hiring support
- Advancement Initiatives
  - Tenure and promotion committee training and development
  - Faculty development workshops on promotion and tenure
  - Tenure clock extension policies
- Resource equity and retention initiatives
  - Salary-equity studies, start-up package and offer letter analyses, and cohort analyses.

Recruitment initiatives were implemented across the *ADVANCE* sites. Strategies included forming a committee to self-study the recruitment process and to make internal recommendations, assisting search committees in identifying and meeting with candidates, training search committees on potential biases and best practices, funding for targeted recruitment, updating and implementing dual-career hiring policies and practices, and providing tools and resources for search committees. The three most frequently used initiatives pertaining to improving faculty recruitment processes are described below:

- Search committee training and support.
- Financial support to help diversify faculty recruitment.
- Dual career hiring support.

(a) *Search committee training and support*: Across *ADVANCE* universities, a number of methods were utilized to train and advise search committees to improve their functioning. A core strategy used was that a trained committee or a qualified individual worked closely with departmental search committees, faculty members, and department and school administrators by providing information, advice, best practices and techniques related to recruitment. For example, the *ADVANCE* project at the University of Michigan created a Committee on Strategies and Tactics for Recruiting to Improve Diversity and Excellence (STRIDE) in 2002 with the purpose of promoting the recruitment of women faculty in STEM (Stewart, LaVaque-Manty, & Malley 2004). STRIDE comprised male and female senior faculty members in STEM fields who were equipped with relevant knowledge (e.g., gender-equitable recruitment and hiring best practices). STRIDE encouraged diversity in search committee composition, and helped committee members develop awareness of nonconscious biases against women applicants and faculty (University of Michigan 2006a). The University of Michigan's *ADVANCE* project created a handbook for faculty searches and hiring describing best practices at each stage in the recruitment process from committee composition and advertisement language to campus visits and negotiating offers (see www.advance. rackham.umich.edu/handbook.pdf).

Similarly, to maximize the quality of potential hires, the Science and Engineering Recruitment Team (SERT) was created at Utah State University. SERT worked with hiring committees and provided information to search committees and departments to aid in recruitment and retention of a diverse faculty. Utah State's SERT committee also worked as informal ambassadors to meet with recruitment candidates to provide them with further information. At the University of Wisconsin, Madison, the Searching for Excellence and Diversity workshops were conducted to train faculty members and search committees, and were evaluated as having a positive impact on hiring women faculty as described in the text box.

At some other *ADVANCE* sites, a trained individual was utilized to support and enhance diversity in faculty hiring, such as a senior faculty equity advisor at the University of California, Irvine, a diversity specialist at Case Western Reserve University, and a college liaison at Virginia Tech. Similar to a committee, utilizing a trained individual in the recruitment process aims at enhancing the faculty search process. For example, liaisons at Virginia Tech met with departmental search committees as well as all female and most male candidates for faculty positions in their respective colleges to inform them of work/life and other programmatic resources at Virginia Tech and answer questions. The liaisons were not members of the search committees, and so were able to discuss potentially sensitive issues with candidates in confidence. During the academic year 2008–2009, the College of Engineering liaison met with 19 candidates for faculty positions in the College of Engineering and shared information on their *ADVANCE* program with eight other candidates via e-mail (Virginia Tech 2009).

Equity advisors (EQAs) were appointed at the University of California, Irvine (UCI) to intervene in and improve the STEM faculty search and recruitment process. Equity advisors provided advice to deans, department chairs, and search committee chairs and members, including information on subtle gender inequities and biases as well as best practices in faculty recruitment. Subsequently, many changes were made regarding faculty recruitment, including: (a) codification of search processes and increased transparency via implementation of search process forms; (b) implementation of a "Train the Trainers" model whereby equity advisors were trained by the *ADVANCE* PIs and then, in turn, trained faculty in their schools on effective practices in recruitment; (c) participation in the university's Academic Planning Group; (d) participation in the Southern California Higher Education Recruitment Consortium (HERC); (e) refinement and expansion of the use of the UCI Career Partners (dual career hiring) Program; and (f) implementation of new position advertisement language to emphasize UCI as an employer that has embraced equity and diversity (University of California, Irvine 2006).

(b) *Financial support to diversify faculty recruitment*: Financial support in the form of small funds to improve faculty recruitment was provided at some *ADVANCE* sites. For example, competitive Departmental

**Searching for Excellence and Diversity Workshops
at University of Wisconsin, Madison**

Purpose:
Improve every stage of the faculty recruitment process by providing
faculty with information, advice, and techniques to help them run
more effective and efficient search committees.

Implementation:
Designed in 2002 and piloted in 2003, Searching for Excellence and
Diversity workshops were implemented in full on the University of Wisconsin, Madison campus beginning in fall 2004. Materials developed
for this workshop included a guidebook and a brochure. These workshops were offered in a variety of formats, using many different campus
experts to inform the chairs of faculty search committees about university policies, best practices, and resources for hiring the best and most
diverse faculty possible.

Participants and Outreach:
As of June 2007, 119 STEM faculty members (10% of the total STEM
faculty) in 49 STEM departments (70% of STEM departments) had
received the training. Approximately 6,343 copies of the brochure
"Reviewing Applicants: Research on Bias and Assumptions" were
requested by 21 institutions across the U.S. and Canada.

Evaluation:
The evaluation reports show that the workshops were useful to the participants, and that departments who send at least one faculty member
to a hiring workshop make more offers to women applicants, and hire
more women applicants. Furthermore, those who attended the workshops were much more likely to disagree that "The climate for faculty
of color in my department is good,", a finding that may indicate greater
awareness of the actual climate experienced by faculty of color.

Source: WISELI—Women in Science and Engineering Leadership
Institute (2007). More information and resources are available at:
http://wiseli.engr.wisc.edu/hiring.php

Transformation Grants were used to improve the hiring and retention of
women STEM faculty at the University of Michigan. Interviews with faculty members in three departments that won these grants suggested that
their departments benefited in four ways: (a) increased understanding,
improved climate and increased transparency of procedures and policies,
(b) direct support to women faculty, (c) improved hiring procedures and
successful recruitment of new faculty, and (d) increased attention to work/
life issues. In contrast, interviews of faculty in two comparison departments that did not receive funding and were characterized by conflict and

lack of transparency indicated that few of these benefits occurred in those departments (University of Michigan 2006b).

Other examples of funding support related to recruitment initiatives included the establishment of endowed professorship funds for the recruitment of senior women faculty in S&E at Columbia University and Case Western Reserve University, an *ADVANCE* research assistantship program for department chairs at the University of Maryland, Baltimore County, recruitment funding (to support departments that were planning to diversify their faculty through the hiring of qualified women and to support newly hired faculty fellows for up to three years) at the University of Rhode Island, start-up package enhancement awards which contributed to breakthrough hires in two departments at New Mexico State University, and a Recruiting to Expand Applicant Pools (REAP) program to support department heads and/or senior faculty on recruiting trips at Kansas State University.

(c) *Dual career hiring support*: A frequently used strategy related to faculty recruitment was the provision of dual-career hiring support. The number of dual-career couples is growing, as more and more women earn doctor degrees in science and engineering. As stated in the Stanford University report, *Dual-Career Academic Couples: What Universities Need to Know*, "new hiring practices are needed to support a diverse professoriate—and one of these practices is couple hiring" (Schiebinger, Henderson, & Gilmartin 2008, 3). To attract and retain talented scholars and outstanding faculty, more and more universities have recognized the importance of supporting dual career partners. The *ADVANCE* institutions have undertaken efforts to convert the so called "two-body problem" into "two-person opportunities" by implementing dual-career hiring programs whose purpose is to assist accompanying partners in searching for appropriate employment opportunities.

ADVANCE initiatives related to dual-career hiring support included creating dual-career hiring policies, supporting funds, creating new structures and positions to support dual-career hiring, and engaging in self-study to result in recommendations. For instance, dual-career guidelines were formally endorsed in February 2008 at University of Rhode Island (see www.uri.edu/advance/work_life_support/dual_career_guidelines.html). Their dual-career accommodation strategies include expedited application for open positions, split positions to meet the needs of several departments/units, shared appointments for faculty dual-career partners in the same academic discipline, soft-money appointments, visiting-professor positions, and lectureships.

The Career Partners Program (CPP) implemented at University of California, Irvine consists of two subprograms: an FTE (full-time equivalency) for Ladder-Rank Faculty Appointments program (see www.ap.uci.edu/programs/careerpart/CareerPartners-FTE.html) and an Interim Funding Assistance program (see www.ap.uci.edu/programs/careerpart/Career-Partners-interim.html). Beginning in 2001, funding for career partners became a three-way partnership: the recruiting unit of the primary appointee provides one-third full-time employee (FTE), the host unit of the partner provides one-third FTE, and the Office of the Executive Vice Chancellor provides one-third FTE. As reported by their *ADVANCE* project, the new funding structure has led to broader buy-in to the program and there has been an increase in the hiring of career partners— since the inception of their *ADVANCE* program, 19 career partners (ten women and nine men) were hired as the primary candidate (University of California, Irvine 2006).

The University of Washington's *ADVANCE* project developed a one-page guide of recommendations to chairs for facilitating dual-career hires (see www.engr.washington.edu/advance/resources/dual_career_hires.html). Similarly, Case Western Reserve University revised its partner hiring policy and created a structure to assist the recruitment and retention of new faculty members and administrators. Between 2004 and 2008, the partner hiring policy at Case Western Reserve University helped recruit and retain 14 faculty members (Case Western Reserve University 2008).

Other efforts related to dual-career hiring include conducting dual-career hiring studies within a particular university and providing related recommendations to department chairs and senior administrators. For example, the *ADVANCE* project at Utah State University formed a dual-career committee to self-study the dual-career issues on campus and make recommendations to the administration regarding the university's dual-career accommodation policy and procedures (Utah State University 2004). In 2004, the *ADVANCE* project at the University of Puerto Rico, Humacao conducted a survey study, *Dual Science Career Couples at UPRH*, results from which were incorporated into the university's Policies for Faculty Recruitment and Retention (Ramos 2004). The *ADVANCE* project at Virginia Tech conducted interviews with dual-career faculty couples at Virginia Tech, University of Wisconsin, New Mexico State University, and Utah State University from fall 2004 through spring 2005. Results were used to identity critical areas for improvement and develop suggestions for handling the challenges associated with dual-career hires issues (Creamer and Glass 2006). The *ADVANCE* project at Columbia University conducted a study of recruiting dual-career academic couples, whose recommendations included (a) establish a centralized coordinating mechanism for dual-career cases, (b) designate a broker within the Office of the Provost with appropriate credibility and influence, (c) provide the broker with the resources necessary to cultivate opportunities inside and outside of Columbia University, and (d) pursue the establishment of a Higher Education Research Consortium for the New York area to serve as an information clearinghouse and support structure for city-wide dual career academic hiring (Earth Institute *ADVANCE* Working Group 2005).

Dual career hiring also posed challenges to the *ADVANCE* institutions. A primary challenge remained the continuation of financial support for academic career partners beyond initial funding, particularly in more difficult economic circumstances. Other challenges included reluctant and slow participation in dual-career hiring programs from departmental faculties who may be afraid that their future open positions may be jeopardized by their support for a dual-career partner hire.

The experience of *ADVANCE* institutions suggests that a dual-career program should involve personnel from multiple levels, including the department chair or center director from the department that the faculty member is being recruited, a dual-career specialist or other designated staff from the school or college, and a specialist or a senior administrator from the office of the university provost. These multilevel involvements, together with clarity and transparency about the financial arrangements related to such appointments, may significantly improve the chances of successful dual-career hiring. In summary, dual-career academic hiring has become increasingly important for a diverse professoriate, and it poses both challenges and opportunities to higher-education institutions. *ADVANCE* universities have created guidelines and documented their successes and challenges with different programs, providing these resources for other institutions.

Overall, the various search committee training and support strategies used across the *ADVANCE* institutions have attempted to create more open, fair, transparent, and inclusive faculty-recruitment structures, practices, and processes.

Advancement initiatives, particularly initiatives to improve the tenure and promotion processes, included special committees to study the processes of promotion and tenure advancement, tools and training for decision makers on evaluation biases and best practices in advancement initiatives, information sessions for faculty to increase transparency in decision making, and special consultants and mentors for women at the tenure or promotion stage. Across *ADVANCE* institutions, the following three types of initiatives were most frequently used to improve faculty advancement structures, practices, and processes:

- Promotion and tenure committee training and development
- Faculty development workshops on promotion and tenure
- Tenure clock extension policies

(a) *Promotion and tenure committee training and development*: Obtaining tenure and getting promoted are key transitions in the academic career pipeline. Each year, promotion and tenure (P&T) committees at the school/college level and university level make decisions about candidates based on their academic performance, research/scholarship materials, and statements of contribution in the research, teaching, and service areas. Many factors may affect equity in their decision-making process, such as the composition of committee members, their knowledge of gender

---

Faculty Advancement Strategies at Georgia Institute of Technology

<u>Goals</u>:
Improve every stage of the faculty recruitment process by providing faculty with information, advice, and techniques to help them run more effective and efficient search committees.

<u>Activities</u>:
PTAC surveyed the faculty to examine academic faculty perceptions concerning promotion and tenure (P&T) at Georgia Tech and to explore a range of areas related to faculty development and evaluation. The committee also identified best practices in unit P&T practices and generated a report that was disseminated to all deans and chairs. They created an Awareness of Decisions in Evaluating Promotion and Tenure (ADEPT) interactive tool (available at www.adept.gatech.edu). ADEPT is a downloadable application that provides case studies and various forms of reference material relevant to P&T evaluations. One of the primary goals of the instrument is to assist users in identifying forms of bias (related to gender, minority status, choice of publication venues, preference for interdisciplinary research, assignment of service activities, allocation of resources, mentoring, disability, etc.) in evaluation processes to achieve fair and objective evaluations. ADEPT is also meant for use by candidates coming up for promotion or tenure, to enhance their ability to prepare their record for evaluation.

<u>Implementation</u>:
ADEPT is now incorporated into the promotion and tenure review process at Georgia Tech, and its completion is required of all members of promotion and tenure committees.

Source: Georgia Tech (2007). See also www.advance.gatech.edu/archive/promotion.html

---

bias, and the role of the committee chair. To enhance the performance of P&T committees, *ADVANCE* institutions have provided training to committee members about potential gender biases in evaluation processes. As described in the text box, Georgia Tech created an online tool to facilitate gender-bias awareness.

Members of the *ADVANCE* project at the University of Texas, El Paso served on the Promotion and Tenure Committee and an ad hoc committee in the College of Science to review their promotion and tenure policy. They implemented a third-year review process which consisted of bringing in each faculty member and his/her mentor to meet with the P&T committee and discuss in an informal and collegial environment the most effective strategies to strengthen the (future) tenure dossier. The dean of science then met with each third-year candidate to discuss the review from the departmental and college levels. Evaluation of the process indicated that it worked very effectively to help with "course corrections" and that it contributed directly to the high number of successful tenure recommendations during the *ADVANCE* award period (University of Texas, El Paso 2008).

Instead of using a committee, the *ADVANCE* project at Utah State University required an ombudsperson to attend each annual P&T meeting. The ombudsperson ensured that all committee members were present and that they have read the file. The ombudsperson also ensured that the candidate had time to ask questions, no inappropriate questions were asked by the committee, the committee stayed on task, and their decision letter reflected the content of the meeting (Utah State University 2007). An ombudsperson training DVD was produced to help make the ombuds process more transparent and understandable to faculty, deans and other top administrators, and disseminated to peer institutions (Utah State University 2008).

(b) *Faculty development workshops on promotion and tenure (P&T)*: Serving as faculty-development sessions, P&T workshops, especially for women and minority faculty but open to all, were introduced and highly visible at several *ADVANCE* sites. These workshops explicitly communicate the requirements and expectations for advancement in the academic

---

Promotion and Tenure Workshops for Faculty at New Mexico State University (NMSU)

Goals:
Partnering with the NMSU Hispanic Caucus and the Provost's Office, the *ADVANCE* project at New Mexico State University offered annual P&T workshops for all faculty members. An annual fall workshop introduced general information about the P&T process and provided an opportunity for faculty across the institution to network. A spring workshop provided the opportunity for faculty members to meet with members of their own school/college's P&T committee and to study successful P&T packets.

Participants:
The annual P&T workshops were well attended on the NMSU campus. In 2008, 54 tenure-track faculty attended the fall university-wide tenure workshop. In 2007, 35 and 52 tenure-track faculty attended the spring and fall university-wide tenure workshops, respectively. In 2006, 45 and 42 tenure-track faculty attended the spring and fall university-wide tenure workshops, respectively. In 2002, 77 faculty members from across the university participated in a P&T workshop.

Source: New Mexico State University (2009). See also www.advance.nmsu.edu/Initiatives/PT/index.html.

pipeline. Typically, P&T workshops provide faculty members with relevant knowledge and information about the P&T process on their campus. For example, the text box provides information on annual fall and spring P&T workshops conducted at New Mexico State University.

The *ADVANCE* program at Georgia Tech created an Annual Career Coaching Workshop (see www.advance.gatech.edu/initiatives.html) which brings together junior and senior tenure-track and tenured faculty in informal discussion. Each prospective candidate for promotion and/or tenure meets one-on-one with a senior colleague to discuss his/her career-related issues. During the workshop each candidate receives advice from approximately four senior faculty members who are available after the workshop if further advice is needed. At the University of Maryland, Baltimore County, each year the Faculty Sponsorship Committee, a committee of senior STEM women, identified and advised junior STEM women faculty who were nearing third-year review or tenure and promotion review about dossier preparation, sharing successful self-assessment documents and informational materials about the P&T process. The committee identified a mentor from the department if one did not already exist, and invited them to work with the junior faculty member during the process (University of Maryland, Baltimore County 2007).

Most of the P&T faculty development workshops conducted at the 19 *ADVANCE* institutions we studied specifically targeted the third-year review or promotion and tenure review for current assistant professors. A few universities offered workshops to and prepared information for dissemination to associate professors detailing promotion strategies and tips (e.g., Utah State University and Hunter College, CUNY). More recently, *ADVANCE* institutions in the first two cohorts and beyond have recognized the importance of providing information, development, and supports to posttenure associate professors seeking promotion to the professor rank. For example, the University of Michigan conducted focus groups of 53 associate professors in 2009 and determined common themes in the positive and negative experiences of faculty in this rank as well as suggestions for improvement (i.e., what is needed to thrive as associate professors?) and promotion (http://sitemaker.umich.edu/advance/files/assocproffocusgroup09reporfinal.pdf). Researchers at Rensselaer Polytechnic Institute documented both a differential rate of promotion to full professor for women and differential access to the knowledge and advice necessary to advance in the academic hierarchy—and geared their *ADVANCE* institutional transformation project, Reforming Advancement Processes through University Professions (RAMP-Up), to address these differentials (see http://rampup.rpi.edu/Documents/ProjectDescription.pdf).

(c) <u>*Tenure clock extension policies*</u>: Many *ADVANCE* universities revised their tenure clock policies to enable a faculty member to take a medical and/or family leave (such as leave surrounding the birth or adoption of a child) and accordingly extend the mandatory tenure evaluation period. Some universities have made this extension an automatic event. For example, the University of Washington instituted the policy that if a leave of six months or more is taken, faculty are automatically entitled to not count that year toward mandatory tenure review, and in the case that a faculty member did not take leave or did not take enough leave to trigger an automatic tenure clock extension, the faculty member can still request a year tenure extension any time prior to the year of review (see http://www.washington. edu/admin/acadpers/policies/leaves-MedFamTen.html). At Virginia Tech, modified duties and stop-the-clock policies were reviewed and updated. Both policies are available to men and women and provide flexibility in the case of illness, childbirth, or family emergencies. Stop-the-clock polices are automatic in the case of childbirth or adoption, and modified duties policies are available in the event of unexpected personal or family circumstances (Virginia Tech 2008). Results from an interview study at Virginia Tech indicated that the majority of newly hired faculty members were aware of the existence of these policies and that the availability of these policies influenced some new faculty members' decisions to accept a position at the university (Virginia Tech 2008).

By creating centrally administered policies around family leave available to women and men faculty, these universities have minimized variations in implementation of stop-the-clock and family leave packages across departments. Other best practices around family leaves that assist in the advancement of faculty include intolerance for any bias or stigma attached to taking such leave, being sensitive to everyday family needs, and creating a more family-friendly workplace environment (e.g., to ensure that meetings are not scheduled too early or late in the day so as to impinge on day-care drop-off and pickup), providing some student or postdoctoral support to keep the faculty member's research activities and laboratory functioning during the leave period, and providing extra student teaching support and more manageable teaching and service assignments on their immediate return from family leave.

In summary, as described above, *ADVANCE* institutions have focused on faculty advancement through P&T committee training regarding gender biases, making the expectations and requirements for advancement more transparent to women faculty members, and developing centrally administered institutional policies about tenure clock extensions and effective practices around family leave.

Resource Equity and Retention initiatives, also were undertaken at *ADVANCE* institutions. While faculty departure may be linked to many factors, resource inequities may provide the spark that catalyzes a productive scientist's departure. Ensuring resource equity may be an important way to improve climate perceptions (Bilimoria et al. 2006), as well as a significant means to retain both women and men scientists in academia.

An innovative effort to support improved equity on campus is the equity-advisor model (see text box), developed at the University of California, Irvine and adopted by some later *ADVANCE* IT cohort institutions.

TRANSFORMATIONAL INITIATIVES TO ENHANCE INSTITUTIONAL CLIMATE

Climate and culture are key elements requiring institutional transformation. These refer to the patterns of interactions and behaviors among group members, and organizational culture refers to the shared assumptions, norms, practices, processes, structure, physical space layout, stories, and formal statements employed by group members (Schein 1992; O'Reilly & Chatman 1996). Workplace climate is particularly consequential because it "can activate interests, convey standards, and stimulate or stifle performance" (Fox 2010, 1001; see also Blau 1973; Kopelman, Brief, & Guzzo 1990). The climate of a university, school, or department is related to faculty performance and outcome variables such as satisfaction, productivity, advancement, and retention (Carr, Schmidt, Ford, & DeShon 2003; August & Waltman 2004). In this section we identify the *ADVANCE* institutions' initiatives to enhance the everyday structures, processes, and practices of the micro and macro work climates prevalent in a university—to make each academic workplace more hospitable to women and minority S&E faculty and more facilitative of their career development and advancement.

Institutional climate may be enhanced by improving the awareness of a critical mass of faculty and decision makers. Intervention practices include improving the awareness and practices of faculty through education, training, and development; engaging in efforts to make departments (microclimates) more collegial, egalitarian, equitable, and transparent; and increasing organizational awareness of diversity and inclusion issues (Peterson & Spencer 1991; Schein 1992; Blakemore et al. 1997; Rosser 1999). Next, we address some of the climate-improvement initiatives implemented at micro (department) level and at the macro (university) level.

Improving Micro (Departmental) Climates

Department climate is an area of focus for institutional transformation efforts. Since individuals experience climate in their immediate workplace, perceptions about department climate are key determinants for faculty satisfaction and retention, and improving department climate is critical for the retention and advancement of women faculty (Callister, Williams, & Fine 2009). A number of campus surveys show that women faculty members experience a more negative departmental climate than their male colleagues. For example, the results of survey of STEM junior faculty across a

Equity Advisors at the University of California, Irvine (UCI)

Goals:
Equity Advisors (EQAs) are senior faculty and respected scholars who serve as faculty assistants to their deans. They work with their constituent faculty to improve faculty recruitment and hiring in particular, as well as advancement and retention. Since they work closely with deans they may be privy to confidential material and meetings.

Selection and Training of EQAs:
Each EQA was nominated by the dean in each of the ten schools in UCI's *ADVANCE* project and approved by the PIs and director. Each was particularly familiar with his/her school constituency including the particular equity issues within the school's disciplines. EQAs were paid $15,000 per year, (either as a stipend or research allowance) for their two- or three-year term, and each school provided access to a $5,000 budget for items and events that are needed to implement relevant school-specific programming.

New EQAs were trained via meetings with the *ADVANCE* project director and interactions with the other EQAs in formal settings such as the monthly two-hour *ADVANCE* Program Advisory Committee (APAC) meetings and informally by collaborating within and across schools. In addition to the committee meetings, the project director met every month with the EQAs from each school. The purpose of these meetings was to assist in problem solving, to facilitate the EQAs' functions, and to share information among the EQAs, project PIs, and university administration.

Activities and Evaluation:
EQAs have become essential partners with deans regarding faculty recruitment, advancement, and retention. An external evaluation site visit found that EQAs were widely regarded as valued resources who contribute to gender equity and diversity of applicant pools. In addition to their central role in improving faculty-hiring processes, EQAs coordinated the mentoring programs in their respective schools, and some participated in salary equity reviews. These additional roles have sometimes been viewed as concerning to department chairs and other faculty for whom EQA reporting lines may not be clear. Additionally, some deans suggested that the structuring of the EQA role (part-time, rotating) does not lend itself well to the complexities of faculty mentoring and salary equity reviews.

Source: University of California, Irvine (2006).

sample of 56 universities (587 women and 1222 men) indicated that women faculty were significantly less satisfied than men faculty with three departmental climate factors (fair treatment of junior faculty in the department, sense of "fit," and opportunities to collaborate with senior colleagues) and seven factors measuring the nature of work including the number of courses taught, amount of time for research, amount of external funding expected, and access to teaching facilities and research assistants (Trower 2008). Additionally, in this survey women faculty reported a significantly lower sense of inclusion in their home units, significantly lower access to equipment and significantly lower recognition from faculty in home units. In another survey of 765 faculty respondents from nine research universities during 2002–2004, women faculty were significantly less likely than men faculty to characterize their home units as helpful, informal, exciting, creative, and inclusive and significantly more likely to characterize their units as stressful (Fox 2010).

Since women faculty in STEM departments often are solo faculty or one of a very small minority, it is not surprising that they may feel isolated. The *ADVANCE* institutions have used a number of initiatives to improve departmental climates, including department climate interventions, funding for departmental transformation projects, assistance to departmental strategic planning efforts, department-specific seminars and workshops, and department chair training and coaching. Below we address the following four initiatives that were most frequently used to improve the departmental climates across *ADVANCE* universities:

- Climate improvement through faculty surveys.
- Small funds for departmental transformation.
- Facilitated microclimate interventions.
- Leadership development and climate awareness training of department chairs.

(a) **Climate improvement through faculty surveys:** Surveys are important tools for changing the organizational climate—they provide robust benchmarks and standards for a range of dimensions of a healthy workplace as well as a process of engaging employees in the development of the organization (Drapeau 2004). Faculty-climate surveys were one of the most widely implemented strategies across *ADVANCE* sites. At the 2006 *ADVANCE* PI meeting, researchers summarized the core climate variables that were investigated in the climate surveys conducted by 14 (*ADVANCE* IT Cohort 1 and Cohort 2) institutions (see http://www.advance.vt.edu/Advance_2006_PI_Mtg/Draft_Core_Climate_Variables.pdf). The most frequently used items included child-care responsibilities and resources (13 universities), treatment by colleagues/supervisors, including items for recognition, respect, collegiality, expectations, sense of being valued, fit, and exclusion (13 universities), spouse employment (12 universities), job/career satisfaction (12 universities), resource equity and access (12 universities), and service and teaching load or time allocation (10 universities).

In the text box, we illustrate how faculty climate surveys were used to improve departmental climates at the University of Wisconsin, Madison.

**Climate Workshop Series for Department Chairs
at University of Wisconsin at Madison**

Goals:
To increase awareness of climate and its influence on the research and teaching missions of a department; to identify various issues that can influence climate in a department; to enable chairs to assess climate in their own departments; to provide chairs with opportunities to enhance climate in their departments by learning from each others' experiences and ideas; and to provide chairs with advice and resources they can use to enhance climate in their departments.

Activities:
Three department chair meeting sessions were conducted interspersed with a survey of department members, as follows. Department chairs were provided advice, supports, and resources to implement changes in their departmental climates based on their survey results.

- *Session 1*: Department chairs engaged in a general discussion of climates and the importance of fostering positive climates. The topics discussed included: definitions of climates, importance and benefits of fostering positive climates, results from the recent studies of faculty and academic staff work life at the university, results from surveys and in-depth interviews with faculty and staff, understanding climate from others' perspectives, research on the influence of unconscious biases and assumptions, and an introduction to the Web-based departmental climate survey.
- *Session 2*: Chairs received the survey results for their individual departments, reviewed these results, and had the opportunity to discuss the survey findings. They shared with each other some positive results of the survey and what they are doing to achieve these results. They solicited advice or suggestions from other chairs, from the facilitator, and/or from provided resource materials on negative results. Chairs learned about resources and people on campus who can help them in their efforts to enhance climate.
- *Session 3*: Chairs met to discuss how they shared survey findings with their departments and how they identified what areas of the department climate need to be improved. Discussion concentrated
Continued

Continued
on the development of an action plan to address areas of concern, and specific topics such as the influence of strategic planning, leadership styles, organizational structure, and decision-making styles on departmental climate.

Evaluation:
Conclusions of the evaluation process were that faculty and staff tend to report more negative perceptions of department climate than graduate students and post-docs/fellows, and that while a majority of faculty and staff report a positive overall department climate, a significant minority reports a negative overall department climate. Data gathered from the climate surveys highlight common issues that department chairs may seek to address in an effort to build a more positive department climate.

Source: http://wiseli.engr.wisc.edu/climate.php; see also http://wiseli.engr.wisc.edu/docs/EvalReport_Climate_2009.pdf.

(b) **Small funds for department transformation:** *ADVANCE* institutions also encouraged decentralized decision making about climate improvements through a variety of department-level transformation grants. These grants were small funds to enable the creation and maintenance of an enriched climate for women and men faculty. Such grants included Department Transformation Grants at the University of Washington, Celebrating Women in Science and Engineering Grant Program at the University of Wisconsin, Madison, Department Enhancement Grants at the University of Colorado Boulder, Department Initiative Grants at Case Western Reserve University, and Internal Advisory Board Initiative Awards at Kansas State University.

For example, Departmental Transformation Grants (DTGs) at the University of Washington were awarded to five departments (Biology, Civil and Environmental Engineering, Electrical Engineering, Mathematics, and Mechanical Engineering) in academic years 2003–04 and 2004–05. The Electrical Engineering Department's DTG was used to improve the department's culture of community and faculty mentoring by holding meetings of senior women faculty with junior women faculty during the winter quarter to advise them in preparing for their spring quarter performance review, developing Web pages with mentoring resources and useful information for new faculty, conducting a quarterly series of panel discussions aimed at graduate student professional development, and undertaking a series of lunch meetings for women graduate students and faculty. The Mechanical Engineering Department used their DTG for strategic planning and activities related to the recruitment, retention, and advancement of women and minority faculty and graduate students, including annual meetings with junior faculty to assist with mentoring and preparation of P&T portfolios, a new series of seminars at which distinguished alumni were invited to speak on their professional lives, an annual mechanical engineering graduate visiting day, and identification of STEM minority databases and other national databases for recruitment (University of Washington 2008).

At the University of Wisconsin at Madison, the Celebrating Women in Science and Engineering grants, funded through contributions from internal STEM schools and colleges, were awarded to student groups, departments, or other groups to bring in outside speakers to address the status of women in STEM. From 2002 through 2006, the *ADVANCE* program awarded 34 grants, and had brought in 66 women speakers to 24 departments/programs in five schools/colleges (WISELI—Women in Science and Engineering Leadership Institute 2007).

Department Initiative Grants were initiated at Case Western Reserve University during 2005–2008. Eight departments were funded and worked on their proposed initiatives. For example, the Department of Physiology and Biophysics initiated a graduate-student senior program, the Department of Biomedical Engineering initiated a faculty mentoring program, and the women's studies area worked on strategic planning. Several other departments were funded to bring in distinguished external women scientists and engineers to spend a few days on the campus and share both their work and life stories with faculty and graduate students. The distinguished woman scholar competitive funding was at first available to science and engineering departments only, but it was soon opened up to all other departments in the university (Case Western Reserve University 2008).

Similarly, at Kansas State University, Internal Advisory Board Departmental Initiative Awards—small grants of $10,000 or less for department activities that promote the goals of *ADVANCE*—were instituted. For example, the Mathematics department used their funds to support visits of prominent mathematicians and provide travel funds for women faculty to gain additional professional exposure. The Physics department used their funding to improve the user-friendliness and content of their departmental Web site as well as host invited lectures from senior women scientists. The Clinical Sciences department implemented a professional development plan for assistant professors to facilitate their transition to successful careers in academic clinical veterinary medicine. The Chemistry department hosted a theatrical performance and discussion on faculty hiring and recruitment practices (see https://www.k-state.edu/advance/Initiatives/IAB%20 Awards%20Summary.pdf).

In general, departmental transformation grants provided individual departments and groups opportunities to reflect on and identify issues and customized solutions related to the climate facing women and minority faculty and students. The funds offered a resource platform to seed departmental changes aimed at improving structures and practices affecting equity, diversity, and inclusiveness.

Facilitated microclimate interventions: A unique initiative was offered at some *ADVANCE* institutions to improve the climate in specific departments through improved internal collaboration, collegial atmosphere, strategic planning, team building, and facilitated interaction. For example, Case Western Reserve University appointed external consultants, experts in team and organizational development, to facilitate faculty retreats, interview faculty members for improvement ideas, and work with certain departments on departmental climate improvement and strategic planning (Case Western Reserve University 2008).

At the University of Washington, results from interviews with 19 STEM department chairs suggested that people-related issues were most significantly needed to improve department climates. In response, the Cross-Department Cultural Change Program (CDCCP) at the University of Washington was designed to help departments enrich communication, enhance collaboration, seek and utilize diversity more effectively, improve faculty recruitment and retention, as well as foster a positive and inclusive environment (University of Washington 2008). The CDCCP provided an opportunity for department chairs and faculty to work together on specific department issues around cultural change. One cohort of four departments participated in CDCCP, which lasted almost a full year. Each CDCCP cohort included four to five department chairs plus two to three faculty members who represented a critical mass of faculty from each department. Over a 12-month period, multiple sessions of meetings (e.g., orientation, communication skills, personality types, conflict management, cross-department conversations, and submeetings of departmental teams) were conducted, with each session lasting two to three hours (Yen & Loving 2005). Overall the program was a positive experience for those involved, particularly because of the cross-departmental nature of the program. The departments that were more engaged gained benefits and saw changes in the attitudes of the participating faculty (University of Washington 2008).

The *ADVANCE* program at Utah State University initiated a unique microclimate intervention program as described in the text box.

Dual Agenda Department Transformation Program
at Utah State University

Sescription and Goals:

The department transformation program was designed to improve faculty effectiveness. The objective was to work internally with a department to ensure that all faculty of the department have the same access to resources and opportunities to succeed. An outside consultant was hired to confidentially interview each faculty member in a department to discover the root concerns leading to ineffectiveness, as well as discuss department climate issues and what steps need to be taken to improve the climate.

Continued

Continued

Participants:
As of 2008, eight STEM departments had participated in a department transformation project.

Learning about Departmental Transformation:
As described in the Utah State University *ADVANCE* 2005 Annual Report, the critical steps for departmental transformation are to collect data from a majority of faculty in the department and report the findings back to them for discussion in a retreat setting, collectively determine innovative ways to create changes that will meet the most critical needs in the department, gain commitment from individuals to prioritize and work on the changes, and hold regular follow-up meetings to keep faculty and the department head focused on change efforts.

Activities and Evaluation:
Through these facilitated micro-climate interventions a variety of efforts were undertaken, including department retreats, customized workshops that met the needs of a department, implementation of the change ideas generated at the retreats, follow-up meetings, and involvement of the department head and associate deans. Outcomes from department transformation projects included improved faculty engagement, initiation of collaborative seed grants, improved mentoring of junior faculty, improved quality of departmental interactions, and very limited backlash.

Source: Utah State University (2008). See also advance.usu.edu/transformation.aspx

In summary, the department transformation experience of *ADVANCE* universities confirms that cultural change is a slow process that requires long-term investments. The department chair's leadership role as a change agent is essential in facilitating climate change in a department. However, involving a critical mass of faculty (grassroots change) is equally important in bringing about successful and sustainable climate transformation within a department. Educating faculty and administrators, problem identification, developing customized change plans and implementation plans, as well as follow-up meetings, are important elements in departmental transformation.

Leadership development and climate awareness training of department chairs: As on-the-ground key change agents within the academic administrative hierarchy, department chairs (or department heads) are crucial for climate improvements in universities. Support from the department chair is especially important for women and minority faculty (Blackmore et al. 1997) as they are key to creating the immediate academic climate (Bemison, Ward, & Sanders 2000; Lucas 2000) and facilitating access to scarce resources (Rowley & Sherman 2003) and collegial mentoring and support (Bilimoria et al. 2006). For these reasons, a frequently used department-level change initiative employed in *ADVANCE* institutions was the leadership development and gender equity training of department chairs.

Examples of leadership development and climate awareness workshops include quarterly leadership development workshops to department chairs at the University of Washington, department head training workshops at New Mexico State University, leadership development lunches at Virginia Tech, an annual leadership retreat for deans and chairs at Case Western Reserve University, senior faculty workshops and chair workshops at the University of Colorado Boulder, and department chair training workshops at the University of Alabama, Birmingham. These workshops were designed for department chairs, deans, administrators, and both men and women faculty members to develop their leadership and managerial skills, as well as to broaden their horizons about academic climate and community building. Leadership development training sometimes occurred as a onetime event, and sometimes as a series of sessions.

At New Mexico State University, department-head training workshops were aimed at heightening awareness and increasing effectiveness of mid-level academic administrators. In 2008, 121 faculty members attended eight department-head training sessions (New Mexico State University 2008). Twenty-one department heads from 20 academic departments attended at least one department-head training event, contributing to the development of the leadership capabilities of women in S&E and a constructive university climate.

The *ADVANCE* program at the University of Washington offered half-day quarterly leadership development workshops for department chairs and emerging faculty leaders to help them become more effective. These sessions provided a regular forum for leadership development and climate-awareness activities using a model of peer-group learning (i.e., peers presenting their own experiences on important topics and engaging others in discussion and skill building). Between November 2002 and June 2007, 15 quarterly workshops were offered to *ADVANCE* departments and more than 30 topics were discussed. The average attendance of invited department chairs was 76.5%; and 98 emerging leaders (46 women) had attended at least one of the 14 workshops (University of Washington 2008). The University of Washington's *ADVANCE* project also conducted two pilot summer two-day workshops for department chairs across the country, covering topics such as the skills and concepts needed to effectively lead a department, facilitating transitions in faculty careers, balancing work and family in higher education, recruiting and retaining a diverse faculty, mentoring faculty throughout their careers, and getting to 'win-win' with faculty and administrators. Subsequently, these pilot workshops were expanded to a national annual leadership development program, Leadership Excellence for Academic Diversity (LEAD) workshops, for department chairs, deans, and emerging leaders in S&E, addressing departmental and university culture and the professional development of faculty (see http://www.engr. washington.edu/lead/).

In summary, while it may take a longer time and requires targeted resources, the *ADVANCE* universities' experience suggests that a department's climate can be improved through initiatives such as utilizing faculty surveys, decentralized change efforts through department transformation funds, facilitated microclimate transformation interventions, and the leadership development and climate awareness training of department chairs.

Improving Macro (School/College and University) Climates

Beyond the climate of individual departments, *ADVANCE* institutions worked on enhancing overall school/college- and campus-wide awareness of gender equity and institutional climate. These universities have established campus-wide advisory councils on women and minorities, brought distinguished senior women scholars on visits to campus, undertaken gender equity awareness training for nonfaculty campus constituencies such as students, held climate awareness workshops for faculty and administrators through interactive theater presentations, and instituted family-friendly policies. We identified the following initiatives used to improve macroclimates across *ADVANCE* sites:

- **Work-life integration policies, academic career flexibility, and family-friendly initiatives.**
- **Child-care initiatives.**
- **Visiting-distinguished-scholars programs.**
- **Targeting the increase of women in administrative (department chair and dean) and faculty leadership (endowed-chair) positions.**
- **Gender equity awareness-training workshops.**
- **Theatrical performances.**

Initiatives improving work-life integration policies, academic career flexibility, and family-friendly environments: *ADVANCE* institutions engaged in a variety of policy and structural changes to improve career flexibility, work-life integration and family-friendly environments, including tenure clock extension, modified duties, paid parental leave, unpaid parental leave, dual career assistance, part-time earning and part-time tenure, job sharing, transitional support programs, on-campus child care available to faculty, financial assistance for child care, lactation facilities, elder care assistance, domestic partner supports, employee and children tuition subsidies, and counseling and referral services (see a summary of work-life policies at *ADVANCE* institutions available at http://www.advance.gatech. edu/archive/2004conf/2b_matrix.xls). Below we describe three related initiatives: reviewing and updating policies and structures related to work-life integration and family-friendly issues, particularly modified work duties, disseminating information about work-life and family-friendly policies, and establishing transition support funds to support faculty undergoing life or career transitions. These initiatives were applicable generally to both women and men faculty, thereby benefiting all faculty.

As described earlier under tenure clock extension policies, *ADVANCE* universities are moving forward to make the academic workplace more family friendly. In addition to stop-the-clock policies, many of these universities implemented modified work duties policies as well. For example, the Active Service Modified Duties Procedure (ASMD) at Georgia Institute of Technology addresses circumstances that significantly alter a faculty member's ability to maintain a standard workload; the procedure allows faculty members dealing with family events (pregnancy, childbirth, adoption, illness of a family member) to request flexible workloads. Between 2003 and 2006, 33 faculty members received funding, and Georgia Tech provided over $290,000 to ASMD with funds over and above those provided by NSF through *ADVANCE* (Georgia Tech 2007). Similarly, the University of Montana developed a new modified-duties policy proposal for tenure-track/tenured faculty that includes a one semester reduction in teaching and service responsibilities following the birth, adoption, or foster care placement of a child, and an automatic tenure clock extension under these circumstances (http://pace.dbs.umt.edu/Policy/default. htm). At Virginia Tech, central funds were committed to provide up to $10,000 to a department for workload reassignment of faculty members approved for a semester of modified duties; during 2008–09, $49,500 was spent in support of modified duties (Virginia Tech 2009). At the University of Rhode Island, a new paid parental-leave policy was approved, due in a large part to the efforts from their *ADVANCE* project (University of Rhode Island 2006).

The *ADVANCE* Work-Life Committee at the University of Rhode Island was actively involved in improving university-wide awareness of work-life issues. Efforts included (a) updating a Web page to include a link to work-life resources and to the *ADVANCE* Work-Life-Family Web site at www. uri.edu/wlfc/, (b) producing a work-life series of brochures covering topics of child care, dual career, family leave, lactation facilities, and work-life-family Web site overview, (c) sponsoring work-life administrators breakfast meetings, (d) sponsoring a series of work-life events including an information session for legislators and the public, *ADVANCE* topical lunches and presentations (e.g., Wellness at Work: Stop, Stretch, and Breathe; Managing Your Life without Stressing Out: Balancing Work, Life, and Family), movies and discussion (e.g., Century of Women: Work and Family), and work-life policy panel discussions (e.g., Building a Balance: Campus & Corporate Work-Life Issues and Challenges). Stemming from these and related efforts, a dual career policy was approved and a parental leave policy was revised and improved (University of Rhode Island 2008).

A few *ADVANCE* institutions explored other avenues of building flexibility into the tenure-track career path such as through proposed policies on part-time tenure earning status and part-time tenure. For example, these proposed innovative policies of the University of Alabama, Birmingham were under consideration at the time of our data collection.

Many *ADVANCE* institutions have noticed a widespread lack of awareness about work-life and family-friendly policies among faculty and department chairs. A significant contribution of *ADVANCE* interventions has been increasing the understanding of the needs for and reasons behind these policies and changing attitudes and perspectives about these policies (University of Washington 2008). *ADVANCE* universities have created different outreach channels to educate and equip faculty and department chairs with relevant knowledge and to encourage them to utilize these policies. For example, the University of Maryland, Baltimore County's *ADVANCE* project developed a campus-wide family-leave brochure, and the *ADVANCE* program at Case Western Reserve University created a booklet that included descriptions of new and ongoing family-friendly policies. These documents/materials have been delivered to faculty candidates, new hires, and current faculty members, as well as department heads, deans, and administrators.

An innovative program undertaken by several *ADVANCE* universities (e.g., Utah State University, Columbia University, University of Washington, and the University of Wisconsin, Madison) was the use of transitional support programs (TSPs). These programs, designed for faculty who are in critical life transitions caused by personal or family reasons, often have been used to balance competing demands of work and life. The transition support award enables women and men faculty to maintain or restart research productivity during life transitions. For example, between 2001 and 2007, the TSP at the University of Washington awarded grants of $5,000 to $38,000 to STEM faculty in the midst of major life transitions such as the arrival of a child, personal illness, family illness, moving into positions of leadership, and/or elder care (University of Washington 2008). Another example of a TSP at the University of Wisconsin, Madison is provided in the text box.

In sum, *ADVANCE* institutions have undertaken a variety of innovative efforts to enhance their macroclimates through improved academic work-life integration, career flexibility, and family-friendly environments.

Child-care initiatives: As part of work-life and family-friendly initiatives, efforts have been made at *ADVANCE* universities to address child care concerns. Child-care initiatives include on-campus or nearby child-care facilities available to faculty, financial assistance for child care, and on-campus lactation rooms. For example, at Virginia Tech each school/college's dean and the university administration pledged five years of annual support from discretionary private funds for a contract with a local day-care provider. In return for this annual subsidy, the provider guaranteed 60% of the 246 new

---

**Vilas Life Cycle Professorship (Transitional Support) Program
at the University of Wisconsin, Madison**

Goal:
The Vilas Life Cycle Professorship (VLCP) program was initiated in
2005 at the University of Wisconsin, Madison to provide competitively -assigned funds to faculty and permanent principal investigators
(including both women and men) who were at critical junctures in
their professional careers and whose research productivity had been
directly affected by personal life events.

Participants:
62 faculty members were funded during 2005–08:
  18 out of 27 applicants were funded in 2005/06
  18 out of 21 applicants were funded in 2006/07
  11 out of 19 applicants were funded in 2007/08
  15 out of 18 applicants were funded in 2008/09

Evaluation:
As described in a 2009 evaluation report, recipients viewed the VLCP
program very positively and indicated that these awards enabled them
to remain at the university, allowed them to address their personal
crises, and provided resources to meet their professional demands.

Source: wiseli.engr.wisc.edu/vilas.php.

---

slots to Virginia Tech families. This expansion of services addressed a long-
term need documented by faculty surveys (Virginia Tech 2009). Columbia
University opened several new lactation facilities across the university during
2008–09. To raise awareness of lactation facilities around the campus for
nursing mothers, their School of Engineering and Applied Science hosted the
launch of a university-wide lactation room initiative in coordination with
their Office of Work Life (Columbia University 2009).

**Visiting scholar programs for distinguished external women scientists and
engineers**: To increase familiarity with and gain mentoring and other benefits
from exposure to women scientists and engineers in senior faculty and leadership positions, the visiting scholar program was one of the most frequently
used initiatives across *ADVANCE* sites. Examples included the *ADVANCE*
Program of Visiting Scientists and Engineers implemented at the University
of Michigan, Distinguished Visiting Professor implemented at New Mexico State University, the Visiting Scholars Program implemented at Virginia
Tech, the *ADVANCE* Distinguished Visiting Scholar Program implemented
at the University of Alabama, Birmingham, the *ADVANCE* Distinguished
Lecture Series implemented at Kansas State University, the Distinguished
Speakers Series implemented at University of Maryland, Baltimore County,

the *ADVANCE* Distinguished Lectureships implemented at Case Western Reserve University, the Marie Tharp Fellowship implemented at Columbia University, and the Visiting Scholar/Mentor Award implemented at the University of Montana. The visits of distinguished women scholars raised the visibility and intellectual authority of women and/or minority faculty on campus and positively influenced the gender equity climate at these institutions. Details of the *ADVANCE* Distinguished Lectureships established at Case Western Reserve University are described in the text box.

**ADVANCE Distinguished Lectureships
at Case Western Reserve University**

Goal:
The goals of the *ADVANCE* distinguished lectureships were to increase the visibility of senior women scientists and engineers on campus, to provide mentoring and networking opportunities for faculty and students while showcasing innovations in STEM to external visitors, and to preview potential hires of women and minority senior faculty.

Implementation:
Distinguished lecturers were invited based on mutual research interests with faculty in a host department for a minimum stay of two days and a maximum stay of two weeks at the university. The visit included three to six seminars and lectures as well as a large public lecture followed by a reception. In addition, many departments scheduled informal discussions with the visitors. The proposals for Distinguished Lectureships were reviewed competitively by the ACES Internal Advisory Board.

Participation:
Forty *ADVANCE* Distinguished Lectureships were offered campus-wide during 2003–2008, significantly increasing the number of women scientists and engineers brought to the university.

Assessment:
Both men and women faculty took advantage of this opportunity to bring senior women to the university. In Years 1–3 (2004, 2005, and 2006), Distinguished Lectureships were offered to the 32 science and engineering departments included in the *ADVANCE* award; in Years 4–5 (2007 and 2008), they were made available to all departments in the university.

Institutionalization:
As part of institutionalization, two lectureships a year have been permanently established in the School of Engineering through the NSF CLiPS Science and Technology Center in collaboration with the Office of the Provost.

Source: Case Western Reserve University (2008)

Initiatives targeting the increase of women in faculty leadership and administrative positions: *ADVANCE* universities have recognized that for gender equity climate change to occur, women need to be in visible positions of leadership, both at the faculty level through endowed chairs or named professorships and at the administrative level as department heads, chairs, and deans. These institutions systematically track faculty leadership and administrative proportions by gender and share this information with their senior university administration to engender change over the longer run. They have also conducted meetings and retreats to enable qualified women faculty to seek and advance into these positions.

The award of an endowed chair or named professorship reflects the prestige and success that a faculty member has achieved over their academic career, and provides them considerable freedom to pursue innovative research avenues. Endowed chairs represent an essential cultural element of recognition by one's peers, especially at research universities. The *ADVANCE* universities have understood this important symbolic and cultural role, have recognized that women and minority faculty are underrepresented as recipients of these prestigious and relatively rare awards, and have worked on increasing the number of women holding endowed chairs through various efforts. For example, termed chairs were created at Georgia Tech to promote the goals of *ADVANCE* and to build networks of communication, mentoring, and exchange among female faculty. Case Western Reserve University created two related goals to address underrepresentation of senior women in S&E areas: the first to increase the overall number of women faculty holding endowed chairs in science and engineering departments over their *ADVANCE* award, and the second to raise funds for five additional chairs to be allocated to women science and engineering faculty. The first goal was realized since the number of women faculty in the science and engineering departments holding endowed chairs nearly doubled (from eight in 2003–04 to 15 in 2007–08). The second goal was partially achieved, with funding established for two new endowed chairs (committed to women faculty) and for a significant proportion of a third new chair at the time when their *ADVANCE* award ended (Case Western Reserve University 2008).

Another example was the *ADVANCE* Term Chairs implemented at the University of California, Irvine. Two distinguished professors were selected to hold these chairs for a period of five years, acting as ambassadors of the *ADVANCE* project. As members of their *ADVANCE* Program Advisory Committee, they assisted in mentoring program development across campus, served as mentors, and assisted in fund-raising for an endowment to fund future term chairs and other aspects of *ADVANCE*. In addition, these eminent scholars were advocates of gender equity with access to other awards committees, providing an institutional mechanism by which awards processes become attentive to gender equity issues (University of California, Irvine 2006).

Gender equity awareness-training workshops for university faculty and students: Equipping faculty members with knowledge of gender equity, diversity, and inclusion issues through awareness training workshops was another frequently used strategy to improve campus climates. Examples include the Equity Action Workshops implemented at Kansas State University that aimed at providing participants with greater understanding of gender issues and how to address those issues, and presentations at the department and college/school levels implemented at Case Western Reserve University. At Virginia Tech, an annual "Advancing Diversity at Virginia Tech" conference was created to improve university-wide awareness. The fifth annual conference, cosponsored with the Office of Multicultural Affairs, was held in January 2009 with almost 200 registered participants. Featured speakers addressed an inclusive excellence model for institutional transformation and the career concerns of pretenure faculty. Workshop sessions also focused on recruiting a diverse faculty and creating department climates that encourage faculty success (Virginia Tech 2008).

The *ADVANCE* project at Case Western Reserve University conducted gender awareness training workshops for undergraduate and graduate STEM students to introduce them to research that indicates that there are gender discrepancies in the treatment of men and women in academia. The training underwent several iterations based on student feedback and faculty reactions, including presentation of the data in and out of classrooms and in forums linked to other career-related speakers and information. The best received training sessions occurred when they were combined with career planning topics and when department-level graduate student groups and/or groups with a solid constituency (such as the graduate-student senate) were integrally involved with the planning (Case Western Reserve University 2008).

Climate change through theatrical performances: *ADVANCE* institutions pioneered the use of a theatrical performance as a distinctive approach to increasing organizational awareness about issues of gender equity, diversity, and inclusion. A theatrical performance works because it combines the best elements of reflection and interpersonal exchanges—characteristic of professional development workshops—with the power and creativity of dramatization (Kaplan, Cook, & Steiger 2006). The theatrical performances used were derived from research conducted on actual faculty experiences during typical events in the academic pipeline (e.g., a promotion review), and enacted by professional stage actors who stayed in role while the audience grappled with the dynamics being presented. The text box describes the theatrical performances employed by the Center for Research on Learning and Teaching (CRLT) Players at the University of Michigan to spread campus-wide awareness and spur climate change around issues of gender equity, diversity, and inclusion.

The success of the CRLT Players at the University of Michigan in raising awareness about campus climate issues inspired other institutions to

The Center for Research on Learning and Teaching (CRLT) Players at the University of Michigan

Description:
The Center for Research on Learning and Teaching (CRLT) Players at the University of Michigan develop and perform sketches that engage faculty in discussions of institutional climate. For example, *Faculty Advising Faculty* explores the junior faculty–senior faculty mentoring process and examines the individual and institutional factors that can hinder or foster effective mentoring. *The Faculty Meeting* depicts a faculty discussion involving a faculty search and how gender and other dynamics and faculty rank influence the conversation and affect the participants. As described by Kaplan, Cook, and Steiger (2006), four strategies were used in the creation of sketches that allow faculty to open up issues with which they would normally resist dealing: (1) serious issues are presented with humor, (2) sketches are emotionally engaging but allow participants to maintain distance, (3) sketches have credibility but take advantage of a willing suspension of disbelief, and (4) mentoring is created through presentation and active learning.

Format:
CRLT presentations generally last one to one and one-half hours and may be integrated into departmental programs, meetings, workshops, or retreats.

Evaluation:
Evaluation results from multiple sources indicate that theater performances affect audience members' awareness and behaviors, as well as make a significant contribution to institutional-level awareness (Kaplan, Cook, & Steiger 2006).

Implementation at Other Universities:
Several other *ADVANCE* universities have invited CRLT players to their campuses. For example, in April 2008, Virginia Tech hosted the CRLT Players at the Lyric Theater to perform *The Faculty Meeting* (Virginia Tech 2008). At the 2005 annual leadership retreat at Case Western Reserve University, the CRLT players also performed *The Faculty Meeting*, followed by a group discussion of hiring processes and climate (Case Western Reserve University 2008).

Source: sitemaker.umich.edu/advance/crlt_players; Kaplan, Cook, & Steiger 2006

undertake similar theatrical development and performance. For example, at Utah State University, the *ADVANCE* Interactive Theatre Project/Performance was modeled after the CRLT players from University of Michigan. Between September 2006 and May 2007, an interactive presentation/

theatrical performance "Third Year Review" (focused on a promotion and tenure meeting) was performed five times. The presentations were designed to increase faculty awareness of issues involved in tenure and promotion including mentoring, gender stereotypes, raising new standards at the meeting, and inappropriate comments. Audiences discussed what happened with the actors and proposed solutions immediately after the show (Utah State University 2007).

At the University of Puerto Rico at Humacao, the *ADVANCE* Theatre Group presented an experimental theatrical performance based on the life of the mathematician Emmy Noether. The performance portrayed Noether's struggle to obtain a faculty position during the first half of the twentieth century and established parallels with the current situation for women in the science faculty. During three performances in April 2007, the University of Puerto Rico Theatre was fully occupied (approximately 800 attendants). As a way of dissemination, a short video summarizing the performance was produced and presented at the 2007 *ADVANCE* PI Meeting (University of Puerto Rico, Humacao 2007).

In summary, theatrical performances were presented in *ADVANCE* institutions based on ordinary events in academic STEM (e.g., daily interactions or a promotion-related decision meeting). The format of these performances gave audiences opportunities to observe and reflect on their own roles in similar situations. As a tool for transforming organizational climate, the theatrical performances thus started with changing individual and group behaviors.

SUMMARY AND CONCLUSIONS

Our analyses of the various individual career-trajectory and institutional-climate transformational initiatives undertaken at the 19 *ADVANCE* institutions studied indicate a pantheon of activities to address gender equity, diversity, and inclusion. Many of these initiatives have been successfully adopted and advanced by subsequent NSF *ADVANCE* awardees, whether through Institutional Transformation (IT) awards, Partnerships for Adaptation, Implementation and Dissemination (PAID) awards, or IT-Catalyst awards, and by other institutions seeking improvements in gender equity, diversity, and inclusion.

Our extensive review reveals that each *ADVANCE* institution implemented a dynamic portfolio of simultaneous, varied, and multilevel initiatives as recommended by Hogue & Lord (2007). These initiatives targeted improvements in the career trajectories of women faculty in the academic pipeline (focusing on programs of change at the individual, unit, and institutional levels) as well as improvements in the institutional workplace climate. Clearly some initiatives worked better in certain environments, and some individual initiatives may have had more finite impact than others. Yet, we conclude from our review that each *ADVANCE* institution employed a coordinated portfolio of organizational change initiatives consisting of simultaneously enacted and varied interventions targeted at multiple levels (individual, unit, and system-wide) within the institution in order to cumulatively effect change. Formative and summative assessments of these initiatives undertaken by the institutions through systematic internal and external evaluations reveal that these initiatives generally have been very well received by participants, and have succeeded in engaging faculty attention on and action to improve gender equity, diversity, and inclusion.

6 Institutionalization of Transformation

In the previous chapter, we described the myriad initiatives undertaken at multiple levels in the 19 institutions studied to repair the leaky pipeline, stem the steady attrition of women scientists and engineers from the academic workplace, and engender improved equity, diversity, and inclusion. In the present chapter we discuss how the successful initiatives were sustained beyond NSF funding and made permanent in the 19 *ADVANCE* universities.

WHAT IS INSTITUTIONALIZATION?

While the antecedents, determinants, and theories of organizational change have been well studied in the literature of higher education transformation, we know little about how and at what level externally funded change initiatives (like the NSF *ADVANCE* program) are institutionalized and sustained within a higher education organization (Litzler, Claiborne, & Brainard 2007). Two related but different concepts are important to understanding enduring transformation: sustainability and institutionalization. Particularly at the final stages of an *ADVANCE* project, but even during its development and implementation, both sustainability and institutionalization of its programmatic initiatives are major considerations. According to Litzler, Claiborne, and Brainard (2007), sustainability of a program may be achieved with external funding and no institutional support, but institutionalization is achieved when the university makes a long-term financial commitment to a project or some of its aspects. However, institutionalization comprises more than just resource commitments from university administrations. Institutionalization of transformation reflects the permanent embedding of changes into the social-structural fabric of the organization. As Clark (1968, 1) notes, institutionalization is a process "whereby specific cultural elements or cultural objects are adopted by actors in a social system." Institutionalization may occur at structural, procedural, and incorporation levels, with incorporation being the highest level (Curry 1991). Four factors affect the degree of institutionalization of a program, including perceived value, leadership, stability, and diffusion

(Litzler, Claiborne, & Brainard 2007). In concert with Litzler, Claiborne and Brainard (2007), we observe that a combination of sustainability (e.g., funding) and institutionalization (infusion of enduring new meaning and value into the system) are necessary for *ADVANCE* projects to continue at the institutional level.

Some have viewed institutionalization as a change outcome (Litzler, Claiborne, & Brainard 2007), while others consider it to be one of three key processes of successful organizational change: (a) mobilization, whereby the system is prepared for change; (b) implementation, whereby change is introduced into the system; and (c) institutionalization, whereby the system is stabilized in its changed state (Kezar 2001; Curry 1992). This latter approach of conceptualizing institutionalization is similar to the third phase of Lewin's (1943) three-phase model of organizational change—unfreezing, change, and refreezing. In our description of *ADVANCE* institutionalization, we acknowledge both the outcome and process facets—the enduring success of transformational projects depends not only on achieving results during the finite periods when they are live, but also on effectively sustaining and leveraging the results into the future, infusing meaning and value into the institutional system for the times to come.

Given the vibrant nature of institutionalization of gender equity, diversity, and inclusion initiatives undertaken at *ADVANCE* universities, below we address their institutionalization outcomes and processes in terms of the following four aspects:

- **Positions: Creation of new positions, offices, and structures.**
- **Policies: Implementation of new and modified policies.**
- **Practices: Long-term supports and resources for new and improved practices.**
- **Programs: Continued funding (sustainability) for effective programs.**

Before describing each of these aspects, it is important to note several factors and challenges that need to be considered in understanding *ADVANCE* institutionalization through our analysis. First, it should be noted that at the time when an *ADVANCE* project funding expired, many initiatives may have been at the stage of being negotiated and institutionalized, and only a few initiatives may have been completely institutionalized. Our reliance on final and annual *ADVANCE* project reports for conclusions about institutionalization may not reflect their most updated status. Second, especially in the case of some Cohort 2 institutions where NSF *ADVANCE* IT funding was extended beyond the initial five years, their projects had not quite ended at the time of our data collection and analyses. Thus information on institutionalization obtained by us may represent an underrepresentation of what may have come about later. Third, given that institutionalization takes time and is subject to all kinds of uncertainties, it is possible that what was proposed to be institutionalized in some final reports may not have been fully realized later. Given these analytic limitations, we describe *ADVANCE* institutionalization with illustrative examples below.

New Positions, Offices, and Structures

As part of the institutionalization of the transformation, several *ADVANCE* universities created new positions and offices such as ombudspersons, equity advisors, endowed chairs, institutional researchers, and provosts/deans for faculty development and diversity to advance equity, diversity, and inclusion on their campuses. New phusical structures, such as child-care facilities, lactation centers for nursing mothers, and faculty development centers were opened at some universities. Other improvements in structures such as institutional research (data collection and analysis systems) were created also through the efforts of *ADVANCE* interventions. Details are presented next.

(a) *New positions and offices related to gender equity, diversity, and inclusion*: As part of institutionalization, several new positions and offices were created at the *ADVANCE* universities focusing on issues of equity, diversity, and inclusion. For example, at Case Western Reserve University, new positions and offices were created including a vice president of diversity, inclusion and equal opportunity at the university level, an associate dean for faculty development at the School of Engineering, a diversity specialist in the Office of Faculty Diversity, a support staff position at the Center for Women, and a support staff position in the Office of Institutional Research. A search also began for an assistant dean of faculty development and diversity in the School of Medicine (Case Western Reserve University 2008).

At New Mexico State University, in 2008 an Office of the Ombuds was created under the office of the president, and four staff and faculty ombudspersons were appointed (New Mexico State University 2009). At the University of Texas, El Paso, in the fall of 2006, the provost appointed a new vice-provost for faculty and academic affairs and convened a new university-wide Chairs' Council (University of Texas, El Paso 2008).

As described earlier, several universities created endowed chairs or paid faculty positions to disseminate the message of gender equity, diversity, and inclusion. At the University of California, Irvine, two *ADVANCE* term chairs were created to provide a tangible demonstration of the value of activities that promote gender equity. At Case Western Reserve University, new funding (external to *ADVANCE* funding from NSF) was raised to establish two new endowed chairs, and partial support was received for a third endowed chair. At the University of Michigan, faculty advocates for gender equity in recruitment were created through the STRIDE Committee, and supported with university funds after the end of their award. At the University of California, Irvine, equity advisors were created to provide resources, guidance, and support to faculty search committees, and supported beyond their *ADVANCE* IT award. At Columbia University, new Lamont Research Professorships were established, creating nontenured endowed research professor positions, carrying many of the benefits that tenure-track faculty positions have at peer institutions.

(b) *New structures supporting gender equity, diversity, and inclusion:* New structures supporting faculty development and work-life integration were created through the influence of *ADVANCE* projects. For example, Georgia Tech established a new office of Faculty Career Development Services (FCDS) in January 2006. Activities were institutionalized within FCDS and the Center for the Study of Women, Science, and Technology. FCDS is responsible for processing all academic faculty personnel transactions, including appointments, reappointments, promotions, tenure, posttenure reviews, leaves of absence, and salary adjustments (Georgia Tech 2007).

At Case Western Reserve University, during the *ADVANCE* award period, interviews with child-care experts in the local metropolitan area were conducted by the President's Advisory Committee on Women and a Web-based survey was sent to all faculty, staff, and students about their likely usage of an on-campus child-care facility. A location was selected and plans were drawn for a new facility, but budgetary problems at the university level precluded its realization. Subsequently, after a faculty senate vote that prioritized child care over other faculty needs, the new president created new funds to support the costs of child care. Two new child-care benefits programs were established, available to all faculty, staff, and students at the university: a Temporary and Back-Up Child Care Program and a Child-Care Support During Travel Program (see http://www.case.edu/finadmin/humres/benefits/childcare.html). Child-care support during faculty travel to conferences was first successfully implemented by the *ADVANCE* IT project at Case Western Reserve University as part of its popular opportunity grants program for women faculty in S&E, and it was subsequently expanded and institutionalized beyond *ADVANCE* as a human-resources benefit available to all faculty, staff, and students at the university.

Other structures were also established as part of the introduction of new family-friendly structures at *ADVANCE* universities. For example, in 2005 the *ADVANCE* program at the University of Washington established a new lactation station on campus, giving priority use to faculty, staff, and students from *ADVANCE* departments (University of Washington 2008). Lactation rooms were also created on the campuses of Utah State University, Columbia University, and the University of Rhode Island, as well as at Case Western Reserve University as part of their ACES+ (Academic Careers in Engineering and Science Plus) project, the institutionalization of their ACES (*ADVANCE* IT) program.

(c) *Improvements to institutional research structures and new data-collection and analysis systems:* Institutional research (primarily data collection and analyses) on varied indicators of gender equity, diversity, and inclusion has been a critical component of *ADVANCE* interventions, and its institutionalization has been a core enhancement to the climate of these universities. New outlets have been identified at these universities to continue and strengthen the institutional data collection and analysis begun during their *ADVANCE* projects. At the University of Puerto Rico, Humacao, the *ADVANCE* baseline data collection and dissemination was institutionalized in the university's Office of Institutional Research (University of Puerto Rico, Humacao 2009). At the University of Texas, El Paso, the *ADVANCE* database moved to the Provost's Office to become part of a larger database beginning in the fall of 2008, and their human-resources department now administers a university-wide faculty exit survey which did not exist prior to their *ADVANCE* project (University of Texas, El Paso 2008). At Case Western Reserve University, the Institutional Research Office and the Provost's Office took over the collection of gender equity indicator data, as well as responsibility for administering or overseeing some of the surveys conducted by the *ADVANCE* program including a faculty climate survey every three years and a biannual junior-faculty survey (Case Western Reserve University 2008).

At Georgia Tech, the new Faculty Career Development Services office was charged with continuing annual or biennial data collection of the 12 NSF data indicators tracked by their *ADVANCE* project (Georgia Tech 2007). At the University of California, Irvine, the function of faculty exit interviews was turned over to the Office of Academic Personnel and the Office of Equal Opportunity and Diversity after their *ADVANCE* project ended (University of California, Irvine 2005). Other institutions have identified new data reports to be produced by their Institutional Research Offices that would be helpful management tools for administrative decision making.

New and Modified University-wide Policies

As described earlier, collectively the *ADVANCE* universities have modified and/or created several new permanent policies to support enhanced equity, diversity, and inclusion of women and other minority faculty groups. As described in Chapter 5, such policies include tenure clock extension policies, dual-career hiring policies, and work-life integration (modified duties or work release) policies. Other family-friendly policies (such as maternity/paternity leave, family medical leave, and domestic partner health benefits) were also created at *ADVANCE* universities.

For example, the *ADVANCE* program at the University of Alabama, Birmingham created and revised family-friendly policies that address tenure clock extension, part-time tenure-track options, and a modified-duties alternative (University of Alabama, Birmingham 2009). Additionally, they also initiated a policy change, implemented in March of 2007, which requests information on the race, ethnicity, and gender of members of every search committee for faculty and upper-level staff positions. In addition, every search committee requires African American representation for tenured/tenure-track faculty searches (University of Alabama, Birmingham

2008). At New Mexico State University, a revised promotion and tenure policy went into effect in August 2008 (New Mexico State University 2008). This umbrella policy serves as a guide for colleges and departments to increase the transparency of the tenure process and to recognize the need for flexibility, particularly with "stopping the tenure clock" and "part-time tenure-track positions" as well as the definition of "scholarship" and the need that candidates should be reviewed on their allocation of effort (see also www.nmsu.edu/~fsenate/ptp/index.html).

At Utah State University, policy changes were made as follows. First, the faculty senate approved a policy change regarding tenure-clock extensions outlining the procedures for extending the clock and for subsequent evaluation of the tenure and promotion dossier (Utah State University 2006). Second, ombudspersons are now institutionalized for all promotion and tenure meetings. Third, promotion advisory committees are now mandated for mentoring associate professors regarding promotion to professor rank; at these mentoring meetings, associate professors are advised on the standards for promotion to professor and develop a plan for going forward (Utah State University 2007).

Long-Term Supports and Resources for New and Improved Practices

In addition to new positions and new policies, several *ADVANCE* innovations and improvements in faculty-related university operational practices have been institutionalized (embedded into the normal way of doing things) through the creation of a variety of guideline documents and support resources. *ADVANCE* universities have systematically documented their effective practices for the benefit of future decision makers in the form of tool kits, guidelines, evaluation forms, training manuals, Web tutorials, presentations, and pamphlets covering the critical aspects of recruitment, tenure and promotion, retention, and leadership development of women and other minority faculty groups.

For example, to institutionalize improvements in the faculty search and recruitment process, *ADVANCE* institutions have created a new *Guide for Affirmative Action in the Recruitment of Faculty Personnel* incorporated into the university's Faculty Manual at the University of Puerto Rico, Humacao; new *Guidelines for Search Committees* sent to all deans and department chairs in the university at Case Western Reserve University; departmental diversity plans for new faculty searches at the University of Maryland, Baltimore County; revisions to the *Faculty Recruitment Handbook* distributed to all chairs, deans, and administrators, and creation of a faculty-recruitment best-practices Web tutorial uploaded on the university's Web site at the University of Rhode Island; revisions to the *Faculty Recruitment Toolkit* at the University of Washington, moving it from the Equal Opportunity Office's Web site to the campus-wide Academic Human Resources Web site; and a new procedure requiring deans to review and validate the diversity of job applicant pools at the University of Montana and at Case Western Reserve University.

Examples of the institutionalization of improvements in other faculty-related operational practices of universities include the creation of a *Faculty Retention Toolkit* distributed to all *ADVANCE* departments, addressing a variety of issues such as faculty development at all career stages, faculty workload, and transparency in operations at the University of Washington; a document, *Resources for Inclusion in Start-Up Packages*, to be used as a guide for discussion of start-up needs for new faculty members, and circulated to all department heads encouraging them to send this document to all candidates invited to campus for interviews at Kansas State University; an *Awareness of Decisions in Evaluating Promotion and Tenure (ADEPT)* interactive training Web tool that has been embedded into the faculty promotion and tenure review process and whose completion is required for all members of promotion and tenure committees at Georgia Tech; a promotion and tenure review training video at Utah State University; a new Work-Life-Family Web site to act as a virtual work-life center and a first step toward the creation of an actual center in the future, and to function as a portal to university, community, and national resources for issues related to work, life and family, education, community, health and well-being, and housing and relocation at the University of Rhode Island; and a new Work/Life Web site advertised to all STEM faculty and staff at Kansas State University.

Continued Funding (Sustainability) for Effective Programs

While *ADVANCE* institutions have experienced that obtaining sustainable funding beyond their initial projects is challenging, several have successfully obtained funding to support all or key aspects of their projects, incorporating the most effective change initiatives into their universities' regular organizational structures and processes. We describe below examples of two different strategies of the continuation of *ADVANCE* programming: the permanent incorporation of entire *ADVANCE* projects within other institutional structures at some universities, and the institutionalization of key *ADVANCE* change initiatives at other universities.

(a) *Incorporation of entire ADVANCE projects within other institutional structures*: With commitment and support from their university administrations, some *ADVANCE* projects were able to be completely institutionalized (embedded within other existing structures and with permanent funding) when their NSF awards expired. Different incorporation models were used at these universities. For example, after the end of NSF funding, the *ADVANCE* program at University of Colorado Boulder (LEAP) was incorporated within the Office of Faculty Affairs and the provost remained committed to its continuation (https://facultyaffairs.colorado.edu/leap). At this same university, the PI of the *ADVANCE* project became the associate vice chancellor for faculty diversity and development after the project ended (Laursen 2009). In 2006, New Mexico State University established its *ADVANCE* project as a permanent program at the university's Teaching Academy, broadening its focus to serve all faculty members, especially underrepresented faculty within the College of Extended Learning (New Mexico State University 2009). The *ADVANCE* project at the University of California, Irvine continued with ongoing support from the Office of the Executive Vice Chancellor and Provost (EVC&P): a new director who was a faculty member at the university was hired, and the EVC&P institutionalized the equity advisors with budgetary support (University of California, Irvine 2006). The *ADVANCE* project at the University of Wisconsin, Madison (WISELI—Women in Science and Engineering Leadership Institute) continues to be funded by a combination of (a) contributions from eight University of Wisconsin, Madison schools, colleges, or units, (b) grant funding from national scientific funding agencies, (c) gift funds, and (d) funds earned through WISELI's income-generating activities (wiseli.engr.wisc.edu).

After NSF funding expired in 2006, the *ADVANCE* project at the University of Michigan received the university's commitment to continue funding for the project through June 2011 at the same annual level as the NSF funding, together with permanent office space at the university's Institute for Research on Women and Gender (sitemaker.umich.edu/advance/). As Dr. Abigail Stewart, the project's PI, described at the 2009 *ADVANCE* PI meeting, the institutionalization of *ADVANCE* initiatives beyond policy changes at University of Michigan included: (a) routine monitoring of data by leadership; (b) a network to *ADVANCE* women scientists and engineers; (c) the Center for Research on Learning and Teaching (CRLT) Players and three "*ADVANCE* sketches" annually presented before tenure discussions; (d) the Committee on Gender in Science and Engineering continues with *ADVANCE* as Convener; (e) departmental climate assessments in the context of five-year departmental reviews; (f) mandatory attendance at STRIDE Committee Faculty Recruitment Workshops for search-committee members in two colleges; (g) required comparison of faculty-search candidate pools and national pools by gender and race/ethnicity in two colleges; and (h) usage of the candidate evaluation tool (Stewart 2009). An external review initiated by the university administration occured in late 2010 to determine the continued impact and contributions of the *ADVANCE* project over the past five years, and funding was extended over another five years.

In preparation of the expiry of their NSF funding, the *ADVANCE* team at Utah State University developed an alliance with the Tri-Council to encourage it to play a crucial role in sustaining and continuing the changes implemented. Their dispersed *ADVANCE* offices moved to a new centralized location on their campus, allowing the sharing of support staff and a closer coordination of activities (Utah State University 2008). Several of their *ADVANCE* faculty-development workshops were taken over by the provost, vice-provosts and deans, such as their assistant-professor workshops, department-head leadership training, and leadership seminars (Utah State University 2008), and ombudspersons were institutionalized for all promotion and tenure meetings (Utah State University 2006).

(b) *Institutionalization of key ADVANCE change initiatives*: At other universities, while *ADVANCE* projects were not retained intact beyond initial funding, institutionalization has occurred with successful and stabilized change initiatives. For example, at Case Western Reserve University, the ACES (Academic Careers in Engineering and Science) project was renamed the ACES+ project and embedded in the Office of the Provost, which took over several of the *ADVANCE* initiatives, including (a) the annual provost's leadership retreat for all deans and chairs in the university, (b) the summer internship program for minority women S&E students absorbed under an existing funded minority-student internship program, (c) academic coaching for new women S&E faculty and all new deans and chairs in the university, (d) a continued partnership for student exchange with Fisk University, and (e) opportunity grants for faculty, expanded to all faculty (male and female, S&E and non-S&E) across the university. Other institutionalized initiatives include: (a) a required cultural competency awareness training for all new faculty, (b) continued resources for faculty search-committee training and support, (c) an annual Spotlight Series on Women's Scholarship & Women of Achievement luncheon, (d) the WISER (Women in Science & Engineering Roundtable) program embedded in the Flora Stone Mather Center for Women, and (e) a faculty work-life brochure of policies and resources printed annually (Case Western Reserve University 2008).

At the University of Texas El Paso, as part of *ADVANCE* institutionalization, the Faculty Mentoring Program for Women evolved into the Collaborative Faculty Mentoring Program hosted by the Center for Effective Teaching and Learning (CETaL) together with their IMPACT Seminar (University of Texas, El Paso 2008). Faculty recruitment and retention activities became the shared responsibility of the associate provost, the CETaL director, and the associate dean of faculty in each of the *ADVANCE* colleges. Funding for start-up and dual-career hires were sought through the STARS program, a University of Texas system initiative that provides funding to attract and hire outstanding researchers (University of Texas, El Paso 2008).

At Virginia Tech, the provost and deans committed to providing financial support to specific AdvanceVT programs following expiration of the grant (Virginia Tech 2009). At the University of Montana, the PACE Outstanding Mentoring Award was institutionalized as an annual university award (not restricted to faculty in the science departments), which provides recognition to a tenured or tenure-track professor who has served as an outstanding mentor to untenured faculty in his/her department (see http://pace.dbs.umt.edu/Mentoring/Awards.html).

SUMMARY AND CONCLUSIONS

The descriptive analyses of the institutionalization undertaken at the *ADVANCE* universities provide illustrative examples of the generation of new permanent positions, offices and structures, new or modified policies, new practices and processes, and new support for continued funding of effective programs beyond *ADVANCE* funding. While different universities have implemented different forms of institutionalization as illustrated in this chapter, all have attempted to sustain their programs beyond their initial investments, to learn from things that have not worked, to institutionalize successes in new or existing workplace structures, and to embed the changes engendered into the social fabric of their institutional cultures and climates.

7 Gender Diversity Outcomes
Changes in the Academic Workforce Participation of Women Faculty in STEM

In this chapter, we examine the diversity outcomes brought about by institutional transformation efforts at the 19 *ADVANCE* universities. Diversity refers to the distribution of the workforce composition, or commonly, the representation of minority-group members within the workforce. Specifically, we answer the question Have targeted gender diversity, equity, and inclusion initiatives made a difference in the workforce participation of women at all ranks in the academic pipeline? To accomplish this, we examine changes in the composition of tenure-track women faculty at all ranks in STEM at the *ADVANCE* universities over their award periods. We specifically examine changes in STEM faculty composition by gender and rank over *ADVANCE* award durations, the number of institutions (out of 19) reporting percentage changes in STEM women faculty, and the average annual proportion of women faculty in STEM at *ADVANCE* universities in comparison with national reference groups.

DEFINITION OF STEM FIELDS

As described in Chapter 3, for purposes of the analyses reported in this chapter we define STEM as science, technology, engineering, and mathematics fields only (see Appendix 1 for details about the specific STEM schools/colleges included for each institution). Appendix 2 offers a more detailed breakdown by institution of the specific departments/fields in engineering that we included in our definition of STEM, and Appendix 3 details the specific departments/fields by institution in natural sciences that were also included in our definition of STEM.

We excluded all social and behavioral science fields for the analyses of STEM disciplines reported in this chapter. We also excluded management and business science departments since only four of the 19 institutions included these fields in their *ADVANCE* projects. Basic science departments/fields in schools of medicine or veterinary medicine or pharmacy were also excluded from these analyses, again because extremely few institutions (four out of 19) included these disciplines in their projects.

CHANGES IN STEM FACULTY COMPOSITION BY GENDER AND RANK OVER *ADVANCE* AWARD PERIODS

To evaluate changes in STEM faculty composition before and after *ADVANCE* awards, comparisons were made between the initial (first funded) year and the final (last funded) year of each NSF award. Since our overall sample size was small (n = 19), we conducted a nonparametric test for two related samples— the Wilcoxon signed-ranks test—to test differences between paired scores. The Wilcoxon signed-ranks test considers information about both the sign of the differences and the magnitude of the differences between pairs. We used the Wilcoxon signed-ranks test to compare the number of women (or men faculty) at each academic rank, as well as the percentage of women faculty at each rank, between the initial year and the final year of each *ADVANCE* IT project. Table 7.1 presents the means and standard deviations of the numbers of women and men STEM faculty across the 19 universities before and after the implementation of *ADVANCE* initiatives.

As shown in this table, results from the Wilcoxon signed-ranks test showed that the number of women STEM faculty at the assistant and professor ranks, as well as for all women at all (combined) ranks, increased significantly between the *ADVANCE* baseline year and final year. It is possible that the failure to increase the number of women associate professors

Table 7.1 Changes in Numbers of Women and Men STEM Faculty at *ADVANCE* Institutions over Their Award Periods

STEM Faculty (# of Universities with Valid Data)	Initial Year		Final Year		Wilcoxon Signed Rankes Test	
	Mean	SD	Mean	SD	Z	p-value
Women STEM Faculty						
# Women assistant professors (n = 18)	19	18	27	21	3.32	0.001**
# Women associate professors (n = 18)	18	11	20	15	1.16	0.245
# Women professors (n = 18)	17	19	25	22	3.66	0.000***
Total # women faculty at all ranks (n = 19)	53	44	71	55	3.73	0.000***
Men STEM Faculty						
# Men assistant professors (n = 18)	57	44	61	50	1.45	0.148
# Men associate professors (n = 18)	73	49	73	46	0.17	0.868
# Men professors (n = 18)	183	163	187	160	1.21	0.227
Total # men faculty at all ranks (n = 19)	311	240	320	243	1.58	0.115

Notes: **p < 0.01, ***p < 0.001.
Rank data were not available for Columbia University.

reflects the short time periods over which we studied the changes. Several women STEM associate professors may have been promoted to the professor level during their university's *ADVANCE* award period without a corresponding increase in promotion to the associate professor rank (from the assistant professor rank) since the *ADVANCE* time frame (usually five years) that we used to evaluate changes is generally shorter than the six-year probationary (pretenure) period conventionally used to assess tenure and promotion to the associate professor rank.

Interestingly, changes in the number of men STEM faculty at all three levels and for combined ranks over the same time period were not statistically significant. These findings indicate that although the number of men STEM faculty at these universities increased modestly or remained the same during the *ADVANCE* award period, the number of women faculty increased significantly in these same disciplines over the same time period.

While causal attributions to *ADVANCE* IT efforts cannot be made from the data presented in Table 7.1, there is clearly a coinciding period between the changes documented and *ADVANCE* IT award periods. We conclude from Table 7.1 that *ADVANCE* IT initiatives have significantly increased the number of women faculty in STEM disciplines at these universities over their *ADVANCE* award periods.

Table 7.2 presents the means and standard deviations of the proportion of women STEM faculty across the 19 universities before and after the implementation of *ADVANCE* initiatives.

Again, while causal attributions to *ADVANCE* efforts cannot be made from the data presented in Table 7.2, there is clearly a coinciding period between the changes documented and *ADVANCE* IT award periods and we conclude that the findings presented in Table 7.2 confirm the results of Table 7.1: *ADVANCE* initiatives have yielded significant increases in the percentage of women STEM faculty at the assistant professor and professor ranks and for all ranks combined.

Table 7.2   Changes in the Percentages of Women STEM Faculty at *ADVANCE* Institutions over Their Award Periods

Percentage within Rank (# of Universities with Valid data)	Initial Year		Final Year		Wilcoxon Signed Rankes Test	
	Mean	SD	Mean	SD	Z	p-value
% Women assistant professors (n = 18)	25%	9%	33%	11%	2.66	0.008**
% Women associate professors (n = 18)	21%	6%	21%	8%	0.90	0.367
% Women professors (n = 18)	10%	8%	14%	8%	3.57	0.000***
% Women faculty at all ranks (n = 19)	16%	7%	19%	6%	3.80	0.000***

Notes: **p < 0.01, ***p < 0.001.
Rank data were not available for Columbia University.

Number of Institutions Reporting Changes in STEM Faculty Composition over *ADVANCE* Award Periods

Table 7.3 presents the distribution of the percentage increases in STEM faculty composition reported by the 19 *ADVANCE* universities. Although each *ADVANCE* IT project lasted five to seven years, these 19 universities were at different stages of project implementation (ten universities had completed their projects and the other nine universities were in the sixth or seventh years of their projects) at the time of our review and had different numbers of female and male faculty at each rank at the start of their projects. The outcomes reported in Table 7.3 for these 19 universities ranged within a period of four to seven years of the start of their projects.

The last two columns in Table 7.3 indicate that all except one university reported an increase in the overall number of women in their tenure-track STEM pipeline and ten institutions also reported an increase in the overall number of male faculty. Eleven out of 18 institutions represented a 30–69% increase in the overall number of women STEM faculty, and

Table 7.3 Number of *ADVANCE* Institutions Reporting STEM Faculty Percentage Change over Their Award Periods

STEM Faculty Percent Change in 4–7 Years	Assistant Professor (N = 18)		Associate Professor (N = 18)		Professor (N = 18)		All Ranks (N = 19)	
% Increase	Women	Men	Women	Men	Women	Men	Women	Men
1–9%		3	1	2	1	6		7
10–19%		4	3	3	3	2	2	2
20–29%	2	5		1	2	3	5	1
30–39%	2		5	2			4	
40–49%	2	1	1		1		4	
50–59%	2				3		1	
60–69%	1				2		2	
70–79%	2							
80–100%					2			
101–300%	4				3			
# universities with % increase	15	13	10	8	17	10	18	10
# universities with no change	1	1	1	1	0	1	1	4
# univserities with % decrease	2	4	7	9	1	6	0	5

Notes: Rank data were not available for Columbia University.

Table 7.4 Changes in Women as a Percentage of STEM Faculty (All Ranks) at ADVANCE Institutions over Their Award Periods

	AY 2002	AY 2003	AY 2004	AY 2005	AY 2006	AY 2007	AY 2008	AY 2009	Change[a]
University of Maryland, Baltimore County[2]			17%	20%	22%	22%	24%	25%	8%
University of Montana[2]		14%		14%	19%	19%	20%	21%	7%
University of Rhode Island[2]		14%	17%	16%	19%	20%			6%
University of California, Irvine[1]	14%	15%	17%	18%	19%	19%	19%		5%
University of Colorado Boulder[1]		14%					19%		5%
University of Texas, El Paso[2]	13%		16%	14%	16%	19%	18%	20%	4%
University of Washington[1]		15%	15%	15%	15%	17%			4%
University of Wisconsin, Madison[1]		16%	17%	18%	19%	20%			4%
Kansas State University[2]			13%	14%	14%	15%	16%		3%
New Mexico State University[1]		18%	18%	19%	19%	21%	18%	21%	3%
University of Michigan[1]	16%	16%	17%	18%	19%				3%
Utah State University[2]			13%	15%	15%	15%	16%		3%
Virginia Tech[2]			11%	12%	13%	13%	14%	14%	3%
Case Western Reserve University[2]			15%	17%	17%	17%	17%		2%
Columbia University[2]		12%	13%	12%	12%	13%	15%	15%	2%
Georgia Institute of Technology[1]	11%	12%	11%	12%	13%				2%
Hunter College, CUNY[1]		27%	28%	28%	29%	29%			2%
University of Alabama, Birmingham[2]			9%	8%	9%	11%	11%		2%
University of Puerto Rico, Humacao[1]	38%	37%	35%	37%					-1%
Average Percentage Change									3.5%

Notes. [1]ADVANCE IT Cohort 1 institution; [2]ADVANCE IT Cohort 2 institution.
[a]Difference in percentage change between initial year and final year of ADVANCE IT projects.
Faculty members with appointments of assistant, associate, and full professors are reported here for all universities except the University of Columbia, for which rank data were not available.

seven institutions represented a 10–29% increase. For male faculty, all ten institutions showing increases in the percentages of male STEM faculty reported an increase of less than 30%.

The data by rank indicate that there has been a general increase in the number of women in tenure-track STEM ranks at most institutions. Nine institutions reported at least a 50% increase in their number of female STEM assistant professors over their *ADVANCE* awards. Ten institutions reported at least a 50% increase in the number of female full professors over the duration of their *ADVANCE* projects. The percentage increase in the numbers of women STEM associate professors was relatively lower but encouraging, with six institutions reporting a 30–49% increase in the number of female associate professors. For their male faculty counterparts, six institutions represented an increase of less than 30% and two institutions represented an increase in the range of 30–39% of male STEM associate professors.

Table 7.3 also shows that seven institutions reported percentage decreases in their women STEM associate professors. As explained earlier, it is possible that our study's time frame for the evaluation of *ADVANCE* changes (approximately five years) may have been too short to detect promotions of assistant professors to this rank since the normal pretenure period is longer than this. In addition, it is possible that overall numbers of faculty may have declined at some universities due to external factors such as budgetary constraints and the global economic downturn. In conclusion, even considering the limited time frames under study, the data on the number of institutions reporting faculty composition change over *ADVANCE* IT award periods indicate a positive impact of *ADVANCE* initiatives on the representation of women in the STEM tenure-track pipeline.

Change in Percentage of Women STEM Faculty (All Ranks) over *ADVANCE* Award Periods

Table 7.4 presents results of the changes in the percentage of STEM women faculty at each of the 19 *ADVANCE* institutions over their award periods.

Table 7.4 indicates that 18 out of 19 universities reported a percentage increase in the representation of women STEM faculty over their *ADVANCE* award periods, with a 2–8% increase between the baseline year and the final year. The average change in the percentage of women STEM faculty experienced over the 19 institutions over their *ADVANCE* award periods was 3.5%. It should be noted that the two institutions with the highest percentage growth started their *ADVANCE* programs with much smaller numbers of women faculty in STEM areas (29 for the University of Maryland, Baltimore County and 20 for the University of Montana) than many other institutions (see Table 7.5).

Table 7.4 also indicates that women comprised 21% or less of the total STEM faculty in 16 out of 19 institutions over the duration of the *ADVANCE* IT projects; all of these are research universities. The percentage of women faculty of the total was extremely low at four research universities, comprising 15% or less of their total STEM faculty over the duration of the *ADVANCE* IT projects. Three universities achieved a high percentage, 25–38%, of their total STEM faculty in at least one year of the *ADVANCE* IT projects; one of these institutions is a research university while the other two are master's and baccalaureate institutions. In conclusion, the results of Table 7.4 indicate steady while modest change in the percentage of women faculty in STEM between the initial and final years of *ADVANCE* interventions, representing movement in a positive direction. These findings further confirm that targeted *ADVANCE* efforts successfully increased the representation of women faculty in STEM.

Average Annual Growth Rate of Total STEM Faculty by Gender

Table 7.5 presents the average annual growth rates in the number of women and men STEM faculty at the *ADVANCE* institutions between the baseline year and the final year of each project.

The findings of Table 7.5 indicate that over the *ADVANCE* IT awards, the average annual rate of increase was greater for women STEM faculty than for men STEM faculty at 18 out of the 19 institutions studied. In many of these universities, the average annual growth rate of men STEM faculty declined or improved only marginally. The average number of women STEM faculty at these 19 universities grew from 53.26 (14.61% of the total faculty) to 70.58 (18.06% of the total faculty) over their *ADVANCE* award periods, while the average number of men STEM faculty changed from 311.26 (85.39% of the total faculty) to 320.21 (81.94% of the total faculty) over the same time period. Across all 19 universities, the average annual growth rate for women faculty in STEM was 7.18% while the corresponding rate for men faculty in STEM was 0.64%. The average percentage growth rate over the total award periods across these 19 institutions was 39.70% for women faculty and 3.54 % for men faculty in STEM; that is, the number of women STEM faculty at these 19 institutions increased on average over their *ADVANCE* award periods by almost 40% while the number of men STEM faculty increased on average by about 3.5%.

While we cannot show that these differential growth rates were caused only by *ADVANCE* initiatives, their occurrence over the *ADVANCE* award period at each university gives us confidence to infer that targeted initiatives to advance the workforce participation of women STEM faculty through *ADVANCE* have played a significant role. We conclude from these findings that initiatives at *ADVANCE* universities have

Table 7.5   Changes in Number of STEM Faculty (All Ranks) at *ADVANCE* Institutions over Their Award Periods by Gender

		Initial Year	Final Year	*ADVANCE* IT Award Duration in Years	Average Annual Growth Rate[b]
Georgia Institute of Technology[1]	Female	68	91	5	8.46%
	Male	542	605		2.91%
Hunter College, CUNY[1]	Female	21	23	6	1.90%
	Male	56	56		0.00%
New Mexico State University[1]	Female	41	52	7	4.47%
	Male	191	191		0.00%
University of Colorado Boulder[1]	Female	58	85	6	9.31%
	Male	357	369		0.67%
University of California, Irvine[1]	Female	53	86	7	10.38%
	Male	317	364		2.47%
University of Michigan[1]	Female	129	170	5	7.95%
	Male	692	729		1.01%
University of Puerto Rico, Humacao[1]	Female	29	29	4	0.00%
	Male	48	50		1.39%
University of Wisconsin, Madison[1]	Female	199	245	5	5.78%
	Male	1009	983		-0.67%
University of Washington[1]	Female	60	77	6	5.67%
	Male	399	380		-0.95%
Case Western Reserve University[2]	Female	43	50	5	4.07%
	Male	250	236		-1.40%
Columbia University[2]	Female	41	52	6	5.37%
	Male	281	303		1.57%
Kansas State University[2]	Female	67	89	5	8.21%
	Male	431	451		1.16%
University of Alabama, Birmingham[2]	Female	10	13	5	7.50%
	Male	96	105		2.34%
University of Maryland, Baltimore County[2]	Female	29	42	6	8.97%
	Male	137	126		-1.61%
University of Montana[2]	Female	20	29	5	11.25%
	Male	118	106		-2.54%

Continued

Table 7.5   Continued

University of Texas, El Paso[2]	Female	22	37	6	13.64%
	Male	119	145		4.37%
University of Rhode Island[2]	Female	32	49	5	13.28%
	Male	202	202		0.00%
Utah State University[2]	Female	41	52	5	6.71%
	Male	266	267		0.09%
Virginia Tech[2]	Female	49	70	6	8.57%
	Male	403	426		1.14%
Average across 19 Universities	**Femal**	53.26	70.58	5.53	**7.18%**
	Male	311.26	320.21		**0.64%**

Notes: [1]*ADVANCE* IT Cohort 1 institution. [2]*ADVANCE* IT Cohort 2 institution.
[a]*ADVANCE* IT award duration in years inclusive of extensions, for which data were available on this measure, as of our data collection.
[b]Percentage difference in numbers between baseline and final years of *ADVANCE* projects divided by (IT Award Duration − 1).
The specific fields within STEM at each institution included in this table are provided in Appendix 1.
STEM faculty (all ranks) included all STEM faculty at assistant professor, associate professor, and professor ranks.
University of Wisconsin, Madison faculty numbers were reported as full-time equivalent (FTE).
For University of Puerto Rico, Humacao, data were available only for AY 2002, AY 2003, AY 2004, and AY 2005.
For the University of Maryland, Baltimore County, data from the Geography department were not included since these data were not consistently available over all years.

successfully increased the academic workforce participation of women faculty in STEM areas. However, the data also indicate the continued underrepresentation of women faculty (less than 20% of the faculty on average) in STEM disciplines, and signal the ongoing challenge of engaging more women faculty in these disciplines in the nation's colleges and universities.

Trends in the Percentages of Women Faculty in STEM over *ADVANCE* IT Award Periods Compared with National Reference Groups

In this section we compare how head-count changes in the representation of women STEM faculty at *ADVANCE* institutions compare with similar trends across the larger universe of U.S. colleges and universities. Our particular concern is to examine whether and how growth in the representation of women STEM faculty has occurred over the same time period with and without NSF *ADVANCE* funding.

In the absence of a control group of matched universities with which to compare results occurring at *ADVANCE* institutions, we employed biannual comparisons with national samples using NSF's Survey of Doctorate Recipients (SDR) database. The Survey of Doctorate Recipients gathers information from individuals who have obtained a doctoral degree in a science, engineering, or health field. The survey is conducted every two years and is a longitudinal survey that follows recipients of research doctorates from U.S. institutions until age 76 (www.nsf.gov/statistics/srvydoctoratework/). Data from SDR are published biennially in detailed statistical tables in the series "Characteristics of Doctoral Scientists and Engineers in the United States" (www.nsf.gov/statistics/doctoratework/).

We obtained data from NSF about the composition of faculty at four-year colleges and universities, as well as at very high and high research universities (RU/VH and RU/H) only, by field, sex, and rank as represented in the SDR samples for 2001, 2003, and 2006, respectively.[1] In our comparative analyses, data drawn from SDR samples serve as national reference groups of STEM faculty at each rank and each discipline. Since the vast majority (17) of the 19 *ADVANCE* institutions studied were research universities (very high or high), we ran two sets of comparisons: a first national comparison group included the sample of four-year colleges and universities in the SDR database, and a second national comparison group included the sample of all research (very high and high) universities only in the SDR database.

As described in Chapter 3, at the time of our data analysis, SDR data were available for three years (2001, 2003, and 2006). 2008 SDR data, while collected, were not available for public use. Data were drawn from http://sestat.nsf.gov/docs/tally06/nsdrmem.html and http://sestat.nsf.gov/docs/tally03/nsdrmem.html. Data were selected for respondents (1) whose principal employer was an educational institution, (2) who worked at a four-year college or university, other than a medical school, (3) whose faculty rank was assistant, or associate, or full professors, and (4) whose field of study for first U.S. S&E or health PhD (major group) was in one of the following areas: (a) biological, agricultural, and environmental life sciences; (b) computer and information sciences; (c) mathematics and statistics; (d) physical sciences; (e) engineering; (f) psychology; and (g) social sciences. For STEM comparisons, the last two areas were dropped.

Results of the comparisons should be interpreted with caution since our *ADVANCE* sample consists of women STEM faculty from 19 universities only, while data in the SDR database encompass samples of

Table 7.6 Survey of Doctoral Recipients (SDR): Women as a Percentage of Employed Doctoral Scientists and Engineers in STEM by Faculty Rank: 2001, 2003, and 2006

	4-year Institutions			Research Universities		
	2001	2003	2006	2001	2003	2006
SDR: women as % of assistant professors in STEM	27%	28%	31%	24%	25%	27%
SDR: women as % of associate professors in STEM	19%	21%	22%	17%	19%	20%
SDR: women as % of full professors in STEM	9%	10%	11%	8%	7%	9%
SDR: women as % of faculty in STEM (all ranks)	16%	17%	19%	13%	14%	16%

Source: The percentage of women faculty within rank in S&E at 4-year institutions and research universities (2001, 2003, and 2006) were calculated from crosstabs of the Survey of Doctorate Recipients (SDR).

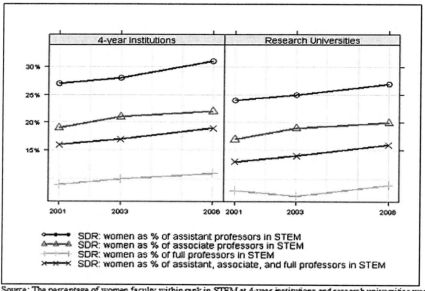

Source: The percentage of women faculty within rank in STEM at 4-year institutions and research universities were calculated from crosstabs of the Survey of Doctorate Recipients, 2001, 2003, and 2006.

Figure 7.1 Women as a percentage of employed doctoral scientists and engineers in STEM by faculty rank: 2001, 2003, and 2006 national samples.

women STEM faculty across much bigger sets of institutions. The SDR samples of four-year institutions and research universities likely include the *ADVANCE* sample of 19 institutions as well. Additionally, it is likely that the population of specific STEM fields represented within the SDR database is considerably larger than the population of specific STEM fields represented within the *ADVANCE* sample used in this study, resulting in possible mismatches in counts, underfavoring the *ADVANCE* sample. Finally, the lack of available SDR data in 2008 provides further reason for caution in interpreting the results provided below.

Results drawn from SDR (2001, 2003, 2006) samples are presented in Table 7.6 and Figure 7.1. Since 17 out of 19 of the *ADVANCE* institutions are research universities, the second set of comparisons (between *ADVANCE* universities and the SDR data samples for research universities only) represented in the right-hand side of the figures on the following pages is most analogous to the study's sample. Hence, we use comparisons with the SDR sample of research universities for most of our conclusions, although we present the findings for the SDR sample of four-year colleges and universities as well.

The results of Table 7.6 and Figure 7.1 indicate that at four-year institutions the biggest increase (4%) between 2001 and 2006 was at the assistant professor rank, followed by a 3% increase at the associate professor rank and 2% increase at the professor rank. Overall, there was a 3% increase in the percentage of women faculty in STEM between 2001 and 2006 at all four-year colleges and universities. Looking at research universities only, a 3% increase in overall women faculty in STEM occurred between 2001 and 2006, with 3% increases at the levels of assistant and associate professors, and a 1% increase in women at the full professor rank. These analyses show that research universities on average have a lower proportion of women STEM faculty than do all four-year colleges and universities.

Comparisons of the *ADVANCE* Sample and National Comparison Groups: The Academic Workforce Participation of Women Faculty in STEM Disciplines (All Ranks)

Table 7.7 and Figure 7.2 present the percentages of women STEM faculty at *ADVANCE* universities relative to national reference groups of women STEM faculty at four-year institutions and at research universities. The findings indicate that *ADVANCE* Cohort 1 institutions started slightly higher and *ADVANCE* Cohort 2 institutions started slightly lower than the overall average percentage of women STEM faculty at the national sample of research universities. Both cohorts of *ADVANCE* universities show increasing trends in the proportions (all ranks) of women STEM faculty, but equivalent comparisons could not be drawn since SDR data were not available for 2008. These findings indicate more rapid growth over the same time period in the overall representation of women STEM faculty (all ranks) at *ADVANCE* schools in comparison with national research universities.

Table 7.7   The Academic Workforce Participation of Women Faculty at *ADVANCE* Institutions over Their Award Periods in STEM (All Ranks)* Compared with National Samples at Four-Year Institutions and Research Universities

	4-year Institutions (n = 17)							Research Universities (n = 16)						
	AY 2002	AY 2003	AY 2004	AY 2005	AY 2006	AY 2007	AY 2008	AY 2002	AY 2003	AY 2004	AY 2005	AY 2006	AY 2007	AY 2008
ADVANCE IT Cohort 1: Women as % of STEM faculty (n = 7)	16%	17%	18%	18%	19%	21%		14%	15%	16%	17%	17%	19%	
ADVANCE IT Cohort 2: Women as % of STEM faculty (n = 10)			14%	14%	16%	16%	17%			14%	14%	16%	16%	17%
SDR: Women as % of STEM faculty	16%	17%			19%			13%	14%			16%		

Notes:
* All Ranks include assistant professors, associate professors, and professors.
1. We excluded two Cohort 1 universities from this analysis for which consistent annual data were not available: University of Colorado and University of Puerto Rico, Humacao. AY 2002 data were not available for two universities: New Mexico State University, and University of Wisconsin, Madison; AY 2007 data were not available for Georgia Institute of Technology and University of Michigan. Hence, for the Cohort 1 comparison with four-year institutions, the average percentage in AY 2002 and AY 2007 was calculated from values of five (out of seven) universities with valid faculty data, respectively.
2. All the ten universities in Cohort 2 are research universities. The average percentage of women faculty at Cohort 2 universities in AY 2004 and AY 2008 was calculated from the percentages of nine universities with valid data, respectively.
3. SDR = Survey of Doctorate Recipients. The percentage of women faculty in STEM at four-year institutions and research universities was calculated from crosstabs of the Survey of Doctorate Recipients, 2001, 2003, and 2006. STEM includes biological sciences, agricultural sciences, and environmental life sciences, computer and information sciences, mathematics and statistics, physical sciences, and engineering. For the SDR sample, the percentages of women faculty in calendar years 2001, 2003, and 2006 were comparable to those of the ADVANCE sample in academic years 2001–02, 2002–03, and 2005–06, respectively.

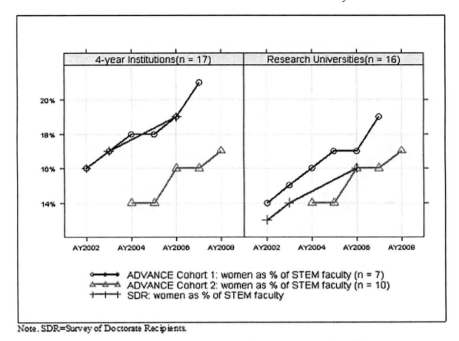

Figure 7.2   The academic workforce participation of women faculty in STEM (all ranks) at *ADVANCE* institutions over their award periods compared with national samples of four-year institions and research universities.

Comparisons of the *ADVANCE* Sample and National Comparison Groups: The Academic Workforce Participation of Women Assistant Professors in STEM

Table 7.8 and Figure 7.3 present percentages of women STEM assistant professors at *ADVANCE* universities relative to the national reference groups of women STEM assistant professors at four-year institutions and at research universities.

Nationwide, women comprised 27–31% assistant professors at four-year institutions and 24–27% assistant professors at research universities in STEM disciplines between 2001 and 2006. For the *ADVANCE* IT Cohort 1 research universities (n = 6), women on average comprised 31% STEM assistant professors in AY 2007, up from 23% in AY 2002. For the *ADVANCE* IT Cohort 2 universities (n = 9), women on average comprised 33% STEM assistant professors in AY 2008, up from 25% in AY 2004. Again, while equivalent comparisons are not possible due to the lack of 2008 SDR data, without question there have been dramatic increases in the percentages of women faculty at the assistant professor rank in STEM in both *ADVANCE* cohorts. These findings indicate more rapid growth over the same time period

Table 7.8   The Academic Workforce Participation of Women Assistant Professors in STEM at *ADVANCE* Universities over Their Award Periods Compared with National Samples at Four-Year Institutions and Research Universities

	4-year Institutions (n = 16)							Research Universities (n = 15)						
	AY 2002	AY 2003	AY 2004	AY 2005	AY 2006	AY 2007	AY 2008	AY 2002	AY 2003	AY 2004	AY 2005	AY 2006	AY 2007	AY 2008
ADVANCE IT Cohort 1: women as % of assistant professors in STEM (n = 7)	22%	23%	26%	29%	31%	35%		23%	25%	25%	27%	27%	31%	
ADVANCE IT Cohort 2: women as % of assistant professors in STEM (n = 9)			25%	27%	31%	32%	33%			25%	27%	31%	32%	33%
SDR: women as % of assistant professors in STEM	27%	28%			31%			24%	25%			27%		

Notes:
1. We excluded two Cohort 1 universities from this analysis for which consistent annual data were not available: University of Colorado and University of Puerto Rico, Humacao. AY 2002 data were not available for two universities: New Mexico State University and University of Wisconsin, Madison; AY 2007 data were not available for Georgia Institute of Technology and University of Michigan. Hence, for the Cohort 1 four-year institutions, the average percentage in AY 2002 and AY 2007 was calculated from values of five (out of seven) universities with valid faculty data, respectively.
2. All the nine Cohort 2 universities reported here are research universities. Columbia University was excluded because its data were not broken down by rank. AY 2004 data were not available for University of Montana, University of Rhode Island, and University of Alabama, Birmingham. AY 2008 data were not available for University of Rhode Island. Thus, for Cohort 2, the average percentage of women faculty in AY 2004 and AY 2008 was calculated from the percentages of six and eight universities with valid data, respectively.
3. SDR = Survey of Doctorate Recipients. The percentage of women assistant professors in STEM at four-year institutions and research universities was calculated from crosstabs of the Survey of Doctorate Recipients, 2001, 2003, and 2006. STEM includes biological sciences, agricultural sciences, and environmental life sciences, computer and information sciences, mathematics and statistics, physical sciences, and engineering. For the SDR sample, the percentages of women faculty in calendar years 2001, 2003, and 2006 were comparable to those of the ADVANCE sample in academic years of 2001–02, 2002–03, and 2005–06, respectively.

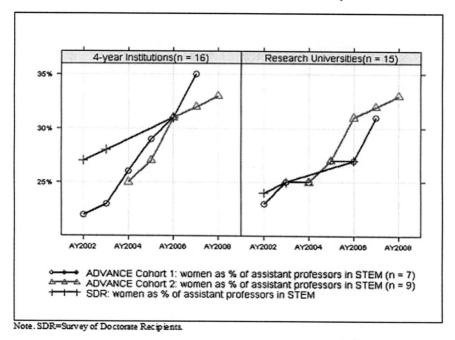

Figure 7.3   The academic workforce participation of women assistant professors in STEM at *ADVANCE* universitites over their award periods compared with national samples of four-year institutions and research universities.

in the representation of women STEM assistant professors at *ADVANCE* institutions in comparison with national research universities.

Comparisons of the *ADVANCE* Sample and National Comparison Groups: The Academic Workforce Participation of Women Associate Professors in STEM

Table 7.9 and Figure 7.4 present the percentages of women STEM associate professors at *ADVANCE* universities relative to national reference groups of women STEM associate professors at four-year institutions and at research universities. The findings indicate that nationwide, women comprised 19–22% STEM associate professors at four-year institutions and 17–20% STEM associate professors at research universities between 2001 and 2006. For *ADVANCE* Cohort 1 four-year universities (n = 7), the percentage of women associate professors ranged between 20 and 23% during AY 2002–07; for Cohort 1 research universities (n = 6), the percentage of women associate professors ranged from 18–24% during AY 2002–07. For Cohort 2 universities (n = 9), the percentage of women associate professors ranged between 16 and 19% during AY 2003–08.

Table 7.9 The Academic Workforce Participation of Women Associate Professors in STEM at *ADVANCE* Universities over Their Award Periods Compared with National Samples at Four-Year Institutions and Research Universities

	4-year Institutions (n = 16)							Research Universities (n = 15)						
	AY 2002	AY 2003	AY 2004	AY 2005	AY 2006	AY 2007	AY 2008	AY 2002	AY 2003	AY 2004	AY 2005	AY 2006	AY 2007	AY 2008
ADVANCE IT Cohort 1: women as % of associate professors in STEM (n = 7)	23%	21%	20%	21%	22%	20%		21%	18%	19%	20%	22%	24%	
ADVANCE IT Cohort 2: women as % of associate professors in STEM (n = 9)			18%	19%	19%	19%	16%			18%	19%	19%	19%	16%
SDR: women as % of associate professors in STEM	19%	21%			22%			17%	19%			20%		

Notes:

1. We excluded two Cohort 1 universities from this analysis for which consistent annual data were not available: University of Colorado and University of Puerto Rico, Humacao. AY 2002 data were not available for two universities: New Mexico State University and University of Wisconsin, Madison; AY 2007 data were not available for Georgia Institute of Technology and University of Michigan. Hence, for the Cohort 1 four-year institutions, the average percentage in AY 2002 and AY 2007 was calculated from values of five (out of seven) universities with valid faculty data, respectively.

2. All the nine Cohort 2 universities reported here are research universities. Columbia University was excluded because its data were not broken down by rank. AY 2004 data were not available for University of Montana, University of Rhode Island, and University of Alabama, Birmingham. AY 2008 data were not available for University of Rhode Island. Thus, for Cohort 2, the average percentage of women faculty in AY 2004 and AY 2008 was calculated from the percentages of six and eight universities with valid data, respectively.

3. SDR = Survey of Doctorate Recipients. The percentage of women associate professors in STEM at four-year institutions and research universities was calculated from crosstabs of the Survey of Doctorate Recipients, 2001, 2003, and 2006. STEM includes biological sciences, agricultural sciences, and environmental life sciences, computer and information sciences, mathematics and statistics, physical sciences, and engineering. For the SDR sample, the percentages of women faculty in calendar years 2001, 2003, and 2006 were comparable to those of the ADVANCE sample in academic years of 2001–02, 2002–03, and 2005–06, respectively.

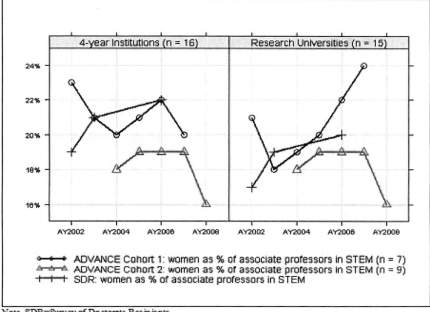

Note. SDR=Survey of Doctorate Recipients.

Figure 7.4   The academic workforce participation of women associate professors in STEM at *ADVANCE* universitites over their award periods compared with national samples of four-year institutions and research universities.

With regard to the trends of change, the percentage of women associate professors at *ADVANCE* Cohort 1 research universities showed an increasing trend from AY 2003 to AY 2007 in comparison with the national percentage of women associate professors, with a dip in AY 2003 from the previous year. The percentage of women associate professors in Cohort 2 lagged behind the national percentage of women associate professors. There was a sharp decrease in the percentage of women associate professors in AY 2008 for Cohort 2 universities. It is very possible that this trend is an artifact of the short time periods used to measure changes—it may be related to the increased number of women full professors (promoted from associate professors) in AY 2008.

Comparisons of the *ADVANCE* Sample and National Comparison Groups: The Academic Workforce Participation of Women Full Professors in STEM

Table 7.10 and Figure 7.5 present the percentages of women STEM full professors at *ADVANCE* universities relative to national reference

Table 7.10   The Academic Workforce Participation of Women Full Professors in STEM at *ADVANCE* Universities over Their Award Periods Compared with National Samples at Four-Year Institutions and Research Universities

	4-year Institutions (n = 16)							Research Universities (n = 15)						
	AY 2002	AY 2003	AY 2004	AY 2005	AY 2006	AY 2007	AY 2008	AY 2002	AY 2003	AY 2004	AY 2005	AY 2006	AY 2007	AY 2008
ADVANCE IT Cohort 1: women as % of full professors in STEM (n = 7)	11%	13%	14%	13%	14%	17%		8%	11%	11%	11%	12%	13%	
ADVANCE IT Cohort 2: women as % of full professors in STEM (n = 9)			6%	7%	8%	9%	10%			6%	7%	8%	9%	10%
SDR: women as % of full professors in STEM	9%	10%			11%			8%	7%			9%		

Notes:

1. We excluded two Cohort 1 universities from this analysis for which consistent annual data were not available: University of Colorado and University of Puerto Rico, Humacao. AY 2002 data were not available for two universities: New Mexico State University and University of Wisconsin, Madison; AY 2007 data were not available for Georgia Institute of Technology and University of Michigan. Hence, for the Cohort 1 four-year institutions, the average percentage in AY 2002 and AY 2007 was calculated from values of five (out of seven) universities with valid faculty data, respectively.

2. All the nine Cohort 2 universities reported here are research universities. Columbia University was excluded because its data were not broken down by rank. AY 2004 data were not available for University of Montana, University of Rhode Island, and University of Alabama, Birmingham. AY 2008 data were not available for University of Rhode Island. Thus, for Cohort 2, the average percentage of women faculty in AY 2004 and AY 2008 was calculated from the percentages of six and eight universities with valid data, respectively.

3. SDR = Survey of Doctorate Recipients. The percentage of women faculty in STEM at four-year institutions and research universities were was calculated from crosstabs of the Survey of Doctorate Recipients, 2001, 2003, and 2006. STEM includes biological sciences, agricultural sciences, and environmental life sciences, computer and information sciences, mathematics and statistics, physical sciences, and engineering. For the SDR sample, the percentages of women faculty in calendar years 2001, 2003, and 2006 were comparable to those of the ADVANCE sample in academic years of 2001–02, 2002–03, and 2005–06, respectively.

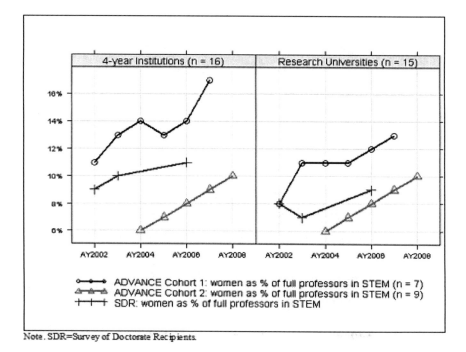

Figure 7.5 The academic workforce participation of women full professors in STEM at *ADVANCE* universitites over their award periods compared with national samples of four-year institutions and research universities.

groups of women STEM full professors at four-year institutions and at research universities.

The findings indicate that nationwide, women comprised 9–11% STEM full professors at four-year institutions and 7–9% STEM full professors at research universities between 2001 and 2006. Over the duration of the *ADVANCE* IT projects, an increasing trend is apparent for both cohorts. For *ADVANCE* Cohort 1 four-year institutions (n = 7), women comprised 17% STEM full professors in AY 2007, up from 11% in AY 2002. For Cohort 1 research universities (n = 6), women comprised 13% STEM full professors in AY 2007, up from 8% in AY 2002. The percentage of women full professors in *ADVANCE* Cohort 1 institutions was greater than the national level of women full professors in all research universities. For *ADVANCE* Cohort 2 universities (n = 9), women comprised 10% of STEM full professors in AY 2008, up from 6% in AY 2004. As of AY 2006, the representation of women full professors in Cohort 2 lagged behind the national levels of women full professors at four-year institutions and research universities. The results thus indicate that *ADVANCE* Cohort 1 universities show a higher proportion of women STEM full professors than comparable national research universities, while Cohort 2 universities show a lower proportion.

OVERALL CONCLUSIONS ABOUT THE DIVERSITY (ACADEMIC WORKFORCE PARTICIPATION) OUTCOMES ENGENDERED THROUGH *ADVANCE* INITIATIVES

From the findings presented in this chapter, we conclude that overall, the *ADVANCE* universities have significantly increased the number of women faculty in STEM at all ranks over the duration of their institutional transformation projects. The targeted efforts of *ADVANCE* universities to increase the number of women STEM faculty were successful; increases in the representation of women STEM faculty occurred during their IT award periods while lesser or no growth occurred in their numbers of men STEM faculty during the same periods. The 19 universities studied engendered a 7.18% average annual growth rate in the numbers of women STEM faculty over their *ADVANCE* award periods; that is, the average number of women STEM faculty at these 19 institutions increased over their *ADVANCE* award periods by almost 40% while the average number of men STEM faculty increased by about 3.5% over the same time period. *ADVANCE* universities were particularly successful in increasing the representation of women assistant and full professors in STEM areas. Comparisons with national samples of research universities from the SDR database suggest that *ADVANCE* universities generally led the pace in increasing the representation of women STEM faculty over the same time periods. However, the data also signal that women faculty continue to be underrepresented in the academic STEM workforce, particularly at the associate professor and professor ranks at the nation's research universities.

8 Equity and Inclusion Outcomes for Women Faculty in Science and Engineering

In this chapter, we examine the equity and inclusion outcomes brought about through *ADVANCE* institutional transformation interventions in three areas: (a) resource equity assessment and improvement through salary equity studies, and offer letter and start-up package analyses, (b) the inclusion of women in faculty leadership and administrative positions, and (c) faculty climate assessment and improvement through surveys, faculty interview and focus group studies, and exit surveys regarding the gender climate at *ADVANCE* institutions. Equity refers to making the playing field level for the performance and success of all workforce participants. Inclusion refers to the social processes that influence one's efficacy and sense of belonging and value in a work system. Inclusion represents a person's ability to participate in and contribute fully and effectively to an organization, and be recognized and valued as contributor to the organization's success. By assessing the efforts to establish resource equity, the promotion of women to leadership positions, as well as the everyday experiences and workplace climate perceptions of women faculty in STEM disciplines, we are able to describe the successes and challenges of the *ADVANCE* institutions in improving equity and inclusion outcomes and creating an inclusive culture in academia.

RESOURCE EQUITY ASSESSMENT AND IMPROVEMENT

To improve resource equity and faculty retention, *ADVANCE* institutions have undertaken reviews of salaries, start-up packages, offer letters, laboratory and office space allocations, and other resources provided to both women and men faculty on each campus. Across the *ADVANCE* sites, the findings of the following most frequently employed equity-related studies, which aim at improving the retention of academic S&E faculty, are described below:

- Salary equity reviews.
- New-hire offer letter and start-up package analyses.

(a) *Salary equity studies:* It is well documented that women faculty members earn less than their male counterparts. For example, the AAUP Faculty Gender Equity Indicators Report reveals that in 2005–06, across all ranks and all institutions, the average salary for women faculty was 81% of the amount earned by men (West & Curtis 2006). Among all full professors at all types of institutions in 2005–06, women earned on average 88% of what men earned. For associate and assistant professors, the overall national figure for women was 93%. The authors of this report note that the salary disadvantage was due to two reasons: women are more likely to have positions at institutions that pay lower salaries, and they are less likely to hold senior faculty rank.

Some of the *ADVANCE* universities employed systematic salary-equity reviews to ascertain and redress pay inequities. For example, a salary equity study conducted early in the *ADVANCE* award period at Case Western Reserve University suggested that (a) Small differences in salary between male and female faculty could not be explained fully by differences in rank, discipline, tenure status, years since hire, years in rank, age, highest degree, and years since attaining the highest degree; (b) Female faculty are predominantly in lower ranks while male faculty are in higher ranks; (c) The differential in tenure and rank status contribute further to disparities in salary; (d) African American, Hispanic, and Native American faculty are underrepresented in most schools and ranks; and (e) Disparities in schools involved within the *ADVANCE* project appear to be smaller than schools not involved with the *ADVANCE* project. Based on these findings, adjustments were made to the S&E salary structure over subsequent *ADVANCE* IT award years, resulting in eliminating the gender pay gap in the schools involved in the *ADVANCE* project as indicated by subsequent salary equity studies (Case Western Reserve University 2008).

The University of California, Irvine (UCI) implemented and institutionalized an annual salary equity study (www.ap.uci.edu/Equity/studies/index.html). In 2009, UCI released a new study, "Campus-Wide Analysis of Median Faculty Salaries by Gender and Ethnicity at UCI for 1998–2008" (see Data and Reports at advance.uci.edu/). The primary research purposes of this study were to investigate campus-wide systematic differences in (a) cross-sectional salaries for each year, (b) starting salaries, and (c) salary increases over time, based on gender or ethnicity. Among other results, the study found that after rank and step were taken into account, there was no gender difference in salaries at the same rank and step (controlling for year of highest degree, year of hire, ethnicity, school, whether the faculty member received administrative pay, and highest degree earned). Longitudinal analyses showed that female salaries increased at a significantly faster rate than males' salaries, even when adjusted for rank and step.

A few other *ADVANCE* universities also conducted salary equity reviews. The University of Michigan conducted salary equity studies in 2001 and 2006 and found small gender differences after accounting for various controls; however, these differences did not increase significantly over the period (sitemaker.umich.edu/advance/publications_and_reports).

Virginia Tech also conducted a salary-equity study in 2007 and found that gender and race/ethnicity did not significantly contribute to salary differentials (www.advance.vt.edu/Measuring_Progress/Measuring_Progress. html). Their conclusions, similar to those of the studies conducted at Case Western Reserve University and the University of Michigan (as well as the AAUP's 2006 gender equity study), highlighted that the key issue confronting research universities is women's underrepresentation in tenure-track ranks, particularly the professor rank.

(b) *Offer letter and start-up package analyses*: Another domain for equity investigations among the *ADVANCE* universities was the start-up packages of new hires. Funding and resources offered in the start-up packages of new S&E faculty members often are the foundation of their subsequent success. Several *ADVANCE* institutions have analyzed gender equity in start-up packages. Due to variations in university, school, and department size, as well as differences in disciplines and geographical regions, it is difficult for us to draw conclusions from these (often descriptive) analyses, but overall we observed that like the salary equity studies described earlier, gender accounted for small or no differences in the start-up packages of newly hired scientists and engineers at the institutions in our sample.

For example, during 2004–2006, the *ADVANCE* project at the University of California, Irvine conducted multiple waves of faculty start-up package analyses (available at Data and Reports of advance.uci.edu/). Analyses of 2006 start-up packages reveal that differences continue to exist in start-up packages, but gender did not account for those differences. Step-level and institutional unit (school) are important determinants of starting salary and total bonus. A significant positive change in 2006 over the previous years was that female hires were hired at roughly the same step levels as males (Stepan-Norris 2008).

Analyses of 109 offer letters detailing the start-up funds of scientists and engineers at Case Western Reserve University between 2003 and 2007 indicated that school/college differences accounted for much of the variance in the amount of start-up funds. Results from independent sample t-tests for base salary and start-up funds suggested that no significant differences between males and females were found within a particular school/college or for the overall sample.

At the University of Washington, the Center for Workshop Development reviewed the contents of new-hire offer letters between 2000 and 2005 to determine if gender differences were evident. One hundred eleven valid offer letters were used for analysis. Descriptive analyses suggested that (a) the largest number of new hires were assistant professors and the female subgroup began at higher mean and median salaries than their male colleagues; (b) male associate and full professors outearned and outnumbered women of similar ranks, although neither the mean nor the median differences were particularly substantial; female assistant professors were offered higher mean and median discretionary funding packages than their male counterparts (University of Washington 2008).

To ensure that equity is well addressed in an offer letter, several *ADVANCE* institutions also reviewed offer letters issued on each campus and made recommendations to department chairs and senior administrators regarding the format and contents to be included in an offer letter. For example, the Gender Equity Project (GEP) at Hunter College, CUNY conducted offer letter analyses in 11 science departments from 1998 through 2004 and 2005–2006. Disparities were found in offer contents. To ensure uniform and complete offer letters, the GEP created a checklist of items that an offer letter should include, a sample narrative template, and a template organized by category (see www.hunter.cuny.edu/genderequity/policies.html). As a result of GEP's efforts, department chairs now receive the checklist and both versions of the template for use in writing offer letters. Similarly at Case Western Reserve University, after reviewing 57 offer letters in S&E, their Resource Equity Committee developed a document titled "Suggested Elements of an Effective Offer Letter," making recommendations for deans and department chairs making new offers to candidates (see www.case.edu/admin/aces/documents/Elements_of_offer_letters.pdf).

In summary, the salary equity studies and analyses of offer letters and start-up packages undertaken at *ADVANCE* institutions represent a diverse range of efforts to create mechanisms of monitoring and addressing equity issues in academic S&E to improve faculty retention. The experience of these institutions suggests the importance of creating internal systems to regularly review the equitable distribution of compensation and other resources to faculty. Our conclusion from the results of various resource equity initiatives is that *ADVANCE* institutions have systematized and improved the assessment of the equity consequences of compensation decisions and resource allocations such as start-up packages to STEM faculty, and made necessary adjustments when gender-related effects have been detected.

THE INCLUSION OF WOMEN IN FACULTY LEADERSHIP AND ADMINISTRATIVE POSITIONS

Women's academic leadership is an important element of culture creation as well as gender equity and inclusion. Institutional leaders such as department chairs and school deans are key to creating the internal academic climate (Bensimon, Ward, & Sanders 2000; Lucas 2000) and facilitating access to scarce resources (Hill & French 1967; Rowley & Sherman 2003) that can impact the career satisfaction of faculty members. The department chair has the power to distribute faculty workload, to establish contacts with higher administrators, to form committees and make committee assignments, to access the inner workings of the internal political system, to provide research assistants, technologies, and supplies, to acquire funds for faculty research, and to maintain good contacts with the community (Hill & French 1967). As pointed out by Rowley and Sherman (2003, 1060),

"At its best, administration facilitates the teaching and research processes by providing the resources, facilities, and technologies necessary to achieve academic excellence." As leaders of their faculty groups, department chairs and deans can serve as mentors and role models, provide vocational and psychological support, and professional network connections to their faculty. They can facilitate workplace environments that are supportive, collegial, respectful, and inclusive of all faculty members. Thus appointment of women to these important administrative positions is a critical indicator of their value and contributions in the academic hierarchy.

Similarly, women's appointment to endowed chairs is a powerful signal of recognition and value for their scholarly achievements and their faculty leadership through their research visibility and contributions. An endowed chair or named research professorship is considered the culmination of significant research and the pinnacle of an academic career. Women faculty, particularly in STEM disciplines, are much less likely to hold endowed chairs than their male colleagues as identified by various university reports on the status of women faculty (see also White 2005; National Academies 2007a).

Results of the analyses of the inclusion of women STEM faculty in faculty leadership (endowed chairs and named professorships) and administrative positions (at departmental, school/college, and university levels) over *ADVANCE* IT award periods are presented in Tables 8.1 and 8.2.

Table 8.1 describes the changes in the numbers of women in faculty and administrative leadership positions at the 19 universities studied before and after their *ADVANCE* IT award periods. The findings indicate that the average number of women faculty with endowed chairs increased marginally over the *ADVANCE* award durations. The number of women department chairs/

Table 8.1 Changes in Numbers of Women in Faculty and Administrative Leadership Positions over *ADVANCE* Award Periods

	N[a]	Initial Year		Final Year		Z[b]
		Mean	SD	Mean	SD	
Number of women with endowed chairs/named professorships	10	8.00	12.03	12.3	18.35	1.895+
Number of women department heads	14	4.86	5.38	6.00	7.43	.763
Number of women deans	14	4.07	3.77	5.07	4.83	1.707+
Number of women central administrators	8	3.13	2.85	4.50	3.93	2.232*
Total number of women in administrative leadership positions	14	10.71	8.42	13.64	11.86	2.140*

[a]N = Number of Institutions.
[b]Wilcoxon Signed-Ranks Test; * $p < .05$, + $p < .10$.

heads did not change significantly through *ADVANCE*; this finding is particularly troubling because departmental administrative leadership is critical for climate improvement, particularly for women faculty (Bilimoria et al. 2006). The number of women deans increased marginally, while the number of women in central administrative positions and the total number of women in administrative leadership positions increased significantly over *ADVANCE* time periods. While causal attributions to *ADVANCE* efforts cannot be made from the data presented in Table 8.1, there is clearly a coinciding period between the changes documented and *ADVANCE* IT award periods. Based on these findings, we conclude that *ADVANCE* has partially succeeded in increasing women in faculty leadership (endowed chair) and administrative (school/college deans and central administrative) positions but that an area for future targeted attention needs to be the increase of women in department chair positions.

Table 8.2 indicates the number of institutions showing positive, negative, or no change in the inclusion of women in faculty leadership and administrative positions over the *ADVANCE* award periods.

The findings presented in Table 8.2 indicate that the vast majority of institutions showed a percentage increase in the inclusion of women in faculty leadership and administrative positions, confirming the earlier conclusion that *ADVANCE* universities have been at least partially successful in improving the inclusion of women in STEM leadership and administrative positions.

We conclude from the combined results of Tables 8.1 and 8.2 that *ADVANCE* institutions have generally had a positive impact on increasing the representation of women faculty in leadership positions. However, a clear area where more still needs to be accomplished is that of departmental leadership; future *ADVANCE* efforts should target increasing the representation of women in STEM departmental chair positions.

Table 8.2   Number of Institutions with Changes in Women's Leadership Positions over *ADVANCE* Award Periods

	Dept. (Chairs, Heads, Associate Heads) n = 14	School/College (Deans, Assoc. Deans) n = 14	University level (Central Administrator) n = 8	Administrative Leadership* n = 14	Endowed Chairs n = 10
# with % increase	7	9	6	10	6
# with no change	3	3	2	1	2
# with % decrease	4	2	0	3	2

Note:
*Administrative leadership includes departmental, school, and university leadership positions. Rank data were not available for Columbia University.

INSTITUTIONAL CLIMATE ASSESSMENT AND IMPROVEMENT

Culture reflects the deeply embedded assumptions, ideologies, and values that members hold about an organization, and climate focuses on current perceptions and attitudes of organizational members. The climate or atmosphere of an organization is perceived by its members and reflected in its structures, policies, practices, the demographics of its membership, the attitudes and values of its members and leaders, and the quality of personal interactions (Moran & Volkwein 1992; Callister, Williams, & Fine 2009). Higher education climate is also a function of the interaction between students, staff, faculty, and administrative policy (Cress & Sax 1998).

The quality of the campus climate rates high on the list of current concerns at most institutions of higher education (Shenkle, Snyder, & Bauer 1998). Through campus climate studies, individual institutions gather data about specific aspects of campus life. Campus officials gather climate information by varying means, ranging from qualitative methods such as focus groups and interviews to quantitative measures using formally designed surveys. Commercial publishers, public service organizations and associations in higher education (e.g., Association of American Universities Data Exchange-AAUDE), and university-affiliated groups (e.g., Collaborative on Academic Careers in Higher Education-COACHE) have also constructed instruments and procedures to collect and report on climate perceptions from university students and employees. Below we describe some of the workplace climate assessments undertaken at *ADVANCE* institutions through interview/focus group studies, climate surveys, and exit interviews/surveys.

CLIMATE ASSESSMENT AND IMPROVEMENT THROUGH FACULTY INTERVIEW AND FOCUS GROUP STUDIES

Several institutions conducted in-depth, qualitative studies based on interviews and focus-group data collections. Table 8.3 presents a summary of selected highlights from various climate assessments through faculty interview and focus group studies conducted at a sample of the *ADVANCE* universities. Since the findings and reports of these *ADVANCE* studies are extensive, we have chosen to highlight findings pertinent to gender equity and inclusion. Some of the interview and focus group studies conducted explored baseline or continuing conditions that reveal different facets of the workplace climate facing women faculty in science and engineering. Others were explicitly evaluative in their goals, being particularly concerned with how *ADVANCE*-related initiatives were being received by the faculty members they seek to serve, and seeking guidance for recommendations and directions for future *ADVANCE* efforts.

The results of the interview and focus-group studies presented in Table 8.3 identify workplace climate factors important to male and female faculty, indicate specific areas where the initiatives undertaken by *ADVANCE*

Table 8.3   Examples and Selected Highlights of Findings of Faculty Interview and Focus Group Studies of Institutional Climate at *ADVANCE* Universities

ADVANCE Institution: Study Purpose, Participants, Methods, and Selected Results of Faculty Interview and Focus- Group Studies

Case Western Reserve University: 2004 Climate for Women Faculty Focus-Group and Interview Study
The purposes of the study were to establish baseline qualitative data about the experiences of women faculty in four test departments at the start of the NSF *ADVANCE* program, and to extend and verify conditions observed in a 2000 focus-group study. Twenty-three faculty members participated in the study for an overall response rate of 24% (with 19% of the male faculty from the test departments, 47% of the female faculty members from the test departments, and 100% of the department chairs participating). Three focus groups, ranging from three to nine participants, were conducted: mixed-rank male faculty, mixed-rank female faculty, and department chairs. Seven additional individual interviews were conducted. Findings included the following trends in perception across both men and women: (a) proportional rarity of women is an issue at the university, (b) female faculty members deal with token dynamics associated with being a statistical minority, (c) the structure of the academic environment is gendered, advantaging men's careers, (d) women perceive their rarity as a disadvantage, whereas men view the rarity as advantageous for women, and (e) the university, as an institution, is resistant to change and improvement efforts. These themes were evident at multiple levels, including departments and schools, the university, and academia as a whole. (*Source:* Case Western Reserve University 2004, 21–22).

Case Western Reserve University: 2005 Science Department Study
The purpose of the study was to identify organizational factors that facilitate both high- quality science and inclusion in a department that was the only STEM department in the university with a female chair. The study used qualitative methods including document and archival research, direct observation, and 29 interviews of departmental members, which included faculty, staff, post-docs, and doctoral students. The study found five factors that contributed to high- quality science and an inclusive departmental culture: *Values and beliefs* about scientists and the goals of science as cooperative and interactive; *constructive interactions* that are collegial, tacit learning–oriented, relational, and generative; *participative departmental activities* such as team teaching, social activities, and participative faculty meetings; *department-wide learning and inclusion processes* including transparent decision making, engagement of faculty across ranks, dissemination of information, sharing of resources, and an open faculty-selection process; and *inclusive leadership practices* of the department chair, including supporting the creation and advancement of good science regardless of who is developing it, seeking input from all affected in decision making, promoting meaningful opportunities for interaction, treating everyone fairly and equitably, and using the role of chair in service of the scientific community within the department. (*Source:* Case Western Reserve University 2008, 34–35). See also http://www.case.edu/admin/aces/documents/science_department.doc, and Jordan and Bilimoria (2007).

Continued

Table 8.3 Continued

Case Western Reserve University: 2005 Faculty-Graduate Student Relationship Interviews

Six focus groups and a few individual interviews were conducted to explore the faculty-graduate student relationship in STEM departments. A total of 19 graduate students (7 males and 12 females) and 35 faculty members (19 males and 16 females) participated in this study. The study found that schemas associated with faculty gender moderate the relationship between faculty selection factors and preferences for advisors. The schemas held about women faculty included perceptions that they are less visible, less credible as scientists, and less committed to research because of the family roles that they have to play, and are expected to be nurturing in interpersonal interactions and work style. Schemas were also associated with junior faculty, senior faculty, international students, and domestic graduate students. Recommendations for improving the advisor-advisee selection process and relationship were provided. (Source: Liang, Joy, and Bilimoria 2008).

Columbia University: 2008 Lamont Senior Scientist Interviews

To obtain the perspective of senior scientists on the achievements and shortcomings of the *ADVANCE* program, semi-structured interviews with 12 Lamont senior scientists (3 women and 9 men) were conducted. These scientists had had direct involvement in *ADVANCE* activities, were collaborators to Marie Tharp Fellows, participants in research workshops, participants in the women's forum, or were current and former associate directors and others involved in the hiring and promotion process on the Lamont campus. The study found that most scientists were generally positive in their overall appraisal of *ADVANCE*, but they also expressed varying degrees of caution about their ability to speak confidently about the full extent of the *ADVANCE* program's impact, particularly with regard to creating a more open and supportive work environment for women. The Marie Tharp Fellowship program received universal praise although senior scientists were more mixed in their assessment of this program. Many of the scientists expressed support for the program's goals but had not attended any of the workshops; only a small number of the scientists had direct involvement in these invited workshops. Those directly involved were generally positive in their evaluations of the importance of the workshops. (Source: Columbia University 2008, 23–29).

Georgia Tech: 2004 Interviews with Georgia Tech Women Faculty

Data were collected in semi-structured interviews with 20 tenured and tenure-track women faculty within NSF funded-fields. Subjects were identified with an aim for distribution across fields, ranks, and racial/ethnic groups. Using these criteria, requests for interviews were sent by email to 24 women faculty so identified; 20 (83%) of those contacted were interviewed in -person or, in the case of three interviewees, by phone. Eight were assistant professors, eight were associate professors, and four were full professors. Study findings pertained to two aspects: participation/performance and advancement. *Participation and performance:* The vast majority of women faculty interviewed said that they value autonomy and freedom in research and teaching, and interaction with students as the most important reasons for having an academic career. For these women

Continued

Table 8.3 Continued

faculty, "success" meant "having recognition and impact in research" and "having positive impact upon students" which frequently was expressed as launching students into graduate education, post-doctoral positions, and careers. *Advancement*: Almost all (95%) of the respondents believed that in promotion from associate to full, standards applied "vary with the candidate." In addition, when asked explicitly about the role of "personal factors" (gender, race, and personality) in academic advancement, almost all (95%) of the respondents believed that these factors influenced advancement. At the same time, 90% said that it was "risky" to discuss the role of such factors because doing so would cause offense or do damage. (Source: Georgia Tech 2007, 12-14).

Utah State University (USU): 2003–04 Faculty Job Satisfaction Interviews
To decide on the projects and activities for the *ADVANCE* grant, STEM faculty women and a matched set of faculty men were interviewed. The 42 female and 40 male faculty members were from the Colleges of Agriculture, Engineering, Natural Resources and Science. Each faculty member was asked about the factors at USU that contributed to their career success and job satisfaction, the factors at USU that were obstacles to success or sources of job dissatisfaction, and the changes they would like to see at USU to improve the recruitment and retention of faculty. Major findings were that: (a) no significant differences (chi-square analyses) between male and female faculty were found in the sources of career success and job satisfaction at USU—the top four of which were interactions with colleagues, campus resources, support of administrators, and positive teaching experiences; (b) the responses of male and female faculty were similar for many of the categories of obstacles to career success and job satisfaction. The most frequently reported sources that did not differ between men and women were lack of resources on campus, negative interactions with administrators, negative teaching experiences, and low salary; and (c) significant gender differences ($p < 0.02$) emerged in four categories of obstacles to success and sources of dissatisfaction: women faculty were more likely to report negative interactions with colleagues; negative experiences with the process of evaluation, promotion and tenure; difficulty balancing work and family life; and overwhelming workloads. (*Source:* Utah State University 2006, 21–23).

Virginia Tech: 2005 Faculty Work/Life Focus Groups
A total of 138 faculty members were invited by letter from the provost to participate in one of five focus groups. Of those invited, 62 faculty members elected to participate. Participants were relatively equally divided among the faculty ranks. Thirty-six participants (58%) were women; 26 (42%) were men. All groups included both men and women and faculty members from a variety of colleges. Four groups were also mixed rank; one group was set aside for assistant professors only, given the importance of work-life issues during the pre-tenure period. The main question asked was "What are the issues of work-life balance that have been, or are currently, concerns for you or for close colleagues?" Three major themes emerged: (a) changing university culture (e.g., lack of clear direction from the administration) and inadequate resources to support the new vision (including

Continued

Table 8.3 Continued

recognition, rewards, and compensation), (b) faculty career issues (e.g., all time is university time, lack of diversity and collegiality, the tenure and promotion process, lack of mentorship), and (c) family and personal health issues. (*Source:* www.advance.vt.edu/Measuring_Progress/Misc_Reports/Faculty_Worklife_Issues_Report_2005.pdf.)

Virginia Tech: 2008 Impact of Work-Life Policies on New Faculty Hires
Twenty-five recently hired faculty members (n = 25) from various departments participated in this study. Three respondents were appointed in fall 2006, six were appointed in spring 2007, and 16 were appointed in fall 2007. The sample consisted of 13 men and 12 women. Three participants were associate professors and 22 were assistant professors. The purpose of the study was to assess the impact of new work-life policies initiated by the *ADVANCE* project, in particular the impact of the dual-career assistance program, family- friendly polices (e.g., stop-the-clock and modified duties), and child- care options. Faculty members were questioned to determine whether they were aware of these programs and policies, had utilized these policies, or had concerns about the impact of these polices in recruiting or retaining them or future faculty members to Virginia Tech. The study found that (a) participants perceived that dual- career hiring policies were important in the recruitment of new hires, (b) a majority of participants (n = 20) were aware that family-friendly policies existed, and (c) six participants indicated that child care was an issue for them before accepting their positions. Of all of the issues discussed, child care seemed to be the issue that concerned participants the most. Some noted that child care was not a concern at the time of their hire, but will become a concern if they decide to have children. (Source: www.advance.vt.edu/Measuring_Progress/Misc_Reports/New_Faculty_Policy_Impact_2008_rev.pdf.).

institutions have been more or less successful, and provide guidance and direction to future *ADVANCE* efforts. Some of these studies reveal that women faculty experience their workplaces less positively than their male colleagues. Others indicate the successful and less successful aspects of specific *ADVANCE* initiatives. We conclude from the findings of the various interview and focus group studies that *ADVANCE* projects have been effective in identifying and addressing specific gender equity and inclusion issues at these universities.

CLIMATE ASSESSMENT AND IMPROVEMENT THROUGH FACULTY CLIMATE SURVEYS

Faculty surveys have been most frequently used by *ADVANCE* institutions to assess and address workplace climate issues. The objectives of conducting a faculty climate survey at a university include: (a) assessing the experiences and perceptions of being a faculty member, (b) assessing the quality

Table 8.4 Summary of Response Rates of Faculty Climate Surveys Conducted by *ADVANCE* Universities

ADVANCE University	Survey Name	Time 1: Response Rate	Time 2: Response Rate
Georgia Tech[1]	Survey of Faculty Perceptions, Needs, and Experiences	76%	71%
University of Michigan[1]	Survey of Academic Climate and Activities	41%	31%
University of Wisconsin, Madison[1]	Study of Faculty Work Life	60%	56%
New Mexico State University[1]	Employee Climate Survey	41%	—
Hunter College, CUNY[1]	Science Faculty Survey	46%	—
University of California, Irvine[1]	Faculty Climate Survey	32% (2002)	22% (2009)
University of Puerto Rico, Humacao[1]	Climate Study	25%	—
University of Colorado Boulder[1]	Faculty Climate Survey	78%	Not available
Utah State University[2]	Work-Life Survey (Department Climate Survey)	70%	Completed
University of Texas, El Paso[2]	Work-Life Survey	42%	46%
University of Alabama, Birmingham[2]	Academic Climate Survey	30%	54%
Case Western Reserve University[2]	Faculty Climate Survey	39%	39%
Virginia Tech[2]	Faculty Work-Life Survey	59%	53%
Kansas State University[2]	Community and Climate Survey		49%
University of Maryland, Baltimore County[2]	Work-Life and Climate Survey	50%	—
Columbia University[2]	Work Environment Survey	50%	Completed
University of Rhode Island[2]	Academic Work Environment Survey	39%	38%
University of Montana[2]	PACE Climate Survey	48%	46%

Continued

Table 8.4 Continued

Note:
[1]*ADVANCE* IT Cohort 1 institution; [2]*ADVANCE* IT Cohort 2 institution.
University of California, Irvine also conducted a faculty climate survey in 2004.
For Case Western Reserve University, School of Medicine was excluded from the calculation of the response rates.
For University of Maryland, Baltimore County, response rates are for STEM tenured and tenure track faculty only.
For Virginia Tech, response rates are for tenured and tenure-track faculty only.
Utah State University and Columbia University had completed their second wave of faculty climate studies but only the first wave of results was available at the time of our data collection.

of the university's academic climate and working environments (e.g., teaching and research, processes of evaluation, and work-family arrangements), (c) providing the opportunity for faculty to voice their concerns, (d) helping departments as well as the university promote equity and inclusion, and (e) helping improve faculty retention and overall satisfaction. Online surveys were the most frequently used method in the collection of faculty responses. Survey questions covered the experience of and satisfaction with multiple aspects of the academic work environment, including research, teaching, mentoring, leadership, evaluation of processes (such as recruitment, tenure, and promotion), work-life balance, service, and support.

Almost all *ADVANCE* universities conducted at least one faculty climate survey during their *ADVANCE* award periods. The majority of universities conducted two rounds of surveys within their IT award durations. At the time of our data collection, one university (University of California, Irvine) had completed three faculty climate surveys (2002, 2004, and 2009). The basic purpose of Time 1 surveys was to establish a baseline estimate of perceptions among faculty members, especially an estimate of gender differences across a number of different measures. Time 2 surveys were undertaken with the objective of assessing changes in faculty climate perceptions. At many institutions, surveys of faculty in all disciplines were undertaken; at others surveys targeted S&E faculty only. As indicated in Table 8.4, most faculty climate surveys had response rates in the range of 30%–50% (similar to many social science surveys), with the highest at 76%.

Table 8.5 summarizes selected findings of the single faculty climate surveys conducted by *ADVANCE* institutions during their award periods. Since the findings and reports of these *ADVANCE* climate studies are extensive, we have chosen to summarize here only those findings specifically pertinent to gender equity and inclusion. These findings reveal various facets of the gendered experience of the academic work environment, and highlight that the everyday work climate for women faculty is a serious concern for these universities.

The findings of the onetime faculty climate surveys reported in Table 8.5 indicate that the academic workplace climate perceived by faculty is gendered and that gender equity and inclusion are concerns for these academic institutions. In particular the findings reveal that women faculty experience

Table 8.5   Examples and Selected Highlights of Findings of Faculty Climate Surveys (One Wave Only) at *ADVANCE* Universities

---

Columbia University: 2005 Work Environment Survey
Women faculty perceived that they get less respect from colleagues and that departmental/unit processes are less fair. They were far more likely to report having heard disparaging remarks about gender and family responsibilities. More female than male respondents believed that their careers have been hindered by their family responsibilities or their gender. While women were less likely to agree that their department/unit is diverse with respect to gender, women and men equally disagreed that their department/unit promotes gender diversity. Women were more likely to report mentoring a junior colleague. Women described more difficulty balancing work and personal life, and were more concerned about securing reliable/flexible child care. Family responsibilities were cited as limiting participation in conferences by twice as many female as male respondents. On average, men reported being away more weeks for research than did women. (*Source:* Columbia University 2006, 32.).

Hunter College, CUNY: Faculty Survey, Fall 2007
Compared to men, women were less satisfied with tenure and promotion processes, were less satisfied with their jobs in general, reported less inclusion, collegiality, and support in their departments, had less discussion with other faculty about teaching, research, and committee work, and reported less recognition for teaching, research, and committee work. (*Source:* www.hunter.cuny.edu/genderequity/facultySurveys.html.)

New Mexico State University: Employee Climate Survey 2004
Women were more likely than males to indicate that the pace and pressure of work interferes with their home life; women were less likely than men to feel that their suggestions were used to improve programs or services; women were much less likely than men to feel that they are given promotion and advancement opportunities comparable to their male colleagues; women were less likely than men to feel that their salary is equitable with their peers and colleagues at the university; and women were much more likely than men to say that they had experienced discrimination based on gender. (*Source:* irpoa.nmsu.edu/EmployeeClimateSurvey/EmployeeClimateSurvey.html.).

University of Puerto Rico, Humacao: 2007 Climate Survey
While no specific gender differences were analyzed, results revealed that there were components of the work climate (e.g., Balancing Personal and Professional Life, Situations and Interactions Facilitating Women's Advancement), both at the institutional and departmental levels, that were un-balanced and urgently needed to be balanced. (*Source:* advance.uprh.edu/Advance_Research_Reports.html.).

Utah State University: 2004 Climate Survey (Results in STEM Colleges)
Women faculty in STEM colleges reported lower levels of job satisfaction, empowerment, and access to information and higher intentions to quit and feelings of isolation than did men faculty. While gender influences job satisfaction and intention to quit (female faculty members report significantly lower job satisfaction and higher intentions to quit), this relationship was completely mediated by

Continued

Table 8.5 Continued

department climate, indicating that female faculty members are more sensitive to negative department climates. When female faculty experience negative department climates they are more likely to experience lower job satisfaction and to consider going elsewhere. (*Source:* Utah State University 2006, 48–75.)

Notes:
Utah State University and Columbia University had completed their second wave of faculty climate studies, but only the first wave of results was available at the time of our data collection.

their workplaces as less supportive and less facilitative of their career development than do their male colleagues. We conclude from these onetime surveys that gender equity and inclusion are of concern in academic S&E workplaces and that *ADVANCE* institutions have identified the main areas for improvement in their specific environments.

Many institutions conducted two (or more) waves of climate studies during their *ADVANCE* IT awards, mostly with an interim period of three to four years. Table 8.6 summarizes selected results from successive waves of faculty climate surveys conducted at the *ADVANCE* universities. Again, since these surveys have extensive findings and reports, we have chosen to report only highlights of findings relevant to gender equity and inclusion.

The findings summarized in Table 8.6 reveal specific areas of improvement in workplace equity and inclusion at *ADVANCE* institutions over a three- to five-year time period. In most cases, these improvements occurred in perceptions of resource equity, work-life integration, and awareness of gender-related issues. In some cases, improvements were seen over successive survey administrations in specific areas of inclusion—the sense of fit or inclusion of women or minority faculty within their departments and in informal collegial networks improved.

However, it appears from Table 8.6 that in many cases institutional climate remained fairly intractable over the short window of *ADVANCE* IT awards; within-institution perceptions held by male and female faculty held generally stable over the two time points of survey administration. While in many aspects perceptions of institutional faculty climate remained low and did not significantly improve over the three- to five-year time period, in some aspects perceptions may have even declined at the second survey administration. A number of reasons may explain the relative stability or deterioration in specific aspects of climate perceptions observed at the *ADVANCE* institutions over time: overall workplace climate perceptions and satisfaction are often influenced by external circumstances such as budgets and resource availabilities, university leadership changes, enrollments and quality of students, and external research funding priorities and availabilities; expectation levels for change may have increased unrealistically in early years; problematic issues that had not been previously exposed may have became more evident through *ADVANCE* interventions; individuals may have felt more empowered to voice their concerns; and the large majority of individuals at these universities not targeted for immediate

Table 8.6 Examples and Selected Highlights of Findings of Successive Faculty Climate Surveys at *ADVANCE* Universities

---

Case Western Reserve University
Gender equity climate remained stable on certain key aspects and improved on others between 2004 and 2007. Similar to 2004, the 2007 survey revealed that women faculty, in comparison with men faculty, continued to report significantly lower ratings of value and inclusion in their primary unit, significantly higher ratings that gender and race make a difference in how faculty are treated in their primary unit, and a significantly greater sense of pressure and restrictions. However, certain key aspects of the climate for women faculty improved as follows. In 2004, women faculty in comparison to men faculty reported: (a) significantly lower community and job satisfaction, (b) significantly lower ratings of the leadership effectiveness of their primary unit head, and (c) significantly lower resources and supports for academic performance from their primary unit head. These significant differences disappeared in the 2007 survey. Additionally, items reflecting university supports for work-life integration (such as partner hiring, tenure clock adjustment, family leave, child care, and flexibility regarding family responsibilities) significantly improved in 2007 as compared with 2004. (*Source:* http://www.case.edu/admin/aces/retreat/2008/Executive_Summary_2007_Faculty_Climate_Study.pdf.).

Georgia Tech
Findings indicate some areas of relative stability between surveys conducted in 2002 and 2005 and other areas of change in the period. Men continued to be more likely to speak daily about research with others in their home unit. Significant changes between the two surveys occurred on the following items. In 2005 compared to 2002, women faculty reported significantly higher mean ratings (improvements) in (a) reasonableness of teaching load; (b) equipment available for research; and (c) space available for research. Among faculty overall, clarity in evaluation was reported as higher in 2005 compared to 2002. Women were significantly more aware and participated significantly more in *ADVANCE* activities. Women faculty's characterizations were less positive than men's for most departmental work environment dimensions, such as "exciting" or "helpful." However, significant differences between the years appear (a) among faculty overall in reports of "fairness" and (b) in reports among men of higher "competitiveness" of units in 2005 compared to 2002. (*Source:* Georgia Tech 2007.)

University of Alabama, Birmingham
Results from the 2004 and 2008 climate surveys showed several indicators of climate change in the schools targeted through the *ADVANCE* program. Observed positive outcomes included (a) a higher percentage of men faculty indicating that more competitive offers were made to women and more female faculty had been hired; (b) a higher percentage of women indicating that their departments had made efforts to recruit qualified women;, (c) a higher percentage of women faculty indicating they had adequate secretarial support; (d) a higher percentage of women and men indicating they had a mentor in the university. The results also indicate some areas that require continued attention with regard to improving the climate for female faculty, specifically, access to teaching assistants and utilization of family-friendly programs. (*Source:* University of Alabama 2008, 64.)

Continued

Table 8.6 Continued

University of California, Irvine

Results of the 2009 survey that were consistent with previous surveys included that women are more familiar than are men with the aims and goals of the *ADVANCE* program; women observed more departmental personnel-related incidents of inappropriate gender-based references to personal life than did men; women experienced more incidents of (a) harassment, intimidation, or assault from staff members that they are too embarrassed to admit, and (b) discouragement from participation at meetings by colleagues or administrators than did men; women experienced more incidents of (a) qualifications-related questions or disparaging remarks from students and faculty, (b) inappropriate references to their personal life from faculty, (c) inappropriate references to their appearance from faculty, (d) overbearing, intimidating, or offensive verbal behavior from students, (e) inappropriate race- or ethnicity-based references to their personal life; women tended to disagree that they face the same opportunities as their male counterparts; women were less satisfied than men with time available for research. (*Source:* http://advance.uci.edu/media/Reports/Climate%20Survey%202009a.pdf.)

University of Colorado Boulder

Comparison of the 2003 and 2007 survey results showed some positive and statistically significant changes in several climate indicators, including (a) an increase in awareness among women (but not among men, whose awareness was higher than women's in both years) that they could negotiate aspects of their job; (b) increases in reported personal commitment to increasing gender and racial/ethnic diversity in their unit, both overall and among men in particular; (c) increases in faculty views of the importance to the institution of increasing diversity—for men, this increase was for both gender and racial/ethnic diversity; for women, it was for racial/ethnic diversity only; (d) an increase among STEM respondents, and separately, among men, in the frequency with which they discuss diversity issues at work; and (e) an overall increase in faculty's positive views of the workplace climate at the university, including an overall increase in perceived support from their main unit—these changes held among respondents as a whole and for tenure-track faculty as a group. In comparison, non-tenure-track teaching faculty assessed the climate as less positive in 2007 than 2003, and research faculty reported declines for some climate indicators and increases for others. (*Source:* Laursen 2009, 13–14.)

University of Michigan

In 2006 as in 2001, the university climate continued to be more positive for men S&E faculty than women S&E faculty and for white S&E faculty than S&E faculty of color. The reported climate was particularly negative for women of color, who rated their departments' climates significantly lower than white women at both times. Rates of overall job satisfaction were lower for white women compared to white men at both times. Reports from both white women and women of color revealed differences with their male colleagues in some areas of career satisfaction, particularly social interaction with department colleagues and their sense of being valued for their work. Women of color were least likely to indicate that they had been nominated by their departments for teaching or research awards at Time 1 and Time 2, and at Time 2 men of color were more likely than

Continued

Table 8.6   Continued

white men to report that their departments had failed to nominate them for awards for which they were qualified. Reports of experiences of unwanted sexual attention showed improvement for women from Time 1 to Time 2 as white women's reports of those experiences, as well as others' reports to them, were significantly lower at Time 2 than Time 1. In addition, for all faculty except women of color, experiences of scholarly isolation were lower at Time 2 than Time 1. Male faculty of color reported fewer disparaging comments about racial-ethnic minorities at Time 2 than at Time 1. (*Source:* Assessing the Academic Work Environment for Science and Engineering Faculty at the University of Michigan in 2001 and 2006, sitemaker.umich.edu/advance/faculty-climate.)

University of Texas, El Paso (UTEP)
The comparison of responses of the two waves (2004 and 2007) of climate surveys revealed that (a) among UTEP faculty, gender differences in assessment of the key climate components in 2004 became negligible in 2007; (b) UTEP faculty, regardless of gender, became more appreciative of gender diversity at all levels; (c) satisfaction with hiring, tenure, and decision-making processes at the department level increased for both sexes, but more so for women; and (d) climate areas that need further improvement were resource allocation, departmental decision-making, and gender diversity at the university level. (*Source:* Ryabov & Darnell 2008.)

University of Wisconsin, Madison
For women faculty in the biological and physical sciences, five of 11 climate indicators used were more positive in 2006 than in 2003. Four items showed no change at all between 2003 and 2006, and two items showed slightly worse experiences for women in 2006. Faculty of color also showed climate improvements for four of 11 items. Of note, there was a decrease in the percentage of faculty of color who reported that they "feel excluded from an informal network in my department." Six items showed no change for faculty of color, and one item showed a slight decline between 2003 and 2006. In 2006, faculty were also asked to report their own perceptions of climate *change* between 2003 and 2006. Women faculty reported positive change more often than they did negative change, as did faculty of color (although not as strongly). Three times as many women faculty indicated the climate for themselves in their departments had improved rather than declined, and two times as many faculty of color reported a climate improvement for themselves rather than deteriorating climate. Women who had a department member participate in *ADVANCE* hiring workshops reported a negative climate change significantly less often than their female colleagues in departments who did not send a faculty member to the workshops. Having at least one faculty member from a department participate in a hiring workshop was correlated with a report of positive climate change for faculty of color. Women faculty overall increased their feelings of departmental "fit" between 2003 and 2006, and this happened significantly more often for women in departments that had participated in hiring workshops, compared to those which did not. For faculty of color, it was departmental participation in the climate workshops that was most highly correlated with feelings of "fit"—faculty of color whose chairs participated did not experience the decline in feelings of fit that other faculty of color experienced. (*Source:* Sheridan et al. 2007; see also wiseli.engr.wisc.edu/facworklife.php.).

Continued

Table 8.6   Continued

Virginia Tech
Comparison of 2008 survey responses with those from 2005 indicated little
  change in faculty perceptions, with the exception of a slight improvement in the
  perceptions of equity and fair treatment. Scores on the work-life balance scale
  remained low across all colleges, and women and underrepresented minority
  faculty continued to have significantly lower scores on many of the scales than
  majority men. Job satisfaction and diversity showed significant positive increases
  between the 2005 and the 2008 surveys; women and African -American faculty
  showed improved perceptions of diversity from 2005 to 2008 (*Source:* Virginia
  Tech 2009, 7.)

benefits from *ADVANCE* initiatives may not yet have experienced sufficient
change or felt deprived in some way.

In summary, Table 8.6 indicates that while faculty climate perceptions
generally remained stable over time, specific aspects of the institutional
climate were reported to improve during *ADVANCE* IT award periods,
while others were reported to deteriorate. Thus we conclude that while
overall climate perceptions remained generally intractable over successive
climate surveys, *ADVANCE* efforts have been positively associated with
improvements in specific aspects of the gender climate and culture at these
universities, particularly gender equity, supports for work-life integration
and gender-related awareness. A challenge for *ADVANCE* remains to document improvements in overall faculty perceptions of workplace climate
through quantitative surveys of all faculty members.

CLIMATE ASSESSMENT AND IMPROVEMENT
THROUGH FACULTY EXIT STUDIES

A few *ADVANCE* universities have sought to assess and improve faculty
climate by conducting faculty exit studies. Some of these studies entailed
phone or face-to-face interviews while others were online surveys of faculty who have left (or are about to leave) the university. Table 8.7 provides
examples of the kinds of findings regarding gender equity and inclusion
obtained through these studies at some *ADVANCE* institutions.

The findings presented in Table 8.7 indicate a number of specific issues identified by the *ADVANCE* institutions as problematic for faculty. While some
studies highlighted gender differences in reasons and considerations for leaving, most studies pointed to general factors pertaining to perceived negative
departmental climate, problems with academic workload expectations and difficulties in performance, work-life integration considerations including partner employment and opportunities, difficulties with university administrators,
and compensation-related issues. In summary, the results of the faculty exit
studies reported in Table 8.7 identified the main reasons for voluntary faculty

Table 8.7 Examples and Selected Highlights of Findings of Faculty Exit Studies at *ADVANCE* Universities

ADVANCE University: Purpose, Participants, Methods, and Selected Results of Faculty Exit Studies
Case Western Reserve University (CWRU): Faculty Exit Survey Study (2005) An online faculty exit survey was designed and implemented in 2005 focusing on three areas: (a) original reasons for accepting the position at CWRU, (b) ratings of experience at CWRU, and (c) reasons for leaving. Surveys were e-mailed to all faculty members who had indicated they were leaving the university at the end of the 2004–05 academic year. Of the 48 respondents, 42 (87.5%) responded that they were leaving CWRU voluntarily, 5 (10.4%) were leaving CWRU involuntarily, and 1 respondent (2.1%) did not answer the question. Although significant differences could not be calculated due to the small sample size of respondents in this study, some differences existed between the 36 men and women in terms of cited reasons for voluntary departure. Specifically, 50% of women said they were leaving because of difficult working conditions, compared to only 35% of men. An unfavorable tenure process was cited by 33% of women but only 13% of men. *Impact:* The information from the faculty exit survey was used by CWRU's Office of Faculty Diversity to identify areas for improvement and trends in attrition. (*Source:* Case Western Reserve University 2006.)
New Mexico State University (NMSU): "A Diamond in the Rough": Faculty Retention at New Mexico State University—A Report on Research Exploring Why Faculty Leave NMSU (November 2008) Thirty-four tenure-track faculty members who left NMSU for other positions between 2005 and 2008 were interviewed by phone and/or face-to-face, for a usual conversation length of one and a half hours, although several interviews were two or more hours. The study found that respondents (a) felt lack of appreciation for their contributions, (b) perceived a large communication gap between the faculty and administrators fueled by a lack of transparency and low faculty involvement in decision making, (c) perceived teaching loads to be unrealistic, (d) lamented a lack of assistance and mentoring, especially during the first year (when the tone often is set for an entire career) and for their partners' or families' adaptation to a new community, and (e) reported that administrators often have superficial or limited understandings of diversity and seldom reflect on their actions in respect to diversity. *Dissemination, impact, and institutionalization of exit interviews:* The report was presented to the Academic Deans Council and in 2009 was presented to the Colleges of Engineering and the Faculty Senate, with plans to present it at the College of Business and other colleges. The *ADVANCE* team was in talks to help integrate the survey into a university-wide exit interview process to be conducted by Employee Relations (*Sources:* New Mexico State University 2009, 13; Eber 2008)
University of Michigan (UM): Faculty Exit Interview Study (2008) Seventy-one out of 118 tenure track faculty members who voluntarily left the university between September 1, 2000, and September 1, 2008 (excluding people who retired, or who were not renewed or denied tenure), participated in an exit

Continued

Table 8.7 Continued

interview study. Interviews were confidential and interviewers were selected who had no direct or indirect relationship with the faculty member with whom they talked or his/her previous school affiliation. Notes were taken of the interviews, and, when permission was granted, interviews were also recorded. Of the 71 faculty interviewed, most were male (68%) and white (71%). Eight of the 18 faculty of color identified as members of underrepresented minority groups. Fewer than half (42%) were assistant professors when they left; 58% were associate or full professors. The study found that important factors in faculty members' decisions to leave included: (a) improved career opportunities for the faculty member, especially in the areas of research, salary, and promotion with new position, (b) improved career opportunities for the faculty member's partner, (c) negatives about their position, including negative climate, problems with leadership, the university's lifestyle and workload, teaching and difficulty working across units, and (d) positives about the new institution, particularly geographic location. Most faculty (73%) reported that the move was a good one for them. (Source: sitemaker.umich.edu/advance/files/exitinterviewfinal.pdf.).

University of California, Irvine (UCI): Exit Interview—Data Analysis of Voluntary Resignations of Regular-Ranks Faculty, University of California Irvine (2004)
Thirty-two former UCI faculty members who had left the institution between 1999 and 2003 were contacted via e-mail requesting an exit interview. A total of 22 faculty (11 female, 11 male) completed a telephone interview (average 33.6 minutes, range 20–60 minutes). The primary reason noted for leaving UCI was an attractive job offer from another university. The most important elements of the competitive offer that participants noted included the following: salary (mentioned by 15 participants), reputation (mentioned by 4), teaching load (mentioned by 3), promotion (mentioned by 3), and research resources (mentioned by 2), and location (mentioned by 2). Equally for men and women, another key factor that influenced their decision to leave was the negative aspects of their departmental/school atmosphere. *Institutionalization of exit interviews:* The Office of Academic Personnel and OEOD will take over the function of faculty exit interviews within the next two years, after the process is refined. (*Sources:* Exit Interview Summary, 2004 advance. uci.edu/images/Exit%20Interview%20for%20web.pdf ; see also Toolkit available at http://advance.uci.edu/images/Faculty%20Toolkit%20Exit%20Interview.final. pdf; and University of California, Irvine 2005, 13.)

University of Wisconsin, Madison (UW-Madison): Faculty Attrition Studies (2005, 2006–07, 2008–09)
Women faculty who left UW-Madison STEM departments from 2001 through 2004 were interviewed in 2005. Following this study, on the request of the Office of the Provost, 35 faculty members who left UW-Madison between 9/1/06 and 8/31/07 were contacted in the fall of 2007and 16 of these individuals (46%) were interviewed using a standardized interview protocol, audiotaping and subsequent transcription and coding. The following emerged as critical areas of concern from the 2006–07 study: (a) issues with research and tenure including "research not supported or understood," "positions misaligned with tenure criteria" and "ineffective mentoring"; (b) economic issues including "financial relationship between the state

Continued

Table 8.7 Continued

and the university,",, "effects on faculty, staff and students,",, and "lack of raises and salary compression"; (c) university and departmental climate issues, including "experiencing discrimination, harassment, and other behaviors" and "lack of recognition and overall morale"; and (d) balancing professional and personal lives, including "respecting the needs of family" and "consideration of the faculty lifestyle." *Impact and institutionalization:* Experience with this study led to a request from the Office of the Provost to implement an annual exit interview study for all UW-Madison faculty who leave. Beginning in 2007 and working with the Office of the Provost and Human Resources, faculty who left UW-Madison in the prior year for reasons other than retirement were identified and interviewed. In 2008/09, the Faculty Attrition Study was expanded to include retirees. (*Source:* Pribbenow 2008.)

departure, established a baseline for faculty climate assessment, and assisted *ADVANCE* programs in developing measures and processes for workplace climate improvement in order to enhance faculty satisfaction. We conclude from these findings that faculty exit studies have assisted *ADVANCE* efforts to identify and address equity and inclusion issues at these universities.

OVERALL CONCLUSIONS ABOUT THE EQUITY AND INCLUSION OUTCOMES ENGENDERED THROUGH *ADVANCE*

Based on our analyses of the resource equity assessment and improvements undertaken, the appointment of women to faculty leadership and administrative positions over *ADVANCE* award durations, and workplace climate assessment and improvement efforts, we conclude that *ADVANCE* has engendered significant equity and inclusion improvements at the universities studied. The most prominent improvements were observed in the areas of (a) increased systematic attention to salary distributions and resource equity between men and women faculty, and intentional efforts to remedy inequities; (b) increases in the inclusion of women in senior leadership positions; and (c) improvements in specific facets of the academic workplace culture and climate such as increased campus-wide awareness of gender issues, improved work-life integration, providing increased voice to women faculty, and improved recognition of and attention to the factors leading to faculty success and retention. Certain challenges remain on these campuses regarding gender equity and inclusion outcomes, particularly the challenge of improving workplace climate as well as reward and recognition systems that are still perceived overall as gendered.

9 Gender Diversity (Workforce Participation) Outcomes by Discipline

In this chapter we examine the diversity (academic workforce participation) outcomes of *ADVANCE* institutional transformation within three specific disciplines—engineering, natural sciences, and social and behavioral sciences at the 19 universities. Engineering and natural sciences disciplines constitute STEM areas, while the social and behavioral sciences (SBS) are included within the larger umbrella of science and engineering (S&E), which also encompasses STEM areas.

THE ACADEMIC WORKFORCE PARTICIPATION OF WOMEN FACULTY IN SCIENCE & ENGINEERING (S&E)

For purposes of these analyses, we classify science and engineering (S&E) disciplines into three areas—engineering, natural sciences, and social and behavioral sciences (SBS). Engineering disciplines include aerospace, aeronautical or astronautical engineering, chemical engineering, civil, architectural or sanitary engineering, electrical or computer hardware engineering, industrial engineering, mechanical engineering, and other engineering. Natural sciences include biological, agricultural, and environmental life sciences, computer and information sciences, mathematics and statistics, and physical sciences. Social and behavioral sciences include social sciences and psychology.

Figure 9.1 presents the percentage profiles of women by earned degree (bachelor, master, and doctoral) in natural sciences, SBS, and engineering, respectively. The figure indicates that from 1993 to 2007, the numbers of degrees awarded to women in natural science, SBS, and engineering at each level are increasing. The percentage of women with degrees in engineering lagged behind natural sciences and SBS. In engineering schools/colleges, women constitute no more than 25% of students who earned degrees between 1993 and 2007. However, women constitute over 45% of the students who earned degrees in SBS since 1993. The percentage of women with degrees in natural sciences is between the profiles of engineering and SBS.

In addition, as discussed in *Key Science and Engineering Indicators: 2010 Digest*, several new developments in S&E education are important to acknowledge. First, the changing field composition of new S&E degrees is gradually altering the composition of S&E jobs and the larger U.S. workforce. Across degree levels, the physical sciences, computer sciences, mathematics, and engineering have had weaker-than-average growth, but engineering doctorates have set records. Second, advanced S&E degrees have risen faster (70%–75%) than bachelor's degrees (about 50%) over the past two decades. Bachelor's and master's degrees in computer sciences have pulled back from their 2004 record highs to levels set in 2000. The biological sciences and psychology have shown the strongest gains (www. nsf.gov/statistics/digest10/trends.cfm#3).

Despite growth in earned degrees in S&E disciplines over the past decades, disparities continue in the representation of women by field of academic occupation. Except in the social sciences, women faculty are generally underrepresented in engineering, mathematics, and computer sciences occupations (see Science and Engineering Indicators 2010, Figures 3.29 and 3.30). Both the award of doctorates to women and the representation

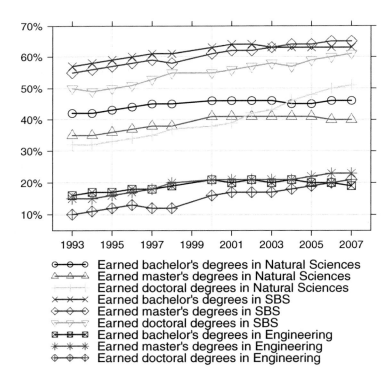

Figure 9.1 Percentage of women by earned degree in natural science, social and behavioral science, and engineering: 1993–2007.
Source: Drawn from Table 2–12, 2–26, 2–28, Science and Engineering Indicators 2010, 222. nsf.gov/statistics/seinf10/appendix.htm#c3.

Table 9.1 Women as a Percentage of Faculty by Discipline and Tenure Status: 1999, 2001, 2003, 2006 (National Sample of Four-Year Colleges and Universities)

S&E Discipline	Women as % of Tenured Faculty within Discipline				Women as % of Tenure-track Faculty within Discipline			
	1999	2001	2003	2006	1999	2001	2003	2006
Engineering	5%	5%	6%	7%	12%	13%	18%	19%
Natural Sciences	14%	16%	17%	18%	28%	29%	28%	30%
Social and Behavioral Sciences (SBS)	26%	28%	30%	34%	45%	46%	49%	50%

Source: Survey of Doctorate Recipients: 1999, 2001, 2003, 2006 (www.nsf.gov/statistics/ doctoratework/). Data drawn from Table 20 and Table 21: Employed doctoral scientists and engineers in four-year educational institutions, by broad field of doctorate, sex, and tenure status: 1999, 2001, 2003, and 2006. Four-year educational institutions include four-year colleges or universities, medical schools (including university-affiliated hospitals or medical centers), and university-affiliated research institutions.

of women faculty were lowest in electrical and mechanical engineering compared to other engineering fields (www.engtrends.com/IEE/0907D. php). Next we discuss the tenure representation of women in S&E academic occupations.

The Tenure Status of Women Faculty within S&E Disciplines

Women faculty are less likely to be tenured in S&E fields than men faculty. Data from the Survey of Doctorate Recipients (SDR) depicting the characteristics of samples of doctoral scientists and engineers in the United States are presented in Table 9.1, which shows employed doctoral scientists and engineers in four-year educational institutions, by broad field of doctorate, sex, and tenure status (1999, 2001, 2003, 2006).

Table 9.1 shows that from 1999 to 2006, the biggest gain (8% increase) of tenured women faculty was in SBS, up from 26% to 34%. The least gain (2% increase) occurred in engineering, up from 5% to 7%; the percentage of tenured women faculty in natural sciences increased from 14% in 1999 to 18% in 2006. In tenure-track positions, the biggest gain (7% increase) was in engineering, with the percentage of women faculty growing from 12% in 1999 to 19% in 2006. The second biggest gain (5% increase) of women faculty was in SBS, which increased from 45% in 1999 to 50% in 2006. Natural sciences represented the least gain (2% increase) of women faculty in tenure-track positions, up from 28% in 1999 to 30% in 2006.

Results from the *ADVANCE* Sample

Given the background described above, we undertook comparisons between the baseline year and the final year of the *ADVANCE* IT projects with regard to the representation of women and men faculty within three

Table 9.2 Changes in the Academic Workforce Participation of Faculty at *ADVANCE* Institutions over Their Award Periods within S&E Disciplines by Gender

Variables (# of Universities)	Initial Year		Final Year		Test Statistic[a]	
	Mean	SD	Mean	SD	Z	p-value
Engineering (n = 16)[b]						
Number of women faculty in engineering	14.1	11.3	19.9	14.6	3.42	.001**
Number of men faculty in engineering	128.3	88.2	134.6	94.1	1.73	.083
Total number of faculty in engineering	142.8	99.0	154.1	108.3	2.85	.004*
Natural Sciences (n = 19)						
Number of women faculty in natural sciences	27.3	10.0	36.5	14.5	3.77	.000***
Number of men faculty in natural sciences	151.4	73.6	154.5	76.8	0.70	.485
Total number of faculty in natural sciences	178.7	80.9	191.0	88.8	2.68	.007**
Social and Behavioral Sciences (n = 13)[b]						
Number of women faculty in SBS	39.8	53.6	48.8	59.9	3.06	.002**
Number of men faculty in SBS	80.3	102.8	78.7	95.6	0.36	.721
Total number of faculty in SBS	120.0	155.9	126.9	154.9	2.32	.021*
Percentage of Women Faculty						
% women faculty in engineering (n = 16)	9.6%	3.7%	12.7%	4.3%	3.11	.002**
% women faculty in natural sciences (n = 19)	16.6%	6.9%	20.5%	6.5%	3.74	.000***
% women faculty in SBS (n = 13)	33.1%	5.4%	39.2%	4.7%	3.06	.002**

[a]Wilcoxon Signed- Ranks Test: * p < .05, ** p < .01, *** p < .001.

[b]Comprises of those universities which included this discipline in their ADVANCE program efforts.

S&E disciplines: engineering, natural sciences, and social and behavioral sciences (SBS). These results are presented in Table 9.2.

Results from the Wilcoxon signed-ranks tests undertaken in Table 9.2 show an average significant increase between the initial year and the final year in the numbers of women faculty in engineering, natural sciences, and SBS, with no corresponding significant change in the numbers of men faculty in these same disciplines over the same time period at these universities. Additionally, women faculty as a percentage of the total faculty at these universities increased significantly over their *ADVANCE* award periods in all three disciplines. While the data cannot show that these differences were caused only due to *ADVANCE* initiatives, there is clearly a coinciding period between the changes documented and *ADVANCE* IT award periods. We conclude from these findings that targeted interventions through *ADVANCE* to increase the workforce participation of women faculty in all three S&E disciplines (engineering, natural sciences, and SBS) have been successful.

Table 9.3 Number of *ADVANCE* Institutions Reporting Faculty Percentage Changes in S&E Disciplines over Their Award Periods

Faculty Percentage Change in 4–7 Years	Engineering (n = 16)		Natural Sciences (n = 19)		Social and Behavioral Sciences (n = 13)	
	Women	Men	Women	Men	Women	Men
1–9%	0	5	0	6	0	2
10–19%	1	1	4	3	4	2
20–29%	4	3	6	0	3	0
30–39%	4	0	2	0	2	0
40–49%	0	0	3	0	2	0
50–59%	3	0	1	0	0	0
60–59%	1	0	1	0	0	0
70–79%	1	0	0	0	0	0
80–100%	0	0	0	0	1	0
101–500%	1	0	1	0	0	0
Total # of universities reporting a % increase	15	9	18	9	12	4
Total # of universities reporting no change	0	1	0	3	1	2
Total # of universities reporting a % decrease	1	6	1	7	0	7

We also undertook analysis of the number of universities (out of 19) reporting changes in the representation of women faculty in these three S&E disciplines. These results are presented in Table 9.3.

The results of Table 9.3 indicate that across all three disciplines, a greater number of universities reported an increase in the representation of women faculty than men faculty. In engineering, 15 universities reported an increase in the number of women faculty, compared to nine universities that reported an increase in the number of men faculty. In natural sciences, 18 universities reported an increase in the number of women faculty, compared to nine universities that reported an increase in the number of men faculty. In SBS, 12 universities reported an increase in the number of women faculty, compared to four universities that reported an increase in the number of men faculty. Additionally, the number of institutions reporting no change or a percentage decrease in the representation of women faculty in the three disciplines was none or one in all cases. These results are consistent with results from the earlier paired t-tests, which showed that the increase in the representation of women faculty was more significant than the increase in the representation of men faculty over the duration of the *ADVANCE* IT projects. These findings confirm that *ADVANCE* initiatives have increased the academic workforce participation of women faculty in all three S&E disciplines (engineering, natural sciences, and SBS).

Next we examine each S&E discipline separately, comparing the changes at the *ADVANCE* universities with changes occurring among other higher-education institutions across the country.

THE ACADEMIC WORKFORCE PARTICIPATION OF WOMEN FACULTY IN ENGINEERING

In Table 9.4, we present results on the representation of women faculty in engineering drawn from the Survey of Doctorate Recipients (SDR) for 2001, 2003, and 2006 for all four-year colleges and universities as well as for research universities only. As described in Chapter 3, SDR data for 2008 were not yet available at the time of our data analyses. According to *Engineering by the Numbers* produced by the American Society for Engineering Education, women constituted 12% of tenured and tenure-track engineering faculty in 2008 nationwide, increasing by 5% since 2001. Also, as addressed in Chapter 7, we provide a comparison to both all four-year institutions and research universities (Carnegie classification Very High and High Research Universities) only since 17 out of the 19 universities studied are research universities. While we provide comparisons with all four-year colleges and universities, we will mainly discuss results pertinent to research universities as they are the most appropriate comparison set for the *ADVANCE* sample we utilized in the present study.

Table 9.4 Women as a Percentage of Employed Doctoral Scientists and Engineers in Engineering at Four-Year Institutions and Research Universities by Faculty Rank: 2001, 2003, and 2006

Engineering	4-year Institutions			Research Universities		
	2001	2003	2006	2001	2003	2006
% Women Assistant Professors	17%	16%	22%	19%	17%	22%
% Women Associate Professors	11%	13%	13%	9%	12%	13%
% Women Full Professors	3%	4%	4%	2%	3%	4%
% Women Faculty at All Ranks	8%	9%	11%	7%	8%	11%

Source: Calculated from Survey of Doctorate Recipients crosstabs, 2001, 2003, and 2006. Reference: National Science Foundation, Division of Science Resources Statistics, 2009. *Characteristics of Doctoral Scientists and Engineers in the United States: 2006.* Detailed Statistical Tables NSF 09-317. Arlington, VA. Available at http://www.nsf.gov/statistics/nsf09317/.

The findings of Table 9.4 indicate increases in the percentage of women engineering faculty at all ranks between 2001 and 2006, with larger increases in the percentage of women assistant and associate professors than full professors, at both four-year institutions and at research universities.

Results from the *ADVANCE* Sample

Sixteen *ADVANCE* universities included engineering as part of their *ADVANCE* efforts; all are research universities. The specific fields included in engineering for each *ADVANCE* university are provided in Appendix 2.

Between 2002 and 2008, seven *ADVANCE* universities had 20 or less women faculty in their engineering schools and nine had no more than 51 women faculty in engineering. Given the small numbers of women faculty in engineering across the *ADVANCE* universities, it is less meaningful to make comparisons by academic rank. Instead, we compare all engineering faculty (combined ranks) to the national sample.

Only four out of seven *ADVANCE* Cohort 1 universities provided valid data for 2002. Given that the average percentage of women faculty at Cohort 1 universities is very sensitive to the values reported by each of the participating universities, we report the average percentage of Cohort 1 from 2003 onwards, which was when all seven Cohort 1 universities provided valid faculty data. This provides us with more consistent, reliable, and meaningful results.

Figure 9.2 presents the percentage profile of women faculty in *ADVANCE* engineering fields relative to the national reference groups of women faculty at four-year institutions and at research universities, respectively.

Figure 9.2 indicates that for *ADVANCE* Cohort 1 universities, the average percentage of women faculty in engineering increased from 11% in AY 2003 to 12% in AY 2007. For *ADVANCE* Cohort 2 universities, the average percentage of women faculty in engineering increased from 9% in

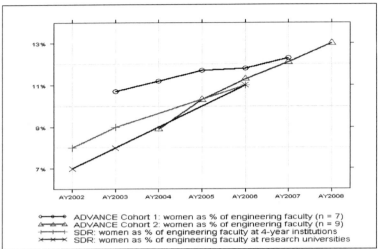

Notes. All *ADVANCE* Cohort 1 and Cohort 2 universities including Engineering are research universities. For Cohort 1, the average percent in AY2007 was calculated based on the percentages of four universities with valid faculty data. For Cohort 2, the average percent in AY2008 was calculated based on the percentages of six universities with valid faculty data. The percentage of women faculty in AY2009 is not reported because only three out of seven universities provided valid faculty data.
SDR=Survey of Doctorate Recipients data for 2001, 2003 and 2006. The percentages of women faculty in calendar years 2001, 2003 and 2006 from SDR data were comparable to those of the *ADVANCE* sample in academic years of 2001-02, 2002-03, and 2005-06, respectively.

Figure 9.2   The academic workforce participation of women faculty (all ranks) in engineering at *ADVANCE* Institutions over their award periods compared with national samples of four-year institutions and research universities.

AY 2004 to 13% in AY 2008. Conclusions regarding comparisons with national reference groups from all four-year institutions and research universities are difficult to draw since 2008 SDR data were not available at the time of our analyses, but *ADVANCE* universities appear to be setting the pace for increases in the representation of women faculty in engineering in comparison with all four-year colleges and universities and other national research universities. The data also confirm the continued severe underrepresentation of women faculty in engineering across the nation at four-year colleges and universities and at research universities.

Our final analysis of the representation of women and men faculty in engineering over the duration of *ADVANCE* IT awards is presented in Table 9.5.

The results presented in Table 9.5 indicate that on average *ADVANCE* universities increased the number of women faculty in engineering over their award periods at a percentage growth rate (8.32% growth per year) higher than that of men faculty (1.00% growth per year). The average growth rate over the total award periods across these 16 institutions was 46.26% for women faculty and 5.56 % for men faculty in engineering; that is, the number of women engineering faculty at these 16 institutions

Table 9.5   Changes in Numbers of Faculty in Engineering at *ADVANCE* Institutions over Their Award Periods by Gender

		Initial Year	Final Year	*ADVANCE* IT Award Duration in Years	Average Annual Growth Rate[b]
Georgia Institute of Technology[1]	Female	41	51	5	6.10%
	Male	333	364		2.33%
New Mexico State University[1]	Female	7	8	7	2.38%
	Male	67	64		-0.75%
University of Colorado Boulder[1]	Female	13	23	6	15.38%
	Male	121	124		0.50%
University of California, Irvine[1]	Female	9	8	7	-1.85%
	Male	71	88		3.99%
University of Michigan[1]	Female	31	39	5	6.45%
	Male	261	270		0.86%
University of Washington[1]	Female	28	36	6	5.71%
	Male	174	167		-0.80%
University of Wisconsin, Madison[1]	Female	16	24.75	5	13.67%
	Male	182.25	172.85		-1.29%
Case Western Reserve University[2]	Female	9	12	5	8.33%
	Male	98	98		0.00%
Columbia University[2]	Female	12	16	6	6.67%
	Male	123	139		2.60%
Kansas State University[2]	Female	9	15	5	16.67%
	Male	98	104		1.53%
University of Alabama, Birmingham[2]	Female	4	6	5	12.50%
	Male	34	41		5.15%
University of Maryland, Baltimore County[2]	Female	15	20	6	6.67%
	Male	63	59		1.16%
University of Rhode Island[2]	Female	6	8	4	6.67%
	Male	58	57		-1.27%
University of Texas, El Paso[2]	Female	1	6	6	100.00%
	Male	47	60		5.53%
Utah State University[2]	Female	4	5	5	6.25%
	Male	71	64		-2.56%

Continued

Continued

Virginia Tech[2]	Female	26	41	6	11.54%
	Male	252	275		1.83%
Average across 16 Universities	Female	14.44	19.92	5.56	8.32%
	Male	128.33	134.1		1.00%

Notes: [1]*ADVANCE* IT Cohort 1 institution. [2]*ADVANCE* IT Cohort 2 institution.
[a]ADVANCE IT award duration in years inclusive of extensions, for which data were available on this measure, as of our data collection.
[b]Percentage difference in numbers between initial and final years of *ADVANCE* projects divided by (IT Award Duration − 1).
16 universities included engineering in their *ADVANCE* projects. The specific fields within engineering at each institution included in this table are provided in Appendix 2.
University of Wisconsin, Madison data were reported as full- time equivalent (FTE).

increased over their *ADVANCE* award periods on average by more than 46% while the number of men engineering faculty increased on average by about 5.5%.

While we cannot show that these differential growth rates were caused only by *ADVANCE* initiatives, their occurrence over the *ADVANCE* award period at each university gives us confidence to infer that targeted initiatives to advance the workforce participation of women faculty in engineering through *ADVANCE* have played a significant role. Table 9.5 also indicates that the numbers of women faculty in engineering at these universities remain extremely small in comparison with the numbers of men faculty. In the initial year of *ADVANCE* awards, the average number of women faculty in engineering at these 16 universities was 14.44, which constituted 10.11% of the total faculty. In the final year of the *ADVANCE* awards, the average number of women faculty in engineering at these 16 universities grew to 19.92, which constituted 12.93% of the total faculty. While the data cannot show that these differences were caused only due to *ADVANCE* initiatives, there is clearly a coinciding period between the changes documented and *ADVANCE* IT award periods. We conclude from the data reported in Table 9.5 that targeted initiatives at the ADVANCE universities have resulted in increases in the numbers of women faculty in engineering over their award periods. However, the percentage of women faculty still remains an extremely small fraction (13%) of the total engineering faculty at these colleges and universities.

THE ACADEMIC WORKFORCE PARTICIPATION
OF WOMEN FACULTY IN NATURAL SCIENCES

As indicated in Table 9.6, the nationwide representation of women faculty in the natural sciences has improved with a 2–5% increase between 2001

Table 9.6 Women as a Percentage of Employed Doctoral Scientists and Engineers in Natural Sciences at Four-Year Institutions and Research Universities by Faculty Rank: 2001, 2003, and 2006

Natural Sciences	4-year Institutions			Research Universities		
	2001	2003	2006	2001	2003	2006
% Women Assistant Professors	29%	30%	34%	26%	27%	30%
% Women Associate Professors	21%	23%	24%	20%	21%	22%
% Women Full Professors	11%	11%	13%	10%	9%	11%
% Women Faculty at All Ranks	18%	19%	22%	16%	16%	18%

Note: Natural Sciences include biological sciences, agricultural sciences, environmental life sciences, computer and information sciences, mathematics and statistics, and physical sciences.
Source: Calculated from Survey of Doctorate Recipients crosstabs, 2001, 2003, and 2006. Reference: National Science Foundation, Division of Science Resources Statistics. 2009. *Characteristics of Doctoral Scientists and Engineers in the United States: 2006.* Detailed Statistical Tables NSF 09-317. Arlington, VA. Available at http://www.nsf.gov/statistics/nsf09317/.

and 2006. Results from SDR indicate that women constituted 34% assistant professors in 2006, up from 29% in 2001. At the associate professor level, the percentage of women increased from 21% in 2001 to 24% in 2006 at four-year institutions; at the full professor level, the percentage of women was 13% in 2006, up from 11% in 2001. At research universities, the representation of women faculty at all three levels is consistently lower than that at four-year institutions between 2001 and 2006. The biggest increase (4%) was at the assistant professor level, followed by the associate professor level (2%). Women full professors at research universities only achieved 1% increase between 2001 and 2006.

The findings of Table 9.6 indicate small increases in the percentage of women faculty at all ranks between 2001 and 2006, with the largest increases occurring in the percentage of women assistant professors, at both four-year institutions and at research universities.

Results from the *ADVANCE* Sample

All 19 universities studied included natural science disciplines in their *ADVANCE* programs. The specific fields included in natural sciences for each *ADVANCE* university are provided in Appendix 3.

Of the 19 *ADVANCE* institutions studied, for this analysis we excluded two Cohort 1 universities (University of Colorado and University of Puerto Rico, Humacao) for which consistent annual data were not available. Sixteen out of 17 *ADVANCE* universities with natural sciences departments are research universities, making the comparison with research universities at the national level (from the SDR database) the most useful for our purposes.

Figure 9.3 presents the percentage profile of women faculty in natural sciences at *ADVANCE* universities relative to the national reference group

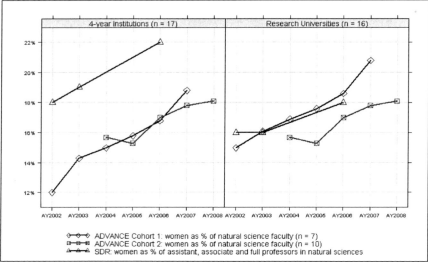

Figure 9.3 The academic workforce participation of women faculty (all ranks) in natural sciences at *ADVANCE* institutions over their award periods compared with national samples of four-year institutions and research universities.

Notes. Natural Sciences include biological, agricultural, and environmental life sciences, computer and information sciences, mathematics and statistics, and physical sciences.

Two *ADVANCE* Cohort 1 universities were excluded from this analysis since consistent annual data were not available: University of Colorado and University of Puerto Rico, Humacao. AY 2002 data were not available for two universities: New Mexico State University and University of Wisconsin, Madison; AY 2007 data were not available for Georgia Institute of Technology and University of Michigan. Hence, the average percentages of women faculty in AY2002 and AY2007 were calculated from five universities with valid faculty data.

All 10 universities in *ADVANCE* Cohort 2 are research universities. AY 2004 data were not available for University of Montana and AY 2008 data were not available for University of Rhode Island. Hence, for the *ADVANCE* Cohort 2 universities, the average percentages of women faculty in AY2004 and AY2008 were calculated from nine universities with valid data.

SDR=Survey of Doctorate Recipients data for 2001, 2003 and 2006. The percentages of women faculty in calendar years 2001, 2003 and 2006 from SDR data were comparable to those of the *ADVANCE* sample in academic years of 2001-02, 2002-03, and 2005-06, respectively.

of women faculty at four-year institutions and at research universities, respectively.

Figure 9.3 indicates that in comparison with national research universities, the average percentage of women faculty in natural sciences at *ADVANCE* Cohort 1 universities increased from 15% in AY 2002 to 21% in AY 2007. For *ADVANCE* Cohort 2 universities, the average percentage of women faculty in natural sciences increased from 16% in AY 2004 to 18% in AY 2008.

The relatively lower representation of women faculty in natural sciences at the *ADVANCE* Cohort 2 universities studied is striking but it appears that the rate of change in this cohort has allowed them to catch up with the national sample levels. It is likely that the scope of natural sciences in the *ADVANCE* sample is much narrower than the scope defined in the national sample. For the SDR sample, natural sciences were defined

Table 9.7 Changes in Numbers of Faculty in Natural Sciences at *ADVANCE* Institutions over Their Award Periods by Gender

		Initial Year	Final Year	*ADVANCE* IT Award Duration in Years	Average Annual Growth Rate[b]
Georgia Institute of Technology[1]	Female	27	40	5	12.04%
	Male	209	241		3.83%
Hunter College, CUNY[1]	Female	21	23	6	1.90%
	Male	56	56		0.00%
New Mexico State University[1]	Female	34	45	7	5.39%
	Male	124	125		0.13%
University of Colorado Boulder[1]	Female	45	62	6	7.56%
	Male	236	245		0.76%
University of California, Irvine[1]	Female	31	64	7	17.74%
	Male	198	232		2.86%
University of Michigan[1]	Female	28	46	5	16.07%
	Male	223	230		0.78%
University of Puerto Rico, Humacao[1]	Female	34	33	4	-0.98%
	Male	55	53		-1.21%
University of Washington[1]	Female	32	41	6	5.63%
	Male	225	213		-1.07%
University of Wisconsin, Madison[1]	Female	29.25	34.75	5	4.70%
	Male	235.37	227.95		-0.79%
Case Western Reserve University[2]	Female	13	16	5	5.77%
	Male	70	65		-1.79%
Columbia University[2]	Female	29	36	6	4.83%
	Male	158	164		0.76%
Kansas State University[2]	Female	43	52	5	5.23%
	Male	283	277		-0.53%
University of Alabama, Birmingham[2]	Female	6	7	5	4.17%
	Male	62	64		0.81%
University of Maryland, Baltimore County[2]	Female	14	22	6	11.43%
	Male	74	67		-1.89%
University of Montana[2]	Female	20	29	5	11.25%
	Male	118	106		-2.54%

Continued

Table 9.7   Continued

University of Rhode Island[2]	Female	31.5	36	6	4.76%
	Male	131	131		0.00%
University of Texas, El Paso[2]	Female	21	31	5	9.52%
	Male	72	85		3.61%
Utah State University[2]	Female	37	47	5	6.76%
	Male	195	203		1.03%
Virginia Tech[2]	Female	23	29	6	5.22%
	Male	151	151		0.00%
Average across 19 Universities	**Femal**	27.30	36.51	5.47	7.54%
	Male	151.34	154.53		0.47%

Notes: [1]*ADVANCE* IT Cohort 1 institution. [2]*ADVANCE* IT Cohort 2 institution.
[a]*ADVANCE* IT award duration in years inclusive of extensions, for which data were available on this measure, as of our data collection.
[b]Percentage difference in numbers between baseline and final years of *ADVANCE* projects divided by (IT Award Duration – 1).
All 19 universities included natural sciences in their *ADVANCE* projects. The specific fields within natural science at each institution included in this table are provided in Appendix 3.
University of Wisconsin, Madison data were reported as full-time equivalent (FTE).

to include biological sciences, agricultural sciences, environmental life sciences, computer and information sciences, mathematics and statistics, and physical sciences. However, for the *ADVANCE* sample, the fields and subfields of natural sciences vary dramatically by institution (see Appendix 3). This might explain why the percentage profile of the *ADVANCE* Cohort 2 sample is lower than the national sample level in natural sciences.

Conclusions regarding comparisons with national reference groups from all four-year institutions and research universities are difficult to draw since 2008 SDR data were not available at the time of our analyses, but *ADVANCE* universities appear to be progressing similarly as or better than other national research universities in increasing the representation of women faculty in natural sciences. The data also confirm the continued low academic workforce participation (around 20%) of women faculty in natural sciences disciplines across the nation, and particularly signal the ongoing challenge of engaging more women faculty in these disciplines at research universities.

Our final analysis of the representation of women and men faculty in natural sciences over the duration of *ADVANCE* IT awards is presented in Table 9.7.

The results presented in Table 9.7 indicate that *ADVANCE* universities increased the number of women faculty in natural sciences over their award periods at an average annual growth rate (7.54%) higher than that of men faculty (0.47%). The average growth rate over the total award periods across these 19 institutions was 41.24% for women faculty and 2.57% for men faculty in natural sciences; that is, the number of women natural sciences faculty at these 19 institutions increased on average over their *ADVANCE* award periods by more than 41% while the number of men natural sciences faculty increased on average by about 2.5%.

While we cannot show that these differential growth rates were caused only by *ADVANCE* initiatives, their occurrence over the identical time period at each university gives us confidence to infer that targeted initiatives to advance the workforce participation of women faculty in natural sciences through *ADVANCE* have played a significant role. Table 9.7 also indicates that the numbers of women faculty in natural sciences at these universities remain small in comparison with the numbers of men faculty. In the initial year of *ADVANCE* awards, the average number of women faculty in natural sciences at these 19 universities was 27.30, which constituted 15.28% of the total faculty. In the final year of the *ADVANCE* awards, the average number of women faculty in natural sciences at these 19 universities grew to 36.51, which constituted 19.11% of the total faculty. We conclude from these data that targeted workforce participation initiatives at the *ADVANCE* universities have resulted in increases in the numbers of women faculty in natural sciences over their award periods. However, the percentage of women faculty still remains less than 20% of the total faculty in the natural science disciplines at these colleges and universities.

THE ACADEMIC WORKFORCE PARTICIPATION OF WOMEN FACULTY IN SOCIAL AND BEHAVIORAL SCIENCES (SBS)

The percentage profile of women faculty in social sciences and psychology at all ranks between 2001 and 2006 at four-year institutions and at research universities is presented in Table 9.8.

Table 9.8 indicates increasing trends for women faculty at all ranks in SBS disciplines. At all four-year colleges and universities, women constituted over 50% of SBS assistant professors in 2003 and 2006. At the associate professor level, the percentage of women SBS faculty was 47% in 2006, up from 38% in 2001; at the full professor level, the percentage of women SBS faculty was 25% in 2006, up from 22% in 2001. The representation of women associate professors represented the biggest increase (9%) between 2001 and 2006.

At research universities, the percentage profile of women faculty in SBS also showed increasing trends at the associate and full professor levels during 2001 and 2006. The increases range from 3–9% between 2001 and 2006 at all three levels. At national research universities, the workforce participation of women SBS faculty in 2006 was similar to (assistant

Table 9.8   Women as a Percentage of Employed Doctoral Scientists and Engineers in Social and Behavioral Sciences at Four-Year Institutions and Research Universities by Faculty Rank: 2001, 2003, and 2006

Social and Behavioral Sciences	4-year Institutions			Research Universities		
	2001	2003	2006	2001	2003	2006
% Women Assistant Professors	49%	51%	52%	47%	53%	52%
% Women Associate Professors	38%	42%	47%	41%	42%	50%
% Women Full Professors	22%	24%	25%	22%	24%	25%
% Women Faculty at All Ranks	33%	35%	39%	33%	36%	39%

Note: Social and behavioral sciences include psychology and social sciences.
Source: Calculated from Survey of Doctorate Recipients crosstabs, 2001, 2003, and 2006.
Reference: National Science Foundation, Division of Science Resources Statistics,. 2009. *Characteristics of Doctoral Scientists and Engineers in the United States: 2006.* Detailed Statistical Tables NSF 09-317. Arlington, VA. Available at http://www.nsf.gov/statistics/nsf09317/.

professors and full professors) or exceeded (associate professors) that at all four-year colleges and universities. These workforce composition data suggest that SBS disciplines, even in research universities, are considerably more welcoming workplaces for women faculty than are engineering and natural science disciplines.

Results from the *ADVANCE* Sample

Only 14 out of the 19 universities studied included SBS departments in their *ADVANCE* projects. However, one institution—Georgia Tech—included faculty data from psychology in their counts of STEM faculty. Since we could not separate this SBS data from other STEM data, we excluded this university from the SBS analyses. The specific fields included in SBS for each *ADVANCE* university are provided in Appendix 4.

Of the *ADVANCE* Cohort 1 institutions, only three out of six universities provided valid data on SBS disciplines in AY 2002. Thus, because the average percentage of women faculty is very sensitive to the percentage in each participating university, we do not report the average percentage of women SBS faculty in Cohort 1 for 2002. Instead, we report the average percentage from AY 2003 when all six universities provided valid faculty data in Figure 9.4. Of the *ADVANCE* Cohort 2 sample that included SBS, six out of seven universities were able to provide valid data for AY 2004; therefore, AY 2004 is viewed as their initial year for this analysis.

Figure 9.4 presents the relative status of women faculty in SBS at *ADVANCE* universities, compared to the national reference groups of women faculty at four-year institutions and at research universities.

For *ADVANCE* Cohort 1 comparisons with all four-year institutions (n = 6), the average percentage of women faculty in SBS was 39% in AY 2007, up from 36% in AY 2003. For *ADVANCE* Cohort 2 universities (n = 7), the average percentage of women faculty in SBS was 37% in AY 2008, up from

29% in AY 2004. Both cohorts showed an increasing trend in women SBS faculty since the inception of their *ADVANCE* programs. In comparisons with national research universities, the percentage of women faculty in SBS at *ADVANCE* Cohort 1 research universities (n = 4) was similar to the national sample in 2006. However, the average percentage of women faculty in SBS at *ADVANCE* Cohort 2 universities (n = 7) was lower than that of the national reference group. It is possible that these findings are an artifact of the small number of *ADVANCE* institutions that included SBS in their projects. It may also be that women's workforce participation and success initiatives at the *ADVANCE* institutions may have targeted engineering and natural science disciplines more than SBS disciplines. We conclude from these comparisons that while the percentage of women SBS faculty has increased in ADVANCE universities over their award periods, overall they had lower percentages of women faculty in SBS disciplines than did national research universities.

Our final analysis of the representation of women and men faculty in social and behavioral sciences over the duration of *ADVANCE* IT awards is presented in Table 9.9.

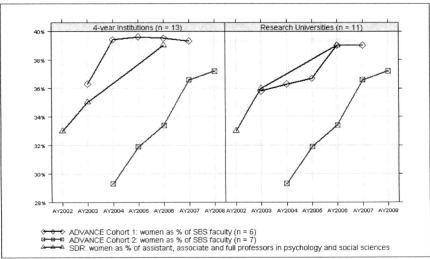

Notes. All seven universities in Cohort 2 are research universities.
For *ADVANCE* Cohort 1 comparisons with four-year institutions, the average percentages of women faculty in AY2006 and AY2007 were calculated from the percentages of four (out of six) universities with valid data.
For *ADVANCE* Cohort 1 comparisons with national research universities, the average percentage of women faculty in AY2006 and AY2007 were calculated from the percentages of three (out of four) universities with valid data.
For *ADVANCE* Cohort 2 universities, six out of seven universities provided valid faculty data for AY2008.
SDR=Survey of Doctorate Recipients data for 2001, 2003 and 2006. The percentages of women faculty in calendar years 2001, 2003 and 2006 from SDR data were comparable to those of the *ADVANCE* sample in academic years of 2001-02, 2002-03, and 2005-06, respectively.

Figure 9.4 The academic workforce participation of women faculty (all ranks) in social and behavioral sciences at *ADVANCE* institutions over their award periods compared with national samples of four-year institutions and research universities.

Table 9.9   Changes in Numbers of Faculty in Social and Behavioral Sciences at *ADVANCE* Institutions over Their Award Periods by Gender

		Initial Year	Final Year	*ADVANCE* IT Award Duration in Years	Average Annual Growth Rate[b]
Hunter College, CUNY[1]	Female	39	44	6	2.56%
	Male	60	65		1.67%
New Mexico State University[1]	Female	21	24	7	2.38%
	Male	30	33		1.67%
University of Colorado Boulder[1]	Female	70	80	6	2.86%
	Male	132	126		-0.91%
University of California, Irvine[1]	Female	53	76	7	7.23%
	Male	108	127		2.93%
University of Puerto Rico, Humacao[1]	Female	5	6	4	6.67%
	Male	9	7		-7.41%
University of Wisconsin, Madison[1]	Female	205.7	230.2	5	2.98%
	Male	392.48	360.23		-2.05%
Case Western Reserve University[2]	Female	14	18	5	7.14%
	Male	24	21		-3.13%
Columbia University[2]	Female	43	62	6	8.84%
	Male	126	131		0.79%
University of Alabama, Birmingham[2]	Female	20	26	5	7.50%
	Male	48	44		-2.08%
University of Montana[2]	Female	13	16	5	5.77%
	Male	23	23		0.00%
University of Rhode Island[2]	Female	13	36	4	12.82%
	Male	26	18		-2.66%
University of Texas, El Paso[2]	Female	14	28	6	20.00%
	Male	51	48		-1.18%
Virginia Tech[2]	Female	6	6	6	0.00%
	Male	14	14		0.00%
Average across 13 Universities	**Female**	**39.75**	**48.78**	**5.54**	**5.01%**
	Male	**80.27**	**78.71**		**-0.43%**

Notes: [1]*ADVANCE* IT Cohort 1 institution. [2]*ADVANCE* IT Cohort 2 institution.
[a]*ADVANCE* IT award duration in years inclusive of extensions, for which data were available on this measure, as of our data collection.

Continued

Table 9.9 Continued

[b]Percentage difference in numbers between initial and final years of *ADVANCE* projects divided by (IT Award Duration – 1).

14 universities included social and behavioral sciences in their *ADVANCE* projects. The specific fields within social and behavioral science at each institution included in this table are provided in Appendix 4.

Georgia Tech was excluded from this analysis because we were not able to separate out faculty in their psychology department.

University of Wisconsin, Madison data were reported as full-time equivalent (FTE).

The results presented in Table 9.9 indicate that on average *ADVANCE* universities increased the number of women faculty in SBS over their award periods at an annual percentage growth rate (5.01%) higher than that of men faculty (–0.43%). The average growth rate over the total award periods across these 13 institutions was 27.75% for women faculty while for men faculty in SBS there was a decline overall by 2.38%. That is, the number of women SBS faculty at these 13 institutions increased on average over their *ADVANCE* award periods by almost 28% while the number of men SBS faculty decreased on average by about 2.4%.

While we cannot show that these differential growth rates were caused only by *ADVANCE* initiatives, their occurrence over the identical time period at each university gives us confidence to infer that targeted initiatives to advance the workforce participation of women faculty in SBS through *ADVANCE* have played a significant role. Table 9.9 also indicates the numbers of women faculty in SBS at these universities in comparison with the numbers of men faculty. In the initial year of *ADVANCE* awards, the average number of women faculty in SBS at these 13 universities was 39.75, which constituted 33.12% of the total faculty. In the final year of the *ADVANCE* awards, the average number of women faculty in natural sciences at these 13 universities grew to 48.78, which constituted 38.26% of the total faculty. We conclude from these data that initiatives at the *ADVANCE* universities have resulted in increases in the numbers of women faculty in social and behavioral sciences over their award periods.

SUMMARY AND DISCUSSION

The findings of our analyses indicate that that targeted interventions through *ADVANCE* to increase the academic workforce participation of women faculty in all three S&E disciplines (engineering, natural sciences, and SBS) have been successful. *ADVANCE* universities have engendered significant growth in the numbers and percentages of women faculty in each of these disciplines. The greatest average percentage growth in the number of women faculty at *ADVANCE* institutions over their award periods occurred in engineering (46%); this higher growth may have occurred because the starting numbers of women faculty in these disciplines were considerably lower than those in natural sciences or SBS. Average percentage growth in the numbers of women faculty at *ADVANCE* institutions over their award periods also occurred in natural sciences (41%) and SBS (28%) in comparison with much smaller increases or even decreases for men faculty on average in these three disciplines over the same time periods. *ADVANCE* universities generally led or equaled national averages for research universities in comparable years in the pace of change in the workforce participation of women faculty in engineering and natural sciences disciplines. However, this was not the case for SBS disciplines, which lagged national samples. Overall, national sample comparisons confirm the continued severe underrepresentation of women faculty in engineering and the ongoing low workforce participation of women faculty in natural sciences.

10 Conclusions

In this chapter we recap the goals of the study and summarize the main findings. We develop a generalizable framework of institutional transformation to enhance gender equity, diversity, and inclusion. This model can be employed by higher education institutions as well as corporate and nonprofit organizations seeking gender equity, diversity, and inclusion transformation. Drawing on these findings, we develop the main conclusions that emerged from our study. We develop the implications of these conclusions and suggest recommendations relevant for higher education institutions as well as other organizations. Study limitations are addressed as well as directions for further research on institutional transformation to increase the workforce participation, equity, and inclusion of women faculty in academic S&E.

The goals of our study were to assess the institutional transformation outcomes of the NSF *ADVANCE* IT program and develop a generalized framework for how institutions of higher education (and other organizations) can enable greater gender equity, diversity, and inclusion. The specific research objectives of the study were to: (1) describe the innovative and "best practice" initiatives that have been employed to enhance gender equity, diversity, and inclusion in *ADVANCE* IT projects at the 19 higher education institutions studied, (2) understand how gender equity changes have been made permanent (i.e., institutionalized by embedding within the structures and cultures) at these institutions, (3) assess the extent to which *ADVANCE* IT has improved the workforce participation of women faculty at all ranks in academic STEM, particularly in senior positions and in leadership at these institutions, (4) investigate whether and how equity and inclusion of women faculty in academic STEM have improved at these institutions, (5) examine the extent to which the workforce participation of women faculty at all ranks has improved in specific science and engineering disciplines (engineering, natural sciences, and social and behavioral sciences) at these institutions, and (6) develop a general framework of successful institutional transformation to enable gender equity, diversity, and inclusion.

To accomplish these objectives, we studied recent organizational change projects undertaken at 19 first- and second-round college and university recipients of NSF's *ADVANCE* IT program. Specifically, we analyzed the results of change projects across these 19 universities and within three specific disciplines, describing their initiatives and institutionalization efforts, and assessing their outcomes relevant to gender diversity, equity, and inclusion. In this final chapter, we summarize the main findings, generate major conclusions of the study, provide a framework for institutional transformation in higher education, and develop implications from this framework for future higher education policy and practice, and research.

The main contribution of this study is that it serves as a comprehensive, stand-alone assessment of ongoing and increasingly widespread approaches to increase the workforce participation and contributions of women in academic science and engineering. While we provide specific insights and recommendations for university administrators and higher-education policy, leaders in business and other nonprofit organizations engaged in promoting organizational change related to equity, diversity, and inclusion likely will benefit also from the experiences of and insights emerging from NSF *ADVANCE* IT efforts.

SUMMARY OF MAIN FINDINGS

As reported in earlier chapters, five categories of research findings emerged from our study: internal and external facilitating factors and research and evaluation in support of institutional transformation (Chapter 4), transformational initiatives (Chapter 5), institutionalization (Chapter 6), workforce participation (diversity) outcomes by rank and by specific discipline (Chapters 7 and 9), and equity and inclusion outcomes (Chapter 8). The main findings in each category are summarized below.

Findings Regarding Factors Facilitating Institutional Transformation

Our study found that changes at the 19 *ADVANCE* institutions studied were facilitated by three major factors. *Internal facilitators* of institutional transformation included senior administrative support and involvement, a transformation champion, collaborative leadership, widespread and synergistic participation, and visibility of actions and outcomes. *External facilitators* included a network of change agents in peer organizations for the sharing of learnings and best practices, and legitimacy and support from an external institutional authority.

Findings Regarding Research and Evaluation in Support of Institutional Transformation

Our study found four important aspects of research and evaluation in support of institutional transformation employed by the 19 *ADVANCE* universities: tracking key indicators of diversity, equity, and inclusion, undertaking workplace climate assessments, conducting research and evaluation in support of change, and improving institutional infrastructure for the collection, analysis, and use of data.

Findings Regarding Transformational Initiatives

Our study found two major categories of initiatives employed at the 19 *ADVANCE* universities to engender equity, diversity, and inclusion. First, these institutions employed initiatives to enhance the individual career trajectories of women in the academic STEM pipeline, including initiatives to increase the inflow of women into the pipeline, initiatives to better equip women to successfully progress in the pipeline, and initiatives to improve institutional structures and processes related to key career transition points in the academic pipeline. Second, the institutions undertook transformational initiatives to enhance micro (department level) and macro (school/ college and university level) climates.

Findings Regarding Institutionalization

Our study found four ways by which institutionalization occurred at the 19 *ADVANCE* universities: new permanent positions, offices and structures, new or modified policies, new and improved practices and processes, and new supports for effective programs.

Findings Regarding Institutional Transformation Outcomes

Finally, our study findings included the outcomes of the transformational activities at the 19 *ADVANCE* universities studied in terms of diversity outcomes (workforce participation of women faculty in STEM and in specific disciplines of S&E), as well as equity and inclusion outcomes. We found that the *ADVANCE* universities have significantly increased the number of women faculty in STEM at all ranks over the duration of their institutional transformation projects; improvements occurred in the career trajectories of women in the academic S&E pipeline. Increases in the representation of women STEM faculty occurred over their *ADVANCE* award periods while lesser or no growth occurred in their numbers of men STEM faculty during the same periods. The 19 universities studied engendered a 7.18% average annual growth rate in the numbers of women STEM faculty over their *ADVANCE* award periods. The number of women STEM faculty at these 19 institutions increased on average over their *ADVANCE* award periods by almost 40% while the number of men STEM faculty increased on average by about 3.5%. *ADVANCE* universities were particularly successful in increasing the representation of women assistant and full professors in STEM areas. *ADVANCE* universities generally led national averages for research universities over comparable years in the pace of change in the workforce participation of women faculty at all ranks. Despite these advances, the data indicate the continued underrepresentation of women faculty, particularly as the associate professor and professor ranks in the academic STEM workforce in research universities.

With regard to diversity outcomes in specific S&E disciplines, the findings of our analyses indicate that targeted interventions through *ADVANCE* to increase the academic workforce participation of women faculty in three S&E disciplines (engineering, natural sciences, and social and behavioral sciences) have been successful. *ADVANCE* universities have engendered significant growth in the numbers and percentages of women faculty in each of these disciplines. The greatest average percentage growth in the numbers of women faculty at the *ADVANCE* universities over their award periods occurred in engineering (more than 46%); this higher growth may have occurred because the starting numbers of women faculty in these disciplines were considerably lower than those in natural sciences or social and behavioral sciences. Average percentage growth in the numbers of women faculty at *ADVANCE* institutions over their award periods also occurred in natural sciences (41%) and SBS (28%) in comparison with much smaller increases or even decreases for men faculty on average in these three disciplines over the same time periods. While the workforce participation of women faculty in engineering and natural sciences disciplines at *ADVANCE* universities led or equaled national averages for research universities in comparable years, this was not the case for SBS disciplines, which slightly lagged national samples. Overall, national sample comparisons confirm the continued severe underrepresentation of women faculty in engineering and the ongoing low workforce participation of women faculty in natural sciences.

In terms of equity and inclusion outcomes, our findings indicate that *ADVANCE* institutional transformation efforts have engendered certain equity and inclusion improvements at the universities studied. The most prominent improvements were observed in the areas of (a) increased systematic attention to salary distributions and resource equity between men and women faculty, (b) increases in the inclusion of women in senior leadership positions, and (c) improvements in specific facets of the academic workplace culture and climate such as increased campus-wide awareness of gender issues, improved work-life integration, providing increased voice to women faculty, and improved recognition of and attention to the factors leading to faculty success and retention. However, certain challenges remain regarding gender equity and inclusion outcomes, particularly the challenge of improving workplace climates, and university evaluation, reward, and recognition systems that are still perceived overall to be highly gendered.

AN INTEGRATIVE FRAMEWORK OF INSTITUTIONAL TRANSFORMATION

Based on the transformational experience of the 19 *ADVANCE* institutions studied, and drawing on an earlier model proposed by Bilimoria, Joy, and Liang (2008), we develop an integrative framework of institutional

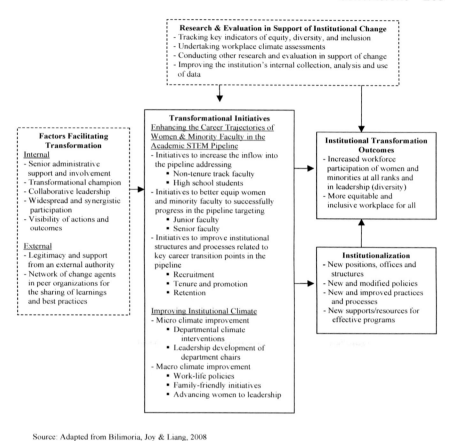

Figure 10.1 An integrative framework of institutional transformation to enhance gender equity, diversity and inclusion in academic science and engineering.

transformation to enhance the workforce participation, equity, and inclusion of women and other minority groups. Figure 10.1 presents a generalized framework of organizational transformation that fuses our five categories of findings: facilitating factors, research and evaluation in support of transformation, change initiatives, institutionalization, and outcomes.

Our framework posits that for successful institutional transformation, all five elements need to operate in unison. With institutional supports that are facilitative of transformation and an active infrastructure of data collection and reporting, initiatives that focus on individual, unit, and organization-wide change imperatives addressing career trajectories and institutional climate can be effectively employed and institutionalized to generate improved gender workforce participation, equity, and inclusion outcomes.

Extending beyond the *ADVANCE* universities, the framework can be applied to academic, corporate, and nonprofit organizations seeking improved equity, diversity, and inclusion of women and underrepresented minority groups. Sharing several features with existing, more generic organizational change models (e.g., Jick 1991; Judson 1991; Kotter 1995; Galpin 1996; Garvin 2000), this framework offers a specific solution for organizations that seek to create a more inclusive workplace. Other change models generally emphasize forces within the organization to drive change initiatives. Adding to the internal facilitating factors mentioned in the literature (particularly Eckel & Kezar 2003), our framework proposes that forces outside the organization (such as partnerships with external legitimizing and funding agencies, and the network of change agents in peer organizations) also can be effective collaborators and drivers of organizational change. Particularly with regard to institutional transformation related to diversity, equity, and inclusion, such networks and partnerships may be especially useful since such transformation requires not only organizational change but also social change.

As discussed by us earlier (Bilimoria et al. 2007), equity, diversity, and inclusion of women and other minorities are not just organization-specific issues. They have social roots, for which wider social change is needed to eliminate systematic, institutional underrepresentation and inequity. For such goals, sector-wide alliances may give greater visibility and legitimacy to change initiatives among organizations employees as well as the general public. Moreover, this kind of a change may benefit entire industry or national/regional sectors, not just single organizations, attracting larger numbers of underrepresented minority group workers and increasing overall talent pools at the industry or national/regional level.

In this regard, newer regional configurations of networks and partnerships are beginning to emerge from NSF's *ADVANCE* program. For example, recently the Midwest Regional *ADVANCE* Meeting (MRAM) was convened to foster information sharing across *ADVANCE* IT and PAID grantee institutions in the Midwest. A number of PAID projects to partner in the adoption, implementation, and dissemination of transformational learnings from IT projects have been developed in recent years; some of these create partnerships between two institutions while others bring together consortia of colleges and universities around a focal region (e.g., Case Western Reserve University's IDEAL project in Northern Ohio, which seeded institutional transformation projects at five other regional research universities) or discipline (e.g., a collaboration between the University of Michigan, Brown University, and University Corporation for Atmospheric Research to create an Earth Science Women's Network) or topic (e.g., MentorNet's creation of a Web community for mentoring of women of color in STEM).

The framework also emphasizes the conduct of research and evaluation to support transformation aimed at improving the workforce participation of women and other underrepresented minority groups. Such research may include conducting studies of best practices and collecting employee survey data regarding resource equity and inclusion. Research helps to avoid assumptions about the experiences of women and other minority group members in the workplace, look at the various aspects of the issue afresh for designing interventions, get feedback on the effectiveness of interventions, and track overall change.

Focusing on the issue of breaking down barriers and creating inclusiveness, our framework contextualizes and expands Kotter's (1995) general steps of organizational transformation: establishing a sense of urgency; forming a powerful guiding coalition; creating and communicating a vision; empowering others to act by removing obstacles and changing systems or structures that undermine the vision; planning for visible performance improvements; consolidating improvements and producing still more change; and institutionalizing new approaches (articulating the connections between the new behaviors and success, and embedding the changes into ongoing structures and practices). Our framework suggests that the implementation and institutionalization of change initiatives that have both an individual and organizational focus collectively lead to successful and sustainable increases in the workforce participation, equity, and inclusion of women and other minority groups, offering the possibility of breaking down barriers to their participation and improving the environment for all. By placing transformation-facilitating factors and research and evaluation in dashed boxes, our framework suggests that these are contingencies of institutional transformation. When internal and external facilitating factors are reduced or missing, or research and evaluation are inadequate to support the transformational initiatives, actions undertaken may be less likely to result in desired transformation outcomes.

OVERALL CONCLUSIONS OF THE STUDY

Below we summarize the conclusions that stand out for us from our extensive study of the initiatives and outcomes of the first two *ADVANCE* cohorts.

1. NSF's *ADVANCE* Institutional Transformation initiative has generated significant improvements in gender equity, diversity, and inclusion at the 19 universities studied. The workforce participation of women faculty improved significantly overall and at the assistant and full professor ranks, in leadership, and across the three science and engineering disciplines studied. Resource inequities and barriers to inclusion were systematically identified and reduced at these institutions. In comparisons with national samples from very high and high research universities, the *ADVANCE* institutions generally equaled or led in increasing the workforce participation of women faculty in STEM.

2. The underrepresentation of women faculty in academic STEM remains an important issue for the future of the U.S. scientific workforce, particularly in engineering and natural science disciplines, and

in research universities overall. Targeted efforts to repair the leaky pipeline and strengthen diversity, equity, and inclusion in academic STEM, especially at research universities, must continue to be prioritized at the national level.

3. Simplistic, ad hoc, or piecemeal solutions cannot eradicate systemic, historical, and widespread gender underrepresentation and inequities in the STEM academic workforce. To overcome existing barriers and inertia, wider and deeper change is needed in our higher education institutions. This requires greater reflexivity about everyday gender practices coupled with systemic actions to transform organizational structures, processes, work practices, mental models, and workplace cultures—to enable equal employment, opportunities, treatment, evaluation, and valuing of women and men so that *all* employees can fully participate, contribute and develop in their careers, and enable their organizations to achieve their goals of effectiveness.

4. Successful institutional change to promote gender equity, diversity, and inclusiveness requires the implementation of a portfolio of simultaneous, varied, and multilevel initiatives. These initiatives must target improvements in the career trajectories of women and minorities in the pipeline (focusing on programs of change at the individual, unit, and institutional levels) as well as improvements in the institutional workplace climate. While some initiatives may work better in certain environments, and each individual initiative may have a finite impact, a conclusion of our study is that a coordinated portfolio of organizational-change initiatives consisting of varied interventions targeted at multiple levels (individual, unit, and system-wide) simultaneously enacted within the institution can cumulatively effect significant and cascading change, and begin to move the needle in the workforce participation, equity, and inclusion of women and underrepresented minority groups.

5. The success of a transformational project is reflected not only by improving diversity, equity, and inclusion within the finite period of the project but also by effectively sustaining and leveraging the results into the future by embedding the changes into the sociocultural fabric of the organization. Starting at early stages of intervention, attention must be paid to postproject institutionalization and sustainability in four distinct areas: generating new permanent positions, offices and structures, implementing new or modified workplace policies, institutionalizing new and improved practices and processes, and developing new supports for effective programs.

6. A data-driven approach to organizational interventions is a most powerful and compelling methodology of institutional change related to gender equity, diversity, and inclusion.

7. Additional targeted attention needs to be paid to increasing the number of women academic leaders in STEM, especially in department-chair positions.

8. Attention needs to be focused in *ADVANCE* universities on the participation and success of women faculty in social and behavioral sciences fields to keep pace with national changes in women's workforce participation in these fields.

9. A network of change agents across *ADVANCE* is disseminating innovations throughout higher education through best-practice sharing, new resource generation, and the creation of an interdisciplinary scholarly community of practice addressing gender equity change in science and engineering.

10. Despite the many positive changes, equity, diversity, and inclusion efforts in academic science and engineering continue to face certain challenges, particularly the unchanging or even backward-sliding perceptions of workplace climate, a slow pace of change in the overall proportions of women and minority faculty, the tenuousness of sustainability of the changes engendered, ongoing difficulties in keeping attention focused on issues of gender equity, diversity, and inclusion, and barriers to the transfer and applicability of knowledge regarding organizational transformation across institutions of higher education. Sustaining such change requires a commitment and dedication—that is strongly supported by senior administrative leaders—to continuously champion, monitor, and support gender equity, diversity, and inclusion.

RECOMMENDATIONS FOR INSTITUTIONAL TRANSFORMATION

In this study, we used the metaphor of the leaky pipeline to identify the problems in women's workforce participation, equity, and inclusion in academic science and engineering. The 19 *ADVANCE* institutions studied have taken deliberate steps and have been successful in improving gender diversity, equity, and inclusion at all ranks overall, and in leadership positions, in academic STEM. From their experiences, we developed a generalizable integrative framework of institutional transformation to guide organizations seeking to improve the workforce participation, equity, and inclusion of women and minority groups. Recommendations for institutional transformation in academic STEM, as well as more general implications for change agents in corporate and nonprofit environments, follow.

RECOMMENDATIONS FOR HIGHER EDUCATION

Institutions of higher education would be well-served to create and support a transformation team composed of senior faculty leaders and administrators to comprehensively tackle the issues of women's underrepresentation in academic science and engineering. Such a team can help align and deploy the internal and external factors that facilitate transformation, as identified in our framework. Colleges and universities should systematically engage in a combination of top-down and grassroots change initiatives, targeting the removal of barriers constraining women at specific transition points in the academic pipeline and improving the macro- and micro-academic climates in which women faculty work. Resources for institutionalizing successful and stable initiatives, as determined by campus-specific research and evaluation, must be generated.

Gender equity data should be tracked and research findings shared regularly among decision makers such as deans, department chairs, faculty search committee members, and promotion and tenure committee members. These individuals should be made aware of the biases and barriers to women's advancement in the academic pipeline. Keeping university administrators and faculty informed about the status of and trends in faculty composition, climate, and resource equity would focus attention on the effectiveness of institutional initiatives in achieving desired outcomes.

Higher education institutions should make a concerted effort to better disseminate information on available gender equity resources. Family-friendly policies, for example, have been in place for many years at many universities, but often faculty members are reluctant to utilize them (Drago 2007) and often administrators are not aware of their existence or understand them fully or clearly (Quinn, Lange, & Olswang 2004). To increase awareness and use of such programs, universities should use multiple communications channels to describe them to employees and to others, and should ensure the elimination of possible backlash to their usage.

Finally, system-wide efforts must be undertaken across academic STEM to develop and institutionalize the data collection and reporting practices that *ADVANCE* IT efforts have suggested are instrumental for transformation in academic institutions. To this end, we recommend that it would be helpful for federal institutional funding agencies, such as the National Science Foundation, the National Institutes for Health, and the Defense Advanced Research Projects Agency as well as other federal and state government departments that fund science and engineering research, to encourage systematic self-study and improved reporting about gender diversity, equity, and inclusion indicators at all academic institutions that receive their funding.

IMPLICATIONS FOR NONACADEMIC ORGANIZATIONS

Although there are differences between academic and nonacademic work environments, the general framework described here is relevant to organizational leaders and human resources practitioners who face similar challenges as they strive to make their work environments more inclusive of women and other underrepresented minority groups. As in higher education transformation efforts, a clear goal and adequate resources are critical in any organizational transformation. Procedures to identify problems, supported by adequate statistical and research resources, should accompany that vision. Organizational change agents must be prepared to field questions and encounter resistance regarding women's underrepresented status and unsatisfactory experiences. They must also identify the resolution of those problems as essential to the long-term success of the organization. It is not enough for employees to recognize the problems as general public concerns.

Rather, organizational leaders and change agents should urgently identify these problems as issues that have serious implications for the long-term success of the organization. Understanding, buy-in, and support from grassroots organizational members regarding the need for and activities of culture change are just as important as strong support from institutional leaders and senior organizational members. Particularly for gender equity-related institutional transformation, engaging male members at all levels of the organization in the culture change effort is particularly critical in trying to achieve gender equality. As Dominguez (1992) points out, it is not women's inabilities that prevent their advancement, but rather their male managers' or peers' inabilities to deal with someone who is different and may not fit their paradigm. As the *ADVANCE* experience highlights, special initiatives and activities encouraging the partnership of men in gender equity changes at all hierarchical levels must be undertaken.

Comprehensive institutional change to promote gender equity and inclusiveness requires simultaneous multi-impact initiatives (Hogues & Lord 2007). There is need for varied kinds of action at multiple levels at the same time. Hence, awareness creation, skill building, empowerment, leadership development, process improvements, new policy creation, and structural changes need to occur simultaneously.

Institutional transformation to advance women and other minorities can be amorphous and contested. The disadvantages that women and underrepresented minority groups experience may be largely invisible to majority or more privileged members (Adler, Brody, & Osland 2000). To demystify gender equity culture change, organizational leaders and human resources practitioners can use metaphors to represent the typical career trajectory and to shed light on the minority experience. The pipeline metaphor is likely to be most relevant to work environments with disproportionate losses of women in higher ranks and structered advancement of women to leadership positions. Although the pipeline is the prevailing metaphor capturing relatively linear academic progression in science and engineering, clearly there is fluidity and dynamism to career trajectories. In nonacademic organizations, career trajectories may involve lateral movements to other functions and divisions in addition to vertical movements; these trajectories may be better served by other metaphors. Pyramids and glass ceilings frequently have been used as metaphors to represent corporate movement. Recently, Mainiero and Sullivan (2005) introduced the kaleidoscope as a metaphor for women's careers, while Eagly and Carli (2007a, 2007b) introduced the labyrinth as a metaphor to describe women's paths to leadership. These latter authors suggest that the complexities of the career decisions and obstacles that women and other minority group members face may be depicted as vestiges and cul-de-sacs where women and minorities get trapped. Change agents may find it useful to track cohorts of women and minorities who joined the organization during different time periods to determine what kinds of vestiges and cul-de-sacs they enter and their subsequent long-term career outcomes.

Finally, transformative change endures after the specific change project ends. To make workforce participation, equity, and inclusion changes sustainable, leaders and human resources practitioners need to be alert to sustaining successful features that promote cultural and structural change and to mobilizing adequate resources to support the changes in the long run.

STUDY LIMITATIONS

Our study data and methods had certain limitations. First, our small sample size of 19 institutions prevented our conducting more extensive statistical analyses. By and large it was difficult, if not impossible, for us to analyze meaningful segmentations of the sample by size and type.

Second, the outcome data were heavily drawn from the *ADVANCE* IT projects' annual and final reports in which data were sometimes reported in inconsistent formats. By relying primarily on these sources of data, we take at face value what was self-reported by the *ADVANCE* institutions to NSF. We observed inconsistencies in the reporting of faculty member counts from year to year within some institutions, possibly due to changes in measurement metrics. Additionally, despite attempts at standardization of the data indicators regarding project progress and outcomes required by NSF to be reported annually, we observed several inconsistencies across institutions. Although we attempted to reconcile the numbers across years within universities, and apply uniform decision rules for inclusion or exclusion of data across universities for any given analysis, in some cases these inconsistencies persisted. We have indicated in table and figure footnotes where these inconsistencies have required certain analytic choices.

Third, the data were sometimes incomplete. In one case we only used data in selected years (e.g., an initial year and a final year for the *ADVANCE* IT project). In other cases, we may have used a period less than five years (i.e., not including the final year) to determine whether significant changes had occurred in the workforce participation of women faculty, possibly underaccounting the likely institutionalization, synergy, and transformation that may have come together in the final year of the project.

Fourth, we encountered inconsistencies and other problems in the implementation of various initiatives and data collection efforts across universities. Generalizing across the variations in initiatives and findings was difficult. For example, although most universities had conducted a faculty-climate survey, not all had conducted it twice during the *ADVANCE* IT award period, making it difficult to identify the nature of changes in institutional climate over the award period. Even for those universities which had conducted faculty climate studies twice over their award periods, generalizable findings were difficult to obtain if different measurement methods were used.

Fifth, our reliance on final and annual *ADVANCE* project reports for conclusions about institutionalization may not reflect their most updated status; many projects were in negotiations to obtain additional support at the time their final reports were written. For others, proposed institutionalization of changes described in final reports may not have come to pass in subsequent months and years due to external, environmental, or budgetary reasons. It may also be possible that since these reports were submitted as a continued funding requirement to an external agency with oversight responsibilities (NSF), initiatives and impact may have been described in their most positive light, minimizing their challenges or downsides.

Sixth, our only comparative group for purposes of investigation of the changes in proportions of women within ranks and disciplines came from Survey of Doctorate Recipients (SDR) samples, which we were only able to obtain for three years: 2001, 2003, and 2006; 2008 SDR data were not available to us at the time of our analyses; therefore, a complete comparison was not feasible. Additionally, we were unable to conduct reliable comparisons of the outcomes of gender equity transformation using a control group of universities. Matching this study's 19 universities with a control sample proved infeasible. Many other colleges and universities (which might have been good matches by public or private type, student size, faculty size, and endowment size) had begun transformational activities in preparation of an IT proposal submission for *ADVANCE* funding or had already submitted *ADVANCE* IT proposals or were otherwise influenced by the efforts of their peer-group institutions already having *ADVANCE* funding at the time of our study, thus contaminating our identification of a suitable control group. Furthermore, detailed outcome (gender diversity, equity, and inclusion indicator) data by rank and discipline such as those emanating from the *ADVANCE* institutions are not as readily available from other institutions, further making appropriate comparisons difficult.

DIRECTIONS FOR FUTURE RESEARCH

In our study we included only the first two cohorts of *ADVANCE* IT universities (i.e., 19 institutions of higher education). As an extension and a replication of this study, we recommend expanding the study to include other *ADVANCE* IT colleges and universities. Given the limitations mentioned above, including Cohort 3 and 4 institutions in future studies would be helpful to continue the systematic study of the nature of organizational change initiatives and their impact on gender equity, diversity, and inclusion.

Although our integrative framework of institutional transformation for gender equity, diversity, and inclusion contributes to existing literature on advancing women in STEM, future research is required to establish the contingencies under which specific transformational initiatives work best. Since the interventions were conducted, by and large, simultaneously within each *ADVANCE* institution without careful attention to experimental conditions, manipulations, or controls, our review could not tease out which solutions worked better than others. Future empirical research should attempt to identify the specific circumstances and structures needed for effective gender equity solutions within a comprehensive change project.

Our study was based on data from higher education institutions in the United States. However, gender equity, diversity, and inclusion in science and engineering fields are emerging as key concerns in other parts of the world as well, and governments particularly in Canada, Australia, Europe, and Asia are investing heavily in the field of gender equity to achieve gains in the workforce participation and contributions of their women scientists and engineers. Much could be learned from comparative analyses of institutional transformation in academc science and engineering from studying systematic and innovative efforts in the higher education sectors of these other countries as well.

In addition, the outcomes of change initiatives should be studied more extensively in different workplace contexts. First, more detailed examination of the context within academic science and engineering may itself be most useful. For instance, how does the type of institution (e.g., public versus private, research versus teaching, urban versus rural, large versus small) affect the goals, nature, and outcomes of the transformational initiatives undertaken? Second, studies of transformation related to gender diversity, equity, and inclusion in other nonacademic workplace contexts such as corporations, nonprofit organizations, and professional associations would shed light on how leading organizations remove barriers and create inclusive work environments. For example, future research could more specifically address the role of external facilitating factors in nonacademic institutions. Our study indicated the powerful facilitating role that external agencies and networks of peer institutions may play in the gender equity-related transformation of higher education institutions. Are there similar effects from external institutions—possibly regulatory, professional, or trade associations—on corporations and other nonprofit organizations? What examples do we have of cooperative and facilitative actions by peer organizations that otherwise typically operate as competitors in corporate environments? Finally, while we studied the profession of academic science and engineering, gender inequalities may exist in other professions as well and their intensive study would benefit women's participation and success in these fields also.

We encourage future research to more specifically address the broader impact of institutional transformation related to gender equity, diversity, and inclusion. How does gender equity-related institutional transformation specifically improve the career trajectory of a woman faculty member in science and engineering? How is science improved by such transformation? To what extent does such institutional transformation increase the attractiveness of science and technology fields for domestic and international students, particularly women and minority students? These and other questions addressing the broader impact of gender equity institutional transformation are yet to be answered. We hope that our study of gender equity, diversity, and inclusion in the specific context of academic science and engineering in U.S. higher education inspires studies of gender inequality in other contexts, as well as investigations of the broader impacts of gender equity transformation in academic science and engineering.

Notes

NOTES TO CHAPTER 1

1. *ADVANCE* program component information provided by Dr. Kelly Mack, program officer, NSF *ADVANCE*, May 2010.

NOTES TO CHAPTER 3

1. Thus, although reported in annual and final project reports, for this study we excluded: The Ivan Allen College of Liberal Arts from Georgia Institute of Technology; the departments of education and humanities from the University of Puerto Rico, Humacao; arts, humanities, education, and school of medicine (clinical sciences) departments from the University of California, Irvine, humanities departments from the University of Wisconsin, Madison, and humanities departments and professional schools/others (e.g., school of journalism and mass communication, school of law) from the University of Colorado Boulder.

2. For Columbia University, we included the natural science departments of Morningside Arts and Sciences and the School of Engineering and Applied Sciences as comprising their STEM fields, and the corresponding faculty data are drawn from the "Table Full-time Faculty Distribution by Gender and Tenure Status" (accessed from www.columbia.edu/cu/opir/abstract/faculty_staff.html on November 3 2009). Faculty distribution by gender and rank was not available from Columbia; therefore, we only report the total number of tenure-line STEM faculty by gender between 2004 and 2008.

NOTES TO CHAPTER 4

1. Our thanks to C. Diane Matt, executive director and CEO, Women in Engineering Proactive Network; Peggy Layne, project director, *ADVANCE* VT; Jenna Carpenter, associate dean, Administration and Strategic Initiatives, and Wayne and Juanita Spinks, professor of mathematics, Louisiana Tech University, for discussing this factor with us.

NOTES TO CHAPTER 7

1. We thank Daniel J. Foley, project officer, Human Resources Statistics Program, National Science Foundation, for providing us with SDR data on faculty composition.

Appendices

Appendix 1   Fields and Subfields of STEM in *ADVANCE* IT Projects

ADVANCE IT University (n = 19)	Fields and subfields of STEM (excluding Social and Behavioral Sciences)
Georgia Institute of Technology[1]	Colleges of Computing, Engineering, and Sciences
Hunter College, CUNY[1]	Natural Sciences (including Biological Science, Chemistry, Computer Science, Mathematics & Statistics, Physics & Astronomy)
New Mexico State University[1]	Colleges of Agriculture and Home Economics, Arts and Sciences (Natural Science departments), Engineering
University of California, Irvine[1]	Biological Sciences, Engineering, Information and Computer Sciences, Physical Sciences
University of Colorado Boulder[1]	Engineering, Physical Sciences, Earth, Atmospheric and Ocean Sciences, Mathematical and Computer Science, Biological and Agricultural Studies
University of Michigan[1]	Engineering and Natural Science departments in the College of Literature, Sciences and Arts
University of Puerto Rico, Humacao[1]	Biology, Applied Physics, Computational Mathematics, Chemistry
University of Washington[1]	College of Arts and Sciences (STEM departments), College of Engineering
University of Wisconsin, Madison[1]	Physical Sciences (including Engineering, Natural Science departments) and Biological Sciences
Case Western Reserve University[2]	College of Arts and Sciences (Natural Science departments), School of Engineering
Columbia University[2]	Natural Science departments of Morningside Arts and Sciences, and School of Engineering and Applied Sciences
Kansas State University[2]	College of Agriculture, College of Arts and Sciences, College of Engineering

Continued

Appendix 1 Continued

University of Alabama, Birmingham[2]	Schools of Natural Science and Mathematics, and Engineering
University of Maryland, Baltimore County[2]	College of Natural and Mathematical Sciences, and College of Engineering and Information Technology
University of Montana[2]	Physical Sciences, Mathematics & Computer Science, and Biological Sciences
University of Rhode Island[2]	College of Arts & Sciences (STEM departments), College of Engineering, College of Environment & Life Sciences (Natural Science departments), Graduate School of Oceanography
University of Texas, El Paso[2]	Biological Sciences, Chemistry, Computer Science, Geological Science, Mathematical Science, Physics, Civil Engineering, Electrical and Computer Engineering, Mechanical and Industrial Engineering, Metallurgical and Materials Engineering
Utah State University[2]	Colleges of Science, Engineering, Natural Resources, and Agriculture
Virginia Tech[2]	College of Science, and College of Engineering

Notes: [1]*ADVANCE* IT Cohort 1 institution; [2]*ADVANCE* IT Cohort 2 institution.

Appendix 2 Fields and Subfields of Engineering As Defined by *ADVANCE* Institutions

ADVANCE IT University (n = 16)	Fields and subfields of Engineering
Georgia Institute of Technology[1]	Aerospace, Biomedical, Chemical, Civil & Environmental, Electrical and Computer, Industrial & Systems, Materials Science, Mechanical, Regional, and Textile & Fiber
New Mexico State University[1]	Electrical and Computer Engineering, Chemical Engineering, Civil and Geological Engineering, Engineering Technology, Industrial Engineering, Mechanical Engineering, and Survey Engineering
University of California, Irvine[1]	Biomedical Engineering, Chemical Engineering & Materials Science, Civil & Environmental Engineering, Electrical Engineering & Computer Science, Mechanical & Aerospace Engineering
University of Colorado Boulder[1]	Aerospace Engineering Sciences, Chemical and Biological Engineering, Civil, Environmental & Architectural Engineering, Electrical & Computer Engineering, Mechanical Engineering, and Other Programs
University of Michigan[1]	Aerospace Engineering; Atmospheric, Oceanic & Space Sciences; Biomedical Engineering; Chemical Engineering; Civil & Environmental Engineering; Electrical Engineering & Computer Science; Industrial & Operations Engineering; Materials Science & Engineering; Mechanical Engineering; Naval Architecture & Marine Engineering; Nuclear Engineering & Radiological Sciences
University of Washington[1]	Aeronautics & Astronautics, Bioengineering, Chemical Engineering, Civil & Environmental Engineering, Computer Science & Engineering, Electrical Engineering, Industrial Engineering, Material Science & Engineering, Mechanical Engineering, Technical Communication
University of Wisconsin, Madison[1]	Biological Systems Engineering, Chemical & Biological Engineering , Civil & Environmental Engineering , Electrical & Computer Engineering, Biomedical Engineering, Industrial Engineering, Mechanical Engineering, Materials Science & Engineering, Engineering Physics, Engineering Professional Development
Case Western Reserve University[2]	Biomedical Engineering, Chemical Engineering, Civil Engineering, Electrical Engineering & Computer Science, Macromolecular Science, Materials Science & Engineering, Mechanical and Aerospace Engineering

Continued

Appendix 2   Continued

Columbia University[2]	Applied Physics & Applied Mathematics, Biomedical Engineering, Chemical Engineering, Civil Engineering & Engineering Mechanics, Computer Science, Earth & Environmental Engineering, Electrical Engineering, Industrial Engineering & Operations Research, Mechanical Engineering, Computer Engineering, Materials Science
Kansas State University[2]	Architectural Engineering and Construction Science, Biological and Agricultural Engineering, Chemical Engineering, Civil Engineering, Computing and Information Sciences, Electrical and Computer Engineering, Industrial and Manufacturing Systems Engineering, Mechanical and Nuclear Engineering
University of Aalabama, Birmingham[2]	Biomedical Engineering, Civil, Construction & Environmental Engineering, Electrical & Computer Engineering, Materials Science & Engineering, Mechanical Engineering
University of Maryland, Baltimore County[2]	Chemical Engineering, Civil Engineering, Computer Science/Electrical Engineering, Information Systems, Mechanical Engineering
University of Rhode Island[2]	Chemical, Civil, Electrical, Industrial, Mechanical, and Ocean Engineering
University of Texas, El Paso[2]	Civil Engineering, Electrical & Computer Engineering, Mechanical & Industrial Engineering, Metallurgical & Materials Engineering
Utah State University[2]	Biological & Irrigation Engineering, Civil & Environmental Engineering, Engineering & Technology Education, Electrical & Computer Engineering, Mechanical & Aerospace Engineering
Virginia Tech[2]	Advanced Research Institute, Aerospace and Ocean Engineering, Biomedical Engineering, Chemical Engineering, Civil & Environmental Engineering, Computer Science, Electrical & Computer Engineering, Engineering Education, Engineering Science & Mechanics, Industrial & Systems Engineering, Materials Science & Engineering, Mechanical Engineering, Mining & Minerals Engineering

Notes: [1]*ADVANCE* IT Cohort 1 institution; [2]*ADVANCE* IT Cohort 2 institution.
*Three universities did not include engineering in their *ADVANCE* IT projects (Hunter College CUNY, University of Montana, and University of Puerto Rico, Humacao); these institutions were excluded from the engineering discipline analyses.

Appendix 3 The Fields and Subfields of Natural Sciences as Defined by *ADVANCE*
Institutions

ADVANCE IT University (n = 19)	Fields and subfields of Natural Sciences
Georgia Institute of Technology[1]	College of Sciences including Applied Physiology, Biology, Chemistry & Biochemistry, Earth & Atmospheric Sciences, Mathematics, Physicals, Psychology; Colleges of Computing (including Computing, Graphics, Visual & Usability)
Hunter College, CUNY[1]	Biological Sciences, Chemistry, Computer Science, Mathematics & Statistics, Physics
New Mexico State University[1]	College of Arts and Sciences (including Astronomy, Biology, Chemistry & Biochemistry, Computer Sciences, Geological Sciences, Mathematical Sciences, Physics); College of Agriculture and Home Economics (Agronomy and Horticulture, Animal and Range Science, Entomology, Plant Pathology and Weed Science, Family and Consumer Science, Fishery and Wildlife Science)
University of California, Irvine[1]	School of Physical Sciences (including Physics & Astronomy, Mathematics, Earth Systems Science, Chemistry), and School of Biological Sciences (including Developmental & Cell Biology, Ecology & Revolutionary Biology, Molecular Biology & Biochemistry, Neurobiology & Behavior); School of Information and Computer Sciences (CS Computing, CS Systems, Informatics, Information & Computer Science, Statistics)
University of Colorado Boulder[1]	Physical Sciences (Astrophysical and Planetary Sciences Chemistry, Physics, and other programs), Earth, Atmospheric & Ocean Sciences (Atmospheric and Oceanic Sciences, Environmental Studies, Geological Sciences, and other programs), Mathematical and Computer Sciences (Applied Mathematics, Computer Science, Mathematics), Biological and Agricultural Studies (Ecology and Evolutionary Biology, Kinesiology, Molecular and Cellular Development Biology)
University of Michigan[1]	Natural Sciences departments in the College of Literature, Sciences, and Arts, including Astronomy, Chemistry, Ecology & Evolutionary Biology, Geological Sciences, Mathematics, Molecular, Cellular & Developmental Biology, Physics, Statistics
University of Puerto Rico, Humacao[1]	Biology, Chemistry, Mathematics, Physics

Continued

Appendix 3 Continued

University of Washington[1]	Applied Mathematics, Astronomy, Atmospheric Sciences, Biology, Chemistry, Earth & Space Sciences, Mathematics, Physics, Statistics
University of Wisconsin, Madison[1]	Physical Sciences (including Soil Science, Astronomy, Chemistry, Computer Sciences, Geology & Geophysics, Mathematics, Atmospheric & Oceanic Sciences, Physics, and Statistics)
Virginia Tech[2]	College of Science including Biological Sciences, Chemistry, Economics, Geosciences, Mathematics, Physics, Statistics
Case Western Reserve University[2]	Astronomy, Biology, Chemistry, Geological Sciences, Mathematics, Physics, Statistics
Columbia University[2]	Natural sciences of Morningside Arts and Sciences, includingAstronomy, Biological Sciences, Chemistry, Earth & Environmental Sciences, Ecology, Evolution & Environmental Biology, Mathematics, Physics, Psychology, Statistics
Kansas State University[2]	College of Arts and Sciences (including Biochemistry, Biology, Chemistry, Geography, Geology, Kinesiology, Mathematics, Physics, Statistics); College of Agriculture (Agricultural Economics, Agronomy, Animal Sciences and Industry, Entomology, Grain Science and Industry, Horticulture, Forestry and Recreation Resources (HFARR), Plant Pathology)
University of Alabama, Birmingham[2]	Biology, Chemistry, Computer & Information Science, Mathematics, Physics
University of Maryland, Baltimore County[2]	College of Natural and Mathematical Sciences including Biology, Chemistry, Mathematics, and Physics
University of Montana[2]	Physical Sciences (including Chemistry, Geology, Physics & Astronomy), Math & Computer Science (including Computer Sciences, Mathematical Sciences), and Biological Sciences (including Biological Sciences, Biomedical & Pharmaceutical Sciences, Ecosystems & Conservation, Forest Management, Society & Conservation)
University of Rhode Island[2]	College of Arts & Sciences (including Chemistry, Computer Science & Statistics, Mathematics, Physics), and College of Environment & Life Sciences (including Biological Sciences, Cell & Molecular Biology, Environmental & Natural Resource Economics, Fisheries, Animal, & Veterinary Sciences, Geosciences, Marine Affairs, Natural Resource Science, Plant Sciences), Graduate School of Oceanography

Continued

Appendix 3 Continued

University of Texas, El Paso[2]	Biological Sciences, Chemistry, Computer Science, Geological Science, Mathematical Science, Physics
Utah State University[1]	College of Sciences including Biology, Chemistry & Biochemistry, Computer Science, Mathematics & Statistics, Geology, Physics; College of Natural Resources (Watershed Sciences, Wildland Resources, Environment & Society), and College of Agriculture (Agricultural Systems Technology & Education, Animal, Dairy, & Veterinary Sciences, Agricultural Economics, Nutrition and Food Sciences, Plants, Soils, & Biometeorology)

Notes: [1]*ADVANCE* IT Cohort 1 institution; [2]*ADVANCE* IT Cohort 2 institution. We were not able to separate out faculty data from the psychology departments of Georgia Tech and Columbia University; therefore, faculty data from their psychology departments are included in the natural sciences discipline analyses for these two universities.

Tenured and tenure-track faculty with appointments of assistant, associate, and full professors at 15 universities were included in the analyses.

For Georgia Tech, faculty with appointments of assistant, associate, professor, and regents professors were included, but their tenure status is unknown.

For New Mexico State University, tenured and tenure-track faculty were included, but their rank status is unknown.

For University of Puerto Rico, Humacao, full-time faculty in non-teaching positions (who do not qualify for tenure or promotion) were excluded.

For University of Colorado Boulder, only tenure-line faculty with appointments of assistant, associate, and full professors in 2003 and 2008 were available.

Appendix 4   Fields and Subfields of Social and Behavioral Sciences (SBS) As Defined by *ADVANCE* Institutions

ADVANCE IT University (n = 13)	Fields and subfields of Social and Behavioral Sciences
Hunter College, CUNY[1]	Anthropology, Economics, Geography, Political Science, Psychology, Sociology
New Mexico State University[1]	Anthropology, Communications, Criminal Justice, Geography, Government, Psychology, Sociology
University of California, Irvine[1]	School of Social Sciences (including Anthropology, Chicano Studies, Cognitive, Economics, Linguistics, Logic, Political Science, Sociology, Social Science); School of Social Ecology (including Psychology & Social Behavior, Planning, Policy & Design, Environmental Health Sciences & Society, Criminology, Law & Society)
University of Colorado Boulder[1]	Social Sciences (including Anthropology, Communication, Economics, Ethnic Studies, Geography, Linguistics, Political Science, Sociology, Speech, Language & Hearing Sciences, Women's Studies), and Psychology
University of Puerto Rico, Humacao[1]	Social Science
University of Wisconsin, Madison[1]	Social Studies (including Agricultural & Applied Economics, Life Sciences Communication, Rural Sociology, Natural Resources-Landscape Architecture, Urban & Regional Planning, School of Business, Counseling Psychology, Curriculum & Instruction, Educational Leadership & Policy Analysis, Educational Policy Studies, Rehabilitation Psychology & Special Education, School of Human Ecology, Law School, Anthropology, Afro-American Studies, Communication Arts, Economics, Ethnic Studies, Geography, School of Public Affairs, School of Journalism & Mass Communication, School of Library & Information, Political Science, Psychology, Social Work, Sociology, Urban & Regional Planning, School of Nursing, Professional Development & Applied Studies)
Case Western Reserve University[2]	Anthropology, Political Science, Psychology, and Sociology
Columbia University[2]	Anthropology, Economics, History, International and Public Affairs, Political Science, Sociology, and Psychology

Continued

Appendix 4   Continued

University of Alabama, Birmingham[2]	Anthropology, Government, History, Justice Sciences, Psychology, Sociology
University of Montana[2]	Psychology, Social Studies (including Economics, Environmental Studies, Geography)
University of Rhode Island[3]	Anthropology, Psychology, Sociology
University of Texas, El Paso[2]	Communication, Languages & Linguistics, Political Science, Psychology, Sociology and Anthropology
Virginia Tech[2]	Psychology

Notes: [1]*ADVANCE* IT Cohort 1 institution; [2]*ADVANCE* IT Cohort 2 institution.
*Only the institutions listed included SBS departments in their *ADVANCE* IT projects. Five universities were excluded from SBS discipline analyses: University of Michigan, University of Washington, Utah State University, University of Maryland, Baltimore County, and Kansas State University.
Georgia Tech was also excluded from this analysis since we were not able to separate out faculty in their psychology department.
Faculty in business or management schools were excluded from these SBS analyses since only four universities (University of California Irvine, Case Western Reserve University, University of Texas, El Paso, and University of Alabama, Birmingham) reported business/management school data.

Bibliography

Acker, Joan. 1990. "Hierarchies, jobs, bodies: A theory of gendered organizations." *Gender and Society* 4(2):139–158.

———. 1992. "Gendering organizational theory," in *Gendering Organizational Analysis*, edited by Albert J. Mills and Peta Tancred, 248–260. Newbury Park, CA: Sage.

Adler, Nancy J., Laura W. Brody, and Joyce S. Osland. 2000. "The women's global leadership forum: Enhancing one company's global leadership capability." *Human Resource Management* 39(2 and 3):209–225.

Allen, Tammy D., Lillian T. Eby, Mark L. Poteet, Elizabeth Lentz, and Lizzette Lima. 2004. "Career benefits associated with mentoring for proteges: A meta-analysis." *Journal of Applied Psychology* 89(1):127–136.

American Association of University Professors. 1993. "The Status of Non-Tenure Track Faculty." Accessed April 27, 2011, from http://www.aaup.org/AAUP/comm/rep/nontenuretrack.htm.

Armenakis, Achilles A., and Arthur G. Bedeian. 1999. "Organizational change: A review of theory and research in the 1990s." *Journal of Management* 25(3):293–315.

Arroba, Tanya, and Kim T. James. 1988. "Are politics palatable to women managers? How women can make wise moves at work." *Women in Management Review* 3(3):123–130.

Association of American Medical Colleges. 2009. "Table 11: Women deans of U.S. medical schools, October 2009." Accessed April 27, 2011, from https://www.aamc.org/download/53494/data/table11_2009.pdf.

Astin, Alexander W., and Associates. 2001. *The Theory and Practice of Institutional Transformation in Higher Education*. Los Angeles: Higher Education Research Institute, University of California, Los Angeles.

Astin, Helen S., and Christine M. Cress. 2003. "A national profile of women in research universities." In *Equal Rites, Unequal Outcomes: Women in American Research Universities*, edited by Lili S. Hornig, 53–88. New York: Kluwer Academic/Plenum Publishers.

August, Louise, and Jean Waltman. 2004. "Culture, climate, and contribution: Career satisfaction among female faculty." *Research in Higher Education*, 45(2):177–192.

Avery, Derek R., Patrick F. McKay, David C. Wilson, and Sabrina D. Volpone. 2008. "Attenuating the effect of seniority on intent to remain: The role of perceived inclusiveness." Paper presented at the 2008 Academy of Management Conference, Anaheim, CA.

Babcock, Linda, Michelle Gelfand, Deborah Small, and Heidi Stayn. 2006. "Gender differences in the propensity to initiate negotiations." In *Social Psychology and Economics*, edited by David D. Crèmer, Marcel Zeelenberg, and J. Keith Murnighan, 239–259. Mahwah, NJ: Lawrence Erlbaum Associates.

Babcock, Linda, and Sara Laschever. 2003. *Women Don't Ask*. Princeton, NJ: Princeton University Press.

Bailyn, Lotte. 2003. "Academic careers and gender equity: Lessons learned from MIT." *Gender, Work, and Organizations* 10:137–153.

———. 2006. *Breaking the Mold: Redesigning Work for Productive and Satisfying Lives*. Ithaca, NY: Cornell University Press.

Barnett, William P., and Glenn R. Carroll. 1995. "Modeling internal organizational change." *Annual Review of Sociology* 21:217–236.

Benschop, Yvonne, and Margo Brouns. 2003. "Crumbling ivory towers: Academic organizing and its gender effects." Gender, Work and Organization 10(2):194–212.

Bensimon, Estela Mara, Kelly Ward, and Karla Sanders. 2000. *The Department Chair's Role in Developing New Faculty into Teachers and Scholars*. Bolton, MA: Anker Publishing.

Bilimoria, Diana, and Kimberly K. Buch. 2010. "The search is on: Engendering faculty diversity through more effective search and recruitment." Change, The Magazine of Higher Learning 42(4):27–32.

Bilimoria, Diana, Margaret M. Hopkins, Deborah A. O'Neil, and Susan Perry. 2007. "Executive coaching: An effective strategy for faculty development." In *Transforming Science and Engineering: Advancing Academic Women*, edited by Abigail J. Stewart, Janet E. Malley, and Danielle LaVaque-Manty, 187–203. Ann Arbor: University of Michigan Press.

Bilimoria, Diana, and Susan Perry. 2005. "Transforming the faculty mindset." Presentation at the 2005 Academy of Management Conference, August: Honolulu, Hawaii. Accessed March 27, 2011, from http://faculty.weatherhead.case.edu/bilimoria/doc/transforming.pps.

Bilimoria, Diana, Susan Perry, Xiang Fen Liang, Patricia Higgins, Eleanor Stoller, and Cyrus Taylor. 2006. "How do female and male faculty members construct job satisfaction? The roles of perceived institutional leadership and mentoring and their mediating processes." *Journal of Technology Transfer* 32(3):355–365.

Bilimoria, Diana, Simy Joy, and Xiang Fen Liang. 2008. "Breaking barriers and creating inclusiveness: Lessons of organizational transformation to advance women faculty in academic science and engineering." *Human Resources Management* 47(3):423–441.

Bilimoria, Diana, and Abigail J. Stewart. 2009. " 'Don't ask, don't tell': The academic climate for lesbian, gay, bisexual and transgender faculty in science and engineering." *National Women's Studies Association Journal* 21(2):85–103.

Bilimoria, Diana, and Virginia Valian. 2006. *Leadership Development at ADVANCE Institutions*. Presentation at NSF *ADVANCE* PI Meeting, Washington, DC.

Blackwell, Lauren V., Lori Anderson Snyder, and Catherine Mavriplis. 2009. "Diverse faculty in STEM Fields: Attitudes, performance, and fair treatment." *Journal of Diversity in Higher Education* 2(4):195–205.

Blakemore, Judith. E. O., Jo Young Switzer, Judith A. DiLorio, and David L. Fairchild. 1997. "Exploring the campus climate for women faculty." In *Subtle Sexism: Current Practice and Prospects for Change*, edited by Nijole V. Benokraitis, 54–71. Thousand Oaks, CA: Sage.

Blau, Peter M. 1973. *The Organization of Academic Work*. New York: Wiley.

Bowles, Hannah R., Linda Babcock, and Lei Lai. 2007. "Social incentives for gender differences in the propensity to initiate negotiations: Sometimes it does hurt to ask." *Organizational Behavior and Human Decision Processes* 103:84–103.

Budden, Amber E., Tom Tregenza, Lonnie Aarssen, Julia Koricheva, Roosa Leimu, and Christopher J. Lortie. 2008. "Double-blind review favours increased representation of female authors." *Trends in Ecology and Evolution* 23:4–6.

Burke, Ronald, J. 2002. "Career development of managerial women." In *Advancing Women's Careers*, edited by Ronald J. Burke and Donna L. Nelson, 139–160. Malden, MA: Blackwell Publishing.

Burnes, Bernard. 1996: *Managing Change: A Strategic Approach to Organizational Dynamics*. London: Pitman Publishing.

Buse, Kathleen R., Sheri Perelli, and Diana Bilimoria. 2010. "Why they stay: The ideal selves of persistent women engineers." Working Paper Series WP-10-04, Department of Organizational Behavior, Case Western Reserve University, Cleveland, Ohio. Accessed April 27, 2011, from http://weatherhead.case.edu/departments/organizational-behavior/workingPapers/WP-10-04.pdf.

Callister, Ronda R. 2006. "The impact of gender and department climate on job satisfaction and intentions to quit for faculty in science and engineering fields." *Journal of Technology Transfer* 30(3):383–396.

Callister, Ronda R., J. Williams, and Eve Fine. 2009. "Managing department climate change." Presentation at 2009 *ADVANCE* PI Meeting, Washington, DC. Accessed April 27, 2011, from http://www.advance.vt.edu/Advance_2009_PI_Mtg/PIMtg2009_Department_Climate_Change.pdf.

Carnegie Foundation. 2011. "Carnegie classifications." Accessed April 27, 2011. from http://classifications.carnegiefoundation.org/descriptions/basic.php.

Carnes, Molly, Jo Handelsman, and Jennifer Sheridan. 2005. "Diversity in academic medicine: A stages of change model." *Journal of Women's Health* 14(6):471–475.

Carr, Jennifer Z., Aaron M. Schmidt, J. Kevin Ford, and Richard P. DeShon. 2003. "Climate perceptions matter: A meta-analytic path analysis relating molar climate, cognitive and affective states, and individual level work outcomes." *Journal of Applied Psychology* 88:605–619.

Carrell, Scott. E., Marianne E. Page, and James E. West. 2010. "Sex and science: How professor gender perpetuates the gender gap." *The Quarterly Journal of Economics* 125 (3):1101–1144.

Case Western Reserve University. 2003. "Resource equity at Case Western Reserve University: Results of Faculty Focus Groups Report." Accessed April 27, 2011, from http://www.cwru.edu/menu/president/resourcequity.doc.

———. 2008. "NSF *ADVANCE* Final Report 2003–2008. Case

———. 2004. "Annual Report for the National Science Foundation *ADVANCE* Project, Academic Careers in Engineering & Science (ACES), Year 1: September 1, 2003–August 31, 2004." Accessed on April 27, 2011 from http://www.case.edu/admin/aces/documents/Annual_Report_YR1.pdf.

———.2006. "Annual Report for the National Science Foundation *ADVANCE* Project, Academic Careers in Engineering & Sciences (ACES), Year 3: September 1, 2005–August 31, 2006." Accessed on April 27, 2011 from http://www.case.edu/admin/aces/documents/Annual_Report_YR3.pdf.

Western Reserve University." Accessed October 15, 2010, from http://www.case.edu/admin/aces/documents/ACESfinalreport.pdf.

Ceci, Stephen J., and Wendy M. Williams. (Eds.). 2007. *Why Aren't More Women in Science? Top Researchers Debate the Evidence*. Washington, DC: American Psychological Association.

Ceci, Stephen J., Wendy M. Williams, and Susan M. Barnett. 2009. "Women's underrepresentation in science: Sociocultural and biological considerations." *Psychological Bulletin* 135(2):218–261.

Chandler, Christy. 1996. "Mentoring and women in academia: Reevaluating the traditional model." *National Women's Studies Association Journal* 8:79–98.

Chao, Georgia T., Anne M. O'Leary-Kelly, Samantha Wolf, Howard J. Klein, and Philip D. Gardner. 1994. "Organizational socialization: Its content and consequences." *Journal of Applied Psychology* 79(5):730–743.

Chen, Tina T., and James L. Farr. 2007. "An empirical test of the glass ceiling effect for Asian Americans in science and engineering." In *Women and Minorities in Science, Technology, Engineering and Mathematics: Upping the Numbers*, edited by Ronald J. Burke and Mary C. Mattis, 128–156. Cheltenham, UK: Edward Elgar Publishing.

Clark, Terry N. 1971. "Institutionalization of Innovations in Higher Education: Four Models." *Administrative Science Quarterly* 13(1):1–25.

Columbia University. 2006. "NSF *ADVANCE* at the Earth Institute at Columbia University Annual Report Year 2: June 2005–May 2006." Accessed October 15, 2010, from http://advance.ei.columbia.edu/sitefiles/file/AnnualReports/columbia_y2_annual_report_public_000.pdf.

————. 2008. "NSF *ADVANCE* at the Earth Institute at Columbia University Annual Report Year 4: June 2007–May 2008." Accessed October 15, 2010, from http://advance.ei.columbia.edu/sitefiles/file/AnnualReports/columbia_y4_annual_report_public(1).pdf.

————. 2009. "NSF *ADVANCE* at the Earth Institute at Columbia University Annual Report Year 5: June 2008–May 2009." Accessed October 15, 2010, from http://advance.ei.columbia.edu/sitefiles/file/AnnualReports/ADVANCE_Columbia_yr5_annual_public.pdf.

Correll, Shelley J., Steven Benard, and In Paik. 2007. "Getting a job: Is there a motherhood penalty?" *American Journal of Sociology* 112:1297–1338.

Creamer, Elizabeth. 1998. "Assessing faculty publication productivity: Issues of equity." *ASHE-ERIC Higher Education Report* 26(2).

Creamer, Elizabeth G., and Valerie Q. Glass. 2006. "*ADVANCE* Dual-Career Hiring Study". Poster presented at the *ADVANCE* PI Meeting, May 18–19, Washington, DC.

Cress, Christine M., and Jeni Hart. 2009. "Playing soccer on the football field: The persistence of gender inequities for women faculty." *Equity and Excellence in Education* 42(4):473–488.

Cress, Christine M., and Linda J. Sax. 1998. "Campus climate issues to consider for the next decade." *New Directions for Institutional Research* 98:65–80.

Croson, Rachel, and KimMarie McGoldrick. 2007. "Scaling the wall: Helping female faculty in economics achieve tenure." In *Transforming Science and Engineering: Advancing Academic Women*, edited by Abigail J. Stewart, Janet E. Malley, and Danielle LaVaque-Manty, 152–169. Ann Arbor: University of Michigan Press.

Curry, Barbara K. 1991. "Institutionalization: The final phase of the organizational change process." *Administrator's Notebook* 35(1).

————. 1992. "Instituting enduring innovations: Achieving continuity of change in higher education." *Eric Digests*. Washington, DC: ERIC Clearinghouse on Higher Education. Accessed October 15, 2010, from http://www.ericdigests.org/1993/higher.htm.

Dean, Donna J., and Anne Flickenstein. 2007. "Keys to success for women in science." In *Women and Minorities in Science, Technology, Engineering and Mathematics*, edited by Ronald J. Burke and Mary C. Mattis, 28–46. Cheltenham, UK: Edward Elgar Publishing.

de Janasz, Suzanne C., Sherry E. Sullivan, and Vicki Whiting. 2003. "Mentor networks and career success: Lessons for turbulent times." *Academy of Management Executive* 17(4):78–91.

DiMaggio, Paul J. 1988. "Interest and agency in institutional theory." In *Institutional Patterns and Organizations: Culture and Environment*, edited by in Lynne G. Zucker, 3–21. Cambridge, MA: Ballinger.

DiMaggio, Paul J., and Walter W. Powell. 1983. "The iron cage revisited: Institutional isomorphism and collective rationality in organizational fields." *American Sociological Review* 48(2):147–160.

Dominguez, Cari M. 1992. "The glass ceiling: Paradox and promises." *Human Resource Management* 31(4):385–392.

Drago, Robert W. 2007. *Striking a Balance: Work, Family, Life*. Boston: Economic Affairs Bureau, Inc.

Drapeau, Suzanne. 2004. "The employee survey: An important tool for changing the culture of an organization." *Journal of Applied Research in the Community College* 11(2):129–136.

Dreher, George F. 2003. "Breaking the glass ceiling: The effects of sex ratios and work-life programs on female leadership at top." *Human Relations* 56:541–562.

Dweck, Carol. 2007. "Is math a gift? Beliefs that put females at risk." In *Why Aren't More Women in Science? Top Researchers Debate the Evidence*, edited by Stephen J. Ceci and Wendy M. Williams, 47–55. Washington, DC: American Psychological Association.

———. 2008. *Mindsets and Math/Science Achievement*. New York: Carnegie Corporation of New York, Institute for Advanced Study, Commission on Mathematics and Science Education. Accessed April 27, 2011, from http://opportunityequation.org/teaching-and-leadership/mindsets-math-science-achievement.

Eagly, Alice H., and Linda L. Carli. 2007a. "Women and the labyrinth of leadership." *Harvard Business Review* 85(9): 63–71.

———. 2007b. *Through the Labyrinth: The Truth about How Women Become Leaders*, Boston: Harvard Business School Publishing.

Earth Institute *ADVANCE* Working Group. 2005. "A Proposal for Recruiting and Retaining Dual-Career Couples." Accessed April 27, 2011, from http://www.mnyscherc.org/site/672/doc_library/Earth%20Institute%20-%20Dual-Career%20Couples.pdf.

Eber, Christine E. 2008. "'A diamond in the rough' - Faculty retention at New Mexico State University: A report on research exploring why faculty leave NMSU." Accessed on April 27, 2011 from http://www.advance.nmsu.edu/Documents/PDF/Retention_Report-Nov08.pdf.

Eckel, Peter D., and Adrianna Kezar. 2003. *Taking the Reins: Institutional Transformation in Higher Education*. Westport, CT: Praeger.

Ehrich, Lisa C., Brian Hansford, and Lee Tennent. 2004. "Formal mentoring programs in education and other professions: A review of the literature." *Educational Administration Quarterly* 40:518–540.

Elam, Carol L., Terry D. Stratton, Frederic W. Hafferty, and Paul Haidet. 2009. "Identity, social networks, and relationships: Theoretical underpinnings of critical mass and diversity." *Academic Medicine* 84(10 Suppl.):S135–140.

Ely, Robin J., and Debra E. Meyerson. 2000a. "Advancing gender equity in organizations: The challenge and importance of maintaining a gender narrative." *Organization* 74:589–608.

———. 2000b. "Theories of gender in organizations: A new approach to organizational analysis and change." Center for Gender in Organizations Working Paper No. 8. Accessed April 21, 2011, from http://dspace.nitle.org/bitstream/handle/10090/18102/SOM_cgo_wp8.pdf?sequence=1.

Erkut, Sumru, Vicki W. Kramer, and Alison M. Konrad. 2008. "Critical mass: Does the number of women on a corporate board make a difference?" In *Women on Corporate Boards of Directors: International Research and Practice*, edited by Susan M. Vinnicombe, Val Singh, Ronald J. Burke, Diana Bilimoria, and Morten Huse, 350–66. Cheltenham, UK: Edward Elgar.

Etzkowitz, Henry, Carol Kemelgor, and Brian Uzzi. 2000. *Athena Unbound: The Advancement of Women in Science and Technology*. New York: Cambridge University Press.

Etzkowitz, Henry, Carol Kemelgor, Michael Neuschatz, Brian Uzzi, and Joseph Alonzo. 1994. "The paradox of critical mass for women in science." *Science* 266:51–54.

Evetts, Julia. 1996. *Gender and Career in Science and Engineering*, London: Taylor & Francis.

Ferris, Gerald R., Sherry L. Davidson, and Pamela L. Perrewé. 2005. *Political Skill at Work: Impact on Work Effectiveness*. Mountain View, CA: Davies-Black Publishing.

Forret, Monica L., and Thomas W. Dougherty. 2004. "Networking behaviors and career outcomes: Differences for men and women?" *Journal of Organizational Behavior* 25(3):419–437.

Foster, William T. 1911. *Administration of the College Curriculum*. Boston: Houghton Mifflin Company.

Fouad, Nadya A., and Romila Singh. 2011. "Stemming the Tide: Why Women Leave Engineering." Accessed April 24, 2011, from http://www.studyofwork. com/wp-content/uploads/2011/03/NSF_Women-Full-Report-0314.pdf.

Fox, Mary Frank. 2008. "Institutional transformation and the advancement of women faculty: The case of academic science and engineering." In *Higher Education: Handbook of Theory and Research*, edited by John C. Smart, 73–103. Dordrecht, Germany: Springer Science + Business Media B.V.

———. 2010. "Women and men faculty in academic science and engineering: Social-organizational indicators and implications." *American Behavioral Scientist* 53(7):997–1012.

Fox, Mary Frank, and Carol Colatrella. 2006. "Participation, performance, and advancement of women in academic science and engineering: What is at issue and why." *The Journal of Technology Transfer* 31(3):377–386.

Fox, Mary Frank, Carol Colatrella, David McDowell, and Mary Lynn Realff. 2007. "Equity in tenure and promotion: An integrated institutional approach." In *Transforming Science and Engineering: Advancing Academic Women*, edited by Abigail J. Stewart, Janet E. Malley, and Danielle LaVaque-Manty, 170–186. Ann Arbor: University of Michigan Press.

Fox, Mary Frank, and Carolyn Fonseca. 2006. "Gender and mentoring of faculty in science and engineering: Individual and organisational factors." *International Journal of Learning and* Change 1(4):460–483.

Frehill, Lisa M. 2006. "Using program evaluation to ensure the success of your *ADVANCE* program." Accessed October 15, 2010, from http://www. advance.vt.edu/Measuring_Progress/Toolkits/Advance_Program_Evaluation_ Toolkit_08May06.pdf.

———. 2009. "*ADVANCE* indicators of the status of women in academia". Presentation at 2009 NSF Joint Annual Meeting, Washington, DC. Accessed on October 15, 2010, from http://www.advance.vt.edu/2009_NSF_HRD_JAM/ JAM09_Advance_Indicators_frehill.pdf.

Frehill, Lisa M., and Jeanette Doeller. 2005. "Indicators and dissemination—Measuring the status of women: Toward cross-institutional analysis to understand institutional transformation." Paper presented at the 2005 NSF *ADVANCE* PI meeting, Washington, DC. Accessed October 15, 2010, from http://www. advance.vt.edu/Advance_2005_PI_Meeting/Panel_2_Toolkit.pdf.

Galpin, Timothy J. 1996. *The Human Side of Change: A Practical Guide to Organization Redesign*. San Francisco: Jossey-Bass.

Garvin, David A. (2000). *Learning in action: A Guide to Putting the Learning Organization to Work*. Boston: Harvard Business School Press.

Georgia Tech. 2007. "NSF *ADVANCE* Institutional Transformation Program Final Report October 1, 2001–December 31, 2006." Georgia Institute of Technology. Accessed April 20, 2011, from http://www.advance.gatech.edu/archive/files/GTADVANCEfinalreport2007.doc.

Gibbons, Michael T. 2009. "Engineering by the numbers." Accessed April 27, 2011, from http://www.asee.org/papers-and-publications/publications/college-profiles/2009-profile-engineering-statistics.pdf.

Gibson, Sharon K. 2004. "Being mentored: The experience of women faculty." *Journal of Career Development* 30(3):173–188.

Ginther, Donna. K., and Shulamit, Khan. 2006. "Does science promote women? Evidence from academia 1973–2001." *National Bureau of Economic Research Working Paper No. 12691*. Accessed March 27, 2011, from http://www.nber.org/papers/w12691.

Goulden, Marc, Karie Frasch, and Mary Ann Mason. 2009. "Staying competitive: Patching America's leaky pipeline in the sciences." Accessed March 21, 2011, from http://www.americanprogress.org/issues/2009/11/women_and_sciences.html.

Hackney, Catherine Eggleston, and Marianne Bock. 2000. "Beyond mentoring: Toward an invitational academe." *Advancing Women in Leadership Online Journal* 3(1). Accessed October 15, 2010, from http://www.advancingwomen.com/awl/winter2000/hackney-bock.html.

Hagedorn, Linda Sera, Winny (YanFang) Chi, Rita M. Cepeda, and Melissa McLain. 2007. "An investigation of critical mass: The role of Latino representation in the success of urban community college students." *Research in Higher Education* 48(1):73–91.

Hall, Roberta M., and Bernice R. Sandler. 1984. "Out of the classroom: A chilly campus climate for women?" Washington, DC: Association of American Colleges. Accessed April 27, 2011, from http://www.hws.edu/offices/provost/pdf/out_classroom.pdf.

Harper, Elizabeth P., Roger G. Baldwin, Bruce G. Gansneder, and Jay L. Chronister. 2001. "Full-time women faculty off the tenure track: Profile and practice." *The Review of Higher Education* 24(3):237–257.

Heilman, Madeline E. 1980. "The impact of situational factors on personnel decisions concerning women: Varying the sex composition of the applicant pool." *Organizational Behavior and Human Performance* 26:286–295.

Herzig, Abbe H. 2004. "Becoming mathematicians: Women and students of color choosing and leaving doctoral mathematics." *Review of Educational Research* 74(2):171–214.

Hewlett, Sylvia Ann, Carolyn Buck Luce, and Lisa J. Servon. 2008. "Stopping the exodus of women in science." *Harvard Business Review* June: 1–2. Accessed March 27, 2011, from http://hbr.org/2008/06/stopping-the-exodus-of-women-in-science/ar/1.

Hewlett, Sylvia Ann, Carolyn Buck Luce, Lisa J. Servon, Laura Sherbin, Peggy Shiller, Eytan Sosnovich, and Karen Sumberg. 2008. *The Athena Factor: Reversing the Brain Drain in Science, Engineering and Technology*, Boston: Harvard Business School Publishing.

Hill, Catherine, Christianne Corbett, and Andresse St. Rose. 2010. "Why so few? Women in science, technology, engineering and mathematics." Washington, DC: American Association of University Women (AAUW). Accessed March 17, 2011, from http://www.aauw.org/learn/research/upload/whysofew.pdf.

Hill, Winston W., and Wendell L. French. 1967. "Perceptions of the power of department chairmen by professors." *Administrative Science Quarterly* 11(4):548–574.

Hogue, Mary and Robert G. Lord. 2007. "A mulit-level, complexity theory approach to understanding gender bias in leadership". *The Leadership Quaterly* 18: 370– 390.

Hollenshead, Carol. 2003. "Women in the academy: Confronting barriers to equality." In *Equal Rites, Unequal Outcomes: Women in American Research Universities*, edited by Lili S. Hornig, 211–225. New York: Kluwer Academic/ Plenum Publishers.

Hult, Christine, Ronda Callister, and Kim Sullivan. 2005. "Is there a global warming toward women in academia?" *Liberal Education* 91(3):50–57.

Isaac, Carol, Barbara Lee, and Molly Carnes. 2009. "Interventions that affect gender bias in hiring: A systematic review." *Academic Medicine* 8(10): 440–446.

Jick, Todd. 1991. "Implementing change." HBS Case 9–491–114. Boston: Harvard Business School Press.

Jordan, C. Greer, and Diana Bilimoria. 2007. "Creating a productive and inclusive academic work environment." In *Transforming Science and Engineering: Advancing Academic Women*, edited by Abigail J. Stewart, Janet E. Malley, and Danielle LaVaque-Manty, 225–242. Ann Arbor: University of Michigan Press.

Judge, Timothy A., and Robert D. Bretz, Jr. 1994. "Political influence behavior and career success." *Journal of Management* 20(1):43–65.

Judson, Arnold S. 1991. *Changing Behavior in Organizations: Minimizing Resistance to Change*. Cambridge, MA: Basil Blackwell.

Kanter, Rosabeth Moss. 1977. *Men and Women of the Corporation*, New York: Basic Books.

Kaplan, Matthew, Constance E. Cook, and Jeffrey Steiger. 2006. "Using theatre to stage instructional and organizational transformation." *Change, the Magazine of Higher Learning* 38(3):33–39.

Kezar, Adrianna J. 2001. "Understanding and facilitating organizational change in the 21st century." *ASHE-ERIC Higher Education Report* No. 28 (4). San Francisco: Jossey-Bass.

Kiopa, Agrita, Julia Melkers, and Zeynep Esra Tanyildiz. 2009. "Women in academic science: Mentors and career development." In *Women in Science and Technology*, edited by Sven Hemlin, Luisa Oliveira, and Katarina Prpic, 55–84. Zagreb, Croatia: Institute for Social Research and SSTNET (Sociology of Science and Technology Network) of European Sociological Association (ESA.).

Kirkman, Ellen E., James W. Maxwell, and Colleen A. Rose. 2005. "2004 Annual Survey of the Mathematical Sciences (3rd Report)." Accessed April 27, 2011, from http://www.ams.org/profession/data/annual-survey/2005Survey-Third-Report.pdf.

Klein, Susan, Patricia Ortman, and Beth Friedman. 2002. "What is the field of gender equity in education? Questions and answers." In *Defining and Redefining Gender Equity in Education*, edited by Janice Koch and Beverly Irby, 2–23. Greenwich, CT: Information Age Publishing.

Koch, Janice, and Beverly Irby. (Eds.). 2002. *Defining and Redefining Gender Equity in Education*. Greenwich, CT: Information Age Publishing.

Kolb, Deborah, Joyce K. Fletcher, Debra E. Meyerson, Deborah Merrill-Sands, and Robin J. Ely. 1998. "Making change: A framework for promoting gender equity in organizations." CGO Insights No. 1, The Center for Gender in Organizations (CGO), Boston. Accessed October 15, 2010, from http://www.simmons.edu/ som/docs/centers/insights1.pdf.

Kopelman, Richard E., Arthur P. Brief, and Richard A. Guzzo. 1990. "The role of climate and culture in productivity." In *Organizational Climate and Culture*, edited by Benjamin Schneider, 282–318. San Francisco: Jossey-Bass.

Kotter, John. 1995. "Leading change: Why transformation efforts fail." *Harvard Business Review* 73(2):59–67.

Kotter, John P. 1996. *Leading Change.* Cambridge, MA: Harvard Business School Press.

Kram, Kathy E. 1985. "Mentoring alternatives: The role of peer relationships in career development." *Academy of Management Journal* 28(1):110–132.

———. 1988. *Mentoring at Work: Developmental Relationships in Organizational Life.* Lanham, MD: University Press of America.

Kramer, Vicki W., Alison M. Konrad, and Sumru Ekrut. 2006. "Critical mass on corporate boards: Why three or more women enhance governance." Working Paper Series, Report No. WCW 11, Wellesley Centers for Women. Accessed April 27, 2011, from http://vkramerassociates.com/writings/CriticalMassExec-Summary%20PDF.pdf.

Laursen, Sandra. 2009. "Summative Report on Internal Evaluation for LEAP, Leadership Education for Advancement and Promotion at Colorado, Boulder." Accessed April 27, 2011, from http://www.colorado.edu/eer/downloads/LEAP-internalSummativeReport2009.pdf.

Laursen, Sandra, and Bill Rocque. 2009. "Faculty development for institutional change: Lessons from an *ADVANCE* project." Change, the Magazine of Higher Learning March/April:19–26.

LaVaque-Manty, Danielle. 2007. "Transforming the science enterprise: An interview with Alice Hogan." In *Transforming Science and Engineering: Advancing Academic Women,* edited by Abigail J. Stewart, Janet E. Malley, and Danielle LaVaque-Manty, 21–27. Ann Arbor: University of Michigan Press.

Leboy, Phoebe. 2008. "Fixing the leaky pipeline: Why aren't there many women in the top spots in academia?" *The Scientist* 22(1):67. Accessed October 15, 2010, from www.the-scientist.com/2008/01/1/67/1/.

Levy, Amir, and Uri Merry. 1986. *Organizational Transformation: Approaches, Strategies, Theories.* New York: Praeger.

Lewin, Kurt. 1943. "Defining the 'field at a given time.'" *Psychological Review* 50:292–310.

Liang, Xiangfen, Simy Joy, and Diana Bilimoria. 2008. "Establishing Advisor-Advisee Relationships: Impact of Decision Factors, Schemas and Time Periods." Paper presented at the Academy of Management Conference, August, Anaheim, CA.

Litzler, Elizabeth, Catherine Claiborne, and Suzanne G. Brainard. 2007. "Five years later: The institutionalization and sustainability of *ADVANCE.*" *American Society for Engineering Education Annual Meeting Proceedings 2007.* Accessed October 15, 2010, from http://icee.usm.edu/ICEE/conferences/asee2007/papers/1172_FIVE_YEARS_LATER__THE_INSTITUTIONALIZATI.pdf.

Long, J. Scott. 1990. "The origins of sex differences in science." *Social Forces* 68(4):1297–1316.

———. 1992. "Measures of sex differences in scientific productivity." *Social Forces* 71(1):159–178.

———. (Ed.). 2001. Scarcity to Visibility: Gender Differences in the Careers of Doctoral Scientists and Engineers. Washington, DC: National Academies Press.

Lucas, Ann F. 2000. *Leading Academic Change: Essential Roles for Department Chairs.* San Francisco: Jossey-Bass.

Madera, Juan M., Michelle R. Hebl, and Randi C. Martin. 2009. "Gender and letters of recommendation for academia: Agentic and communal differences." *Journal of Applied Psychology* 94(6):1591–1599.

Mainiero, Lisa A., and Sherry E. Sullivan. 2005. "Kaleidoscope careers: An alternate explanation for the "opt-out" revolution." *Academy of Management Executive* 19(1):106–123.

Mann, Sandi. 1995. "Politics and power in organizations: Why women lose out." *Leadership and Organization Development Journal* 16(2):9–15.

Margolis, Jane, and Allan Fisher. 2002. *Unlocking the Clubhouse: Women in Computing*. Cambridge: Massachusetts Institute of Technology.

Martell, Richard F., David M. Lane, and Cynthia Emrich. 1996. "Male-female differences: A computer simulation." *American Psychologist* 51:157–158.

Martinez, Elisabeth D., Jeannine Botos, Kathleen M. Dohoney, Theresa M. Geiman, Sarah S. Kolla, Ana Olivera, Yi Qiu, Geetha Vani Rayasam, Diana A. Stavreva, and Orna Cohen-Fix. 2007. "Falling off the academic bandwagon." *EMBO Reports* 8:977–981. Accessed March 27, 2011, from http://www.nature.com/embor/journal/v8/n11/full/7401110.html.

Mason, Mary Ann, and Marc Goulden. 2002. "Do babies matter? The effect of family formation on the lifelong careers of academic men and women." *Academe* 88(6):21–27.

——— 2004. "Marriage and baby blues: Redefining gender equity in the academy." *Annals of the American Academy of Political and Social Science* 596(1):86–103.

Mason, Mary Ann, Angelica Stacy, Marc Goulden, Carol Hoffman, and Karie Frasch. 2005. "Faculty family friendly edge: An initiative for tenure-track faculty at the University of California report." Accessed March 21, 2011, from http://ucfamilyedge.berkeley.edu/ucfamilyedge.pdf.

Massachusetts Institute of Technology. 1999. "A study on the status of women faculty in science at MIT." *The MIT Faculty Newsletter* 11(4). Accessed April 27, 2011, from http://web.mit.edu/fnl/women/women.html.

Mattis, Mary C. 2007. "Upstream and downstream in the engineering pipeline: What's blocking U.S. women from pursuing engineering careers?" In *Women and Minorities in Science, Technology, Engineering and Mathematics*, edited by Ronald J. Burke and Mary C. Mattis, 334–362. Cheltenham, UK: Edward Elgar Publishing.

McCracken, Douglas M. 2000. "Winning the talent war for women: Sometimes it takes a revolution." *Harvard Business Review* 78(6):159–167.

McLean, Denise. 2003. "Creating a workplace culture that attracts, retains and promotes women." Ontario: The Center of Excellence For Women's Advancement, The Conference Board of Canada. Accessed October 15, 2010, from http://www.gnb.ca/0037/report/WorkplacesthatWork-e.pdf.

Mento, Anthony J., Raymond M. Jones, and Walter Dirndorfer. 2002. "A change management process: Grounded in both theory and practice." *Journal of Change Management* 3(1):45–59.

Merton, Robert K. 1942/1973. *The Sociology of Science*. Chicago: University of Chicago Press.

Meyer, John W., and Brian Rowan. 1977. "Institutionalized organizations: Formal structure as myth and ceremony." *American Journal of Sociology* 83:340–363.

Meyerson, Debra E. 2003. *Tempered Radicals: How People Use Difference to Inspire Change at Work*. Boston: Harvard Business School Publishing.

Meyerson, Debra E., and Joyce K. Fletcher. 2000. "A modest manifesto for shattering the glass ceiling." *Harvard Business Review* 78(1):127–136.

Meyerson, Debra E., and Deborah M. Kolb. 2000. "Moving out of the 'armchair': Developing a framework to bridge the gap between feminist theory and practice." *Organization* 7(4): 553–571.

Meyerson, Debra E., and Maureen A. Scully. 1995. "Tempered radicalism and the politics of ambivalence and change." *Organization Science* 6:585–600.

Meyerson, Debra E., and Megan Tompkins. 2007. "Tempered radicals as institutional change agents: The case of advancing gender equity at the University of Michigan." *Harvard Journal of Law and Gender* 30:303–322.

Mills, Julie E., and Mary Ayre. 2003. "Implementing an inclusive curriculum for women in engineering education." *Journal of Professional Issues in Engineering Education and Practice* 129(4):203–210.

Misra, Joy, Jennifer Lundquist, Elissa Dahlberg Holmes, and Stephanie Agiomavritis. 2010. "Associate professors and gendered barriers to advancement—full report." Accessed April 27, 2011, from http://people.umass.edu/misra/Joya_Misra/Work-Life_Research.html.

Monroe, Kristen, Saba Ozyurt, Ted Wrigley, and Amy Alexander. 2008. "Gender equality in academia: Bad news from the trenches, and some possible solutions." *Perspectives on Politics* 6(2):215–233.

Montelone, Beth A., and Ruth A. Dyer. 2008. "Career advancement program for tenured SEM women faculty." *2008 WEPAN Conference Proceedings.* Accessed April 20, 2011, from http://advance.ksu.edu/file_download/5/wepan08.pdf.

Moran, E. Thomas, and J. Fredericks Volkwein. 1992. "The cultural approach to the formation of organizational climate." *Human Relations* 45:19–47.

Mor Barak, Michàlle E. 2000. "Beyond affirmative action: Toward a model of diversity and organizational inclusion." *Administration in Social Work* 23(3/4):47–68.

Muller, Carol B. 2003. "The Underrepresentation of women in engineering and related sciences: Pursuing two complementary paths to parity." In *Pan-Organizational Summit on the U.S. Science and Engineering Workforce: Meeting Summary*, edited by Marye Anne Fox, 119–126. Washington, DC: National Academies Press.

Murray, Fiona, and Leigh Graham. 2007. "Buying science and selling science: Gender differences in the market for commercial science." Industrial and Corporate Change 16(4):657–689.

National Academies. 2003. *Pan-Organizational Summit on the U.S. Science and Engineering Workforce: Meeting Summary.* Washington, DC: National Academies Press.

———. 2007a. *Rising above the Gathering Storm: Energizing and Employing America for a Brighter Economic Future.* Washington, DC: National Academies Press.

———. 2007b. *Beyond Bias and Barriers: Fulfilling the Potential of Women in Academic Science and Engineering,* Washington, DC: National Academies Press.

———. 2010. *Gender Differences at Critical Transitions in the Careers of Science, Engineering, and Mathematics Faculty.* Washington DC: National Academies Press.

National Institutes of Health. 2008. "Funding opportunity: Research on causal factors and interventions that promote and support the careers of women in biomedical and behavioral science and engineering" (RFA-GM-09–012). Accessed October 15, 2010, from http://womeninscience.nih.gov/funding/.

———. 2010. "Recovery act limited competition: The NIH director's ARRA funded Pathfinder Award to Promote Diversity in the Scientific Workforce." Accessed October 15, 2010, from http://grants.nih.gov/grants/guide/rfa-files/RFA-OD-10–013.html.

National Science Foundation. 2001. "Survey of doctorate recipients." Accessed April 27, 2011, from http://www.nsf.gov/statistics/srvydoctoratework/.

———. 2003. "Gender differences in the careers of academic scientists and engineers: A literature review." NSF 03–322. Arlington, VA: Division of Science Resources Statistics.

———. 2004. "Science and engineering indicators 2004." Accessed April 27, 2011, from http://www.nsf.gov/statistics/seind04/.

——— 2005. "Science and engineering indicators: 2004." Accessed October 15, 2010, from http://www.nsf.gov/statistics/seind04/c1/c1h.htm.

————. 2006. "Science and engineering indicators 2006." Accessed April 27, 2011, from www.nsf.gov/statistics/seind06/.

————. 2008. "Science and engineering indicators 2008." Accessed October 15, 2010, from www.nsf.gov/statistics/seind08/c6/c6h.htm.

————. 2009. "Women, minorities, and persons with disabilities in science and engineering: 2009." Arlington, VA: NSF 09–305. Accessed March 27, 2011, from http://www.nsf.gov/statistics/wmpd/.

————. 2010. "Science and engineering indicators 2010." Accessed October 15, 2010, from www.nsf.gov/statistics/seind10/start.htm.

————. 2011. "Women, minorities, and persons with disabilities in science and engineering 2011." Accessed April 27, 2011, from http://www.nsf.gov/statistics/wmpd/.

Nelson, Donna J. 2007. "National analysis of diversity in science and engineering faculties at research universities." Accessed April 27, 2011, from http://chem.ou.edu/~djn/diversity/briefings/Diversity%20Report%20Final.pdf.

Nelson, Donna J., and Christopher N. Brammer. 2010. "A national analysis of minorities in science and engineering faculties at research universities." Accessed March 17, 2011, from http://cheminfo.ou.edu/~djn/diversity/faculty_tables_fy07/07report.pdf.

Newcombe, Nora S. 2007. "Taking science seriously: Straight thinking about spatial sex differences." In *Why Aren't More Women in Science? Top Researchers Debate the Evidence*, edited by Stephen J. Ceci and Wendy M. Williams, 69–78. Washington, DC: American Psychological Association.

New Mexico State University. 2008. "*ADVANCE*: Institutional Transformation Annual Report, January 1, 2008–December 31, 2008." Accessed October 15, 2010, from http://www.advance.nmsu.edu/Documents/PDF/ann-rpt-08.pdf.

————. 2009. "*ADVANCE*: Institutional Transformation Final Report, January 1, 2002–April 30, 2009." Accessed October 15, 2010, from http://www.advance.nmsu.edu/Documents/PDF/ann-rpt-09.pdf.

Nguyen, Hannah-Hanh D., and Ann Marie Ryan. 2008. "Does stereotype threat affect test performance of minorities and women? A meta-analysis of experimental evidence." *Journal of Applied Psychology* 93(6):1314–34.

Nielsen, Joyce McCarl, Robyn Marschke, Elisabeth Sheff, and Patricia Rankin. 2005. "Vital variables and gender equity in academe: Confessions from a feminist empiricist project." *Signs: Journal of Women in Culture and Society* 31(1):1–28.

Niemann, Yolanda F., and John F. Dovidio. 1998. "Relationship of solo status, academic rank and perceived distinctiveness to job satisfaction of racial/ethnic minorities." *Journal of Applied Psychology* 83:55–71.

Niemeier, Debbie A., and Cristina Gonzales. 2004. "Breaking into the guild masters club: What we know about women science and engineering department chairs at AAU Universities." *National Women's Studies Association Journal* 14(1):157–171.

Nishii, Lisa, Robert Rich, and Susan Woods. 2007. "Framework of organizational inclusion." Accessed October 15, 2010, from www.ilr.cornell.edu/wdn/resources/upload/Today_Leadership_development_org_inclusion_concept.pdf.

Nolan, Susan A., Janine P. Buckner, Valerie J. Kuck, and Cecilia H. Marzabadi. 2004. "Analysis by gender of the doctoral and postdoctoral institutions of faculty members at the top-fifty ranked chemistry departments." *Journal of Chemical Education* 81(3):356–363.

Nutt, Paul C., and Robert W. Backoff. 1997. "Crafting vision." *Journal of Management Inquiry* 6(4):308–328.

O'Reilly, Charles A., and Jennifer A. Chatman. 1996. "Culture as social control: Corporations, cults, and commitment." *Research in Organizational Behavior* 18:157–200.

Park, Shelley M. 1996. "Research, teaching, and service: Why shouldn't women's work count?" *Journal of Higher Education* 67(1):46–84.

Pelled, Lisa H., Gerald E. Ledford, and Susan A. Mohrman. 1999. "Demographic dissimilarity and workplace inclusion." *Journal of Management Studies* 36(7):1013–1031.

Perna, Laura W. 2001. "Sex and race differences in faculty tenure and promotion." *Research in Higher Education* 42(5):541–567.

Peterson, Marvin, and Melinda G. Spencer. 1991. "Understanding academic culture and climate." In *Organization and Governance in Higher Education: An ASHE Reader (Fourth Edition)*, edited by Marvin W. Peterson, Ellen E. Chaffee, & Theodore H. White. Lexington, MA: Ginn Press.

Pfund, Christine, Christine Maidl Pribbenow, Janet Branchaw, Sarah Miller Lauffer, and Jo Handelsman. 2006. "The merits of training mentors." *Science* 311(27):473–474.

Plummer, Ellen W. 2006. "Institutional transformation: An analysis of change initiatives at NSF *ADVANCE* institutions." Unpublished dissertation, Virginia Polytechnic Institute and State University. Accessed April 27, 2011, from http://scholar.lib.vt.edu/theses/available/etd-07042006–153209/unrestricted/PlummerDissertation.pdf.

Pohlhaus, Jennifer Reineke, Hong Jiang, Robin M. Wagner, Walter T. Schaffer, and Vivian W. Pinn. 2011. "Sex differences in application, success, and funding rates for NIH extramural programs." *Academic Medicine* 86(6):1–9.

Powell, Abigail, Barbara Bagilhole, and Andrew Dainty. 2007. "The good, the bad, and the ugly: Women engineering students' experiences of UK higher education." In *Women and Minorities in Science, Technology, Engineering and Mathematics*, edited by Ronald J. Burke and Mary C. Mattis, 47–70. Cheltenham, UK: Edward Elgar Publishing.

Preston, Ann E. 2004. *Leaving Science: Occupational Exit from Scientific Careers.* New York: Russell Sage Foundation.

Pribbenow, Christine M. 2008. "Results of the 2006–07 Study of Faculty Attrition at the University of Wisconsin, Madison." Accessed April 27, 2011, from wiseli.engr.wisc.edu/fas.php.

Pribbenow, Christine M., Jennifer Sheridan, Jessica Winchell, Deveny Benting, Jo Handelsman, and Molly Carnes. 2010. "The tenure process and extending the tenure clock: The experience of faculty at one university." *Higher Education Policy* 23:17–38.

Quinn, Kate, Sheila E. Lange, and Steven G. Olswang. 2004. "Family-friendly policies and the research university." *Academe: Balancing Faculty Careers and Family Work* November–December. Accessed April 27, 2011, from http://www.aaup.org/AAUP/pubsres/academe/2004/ND/Feat/ndquin.htm.

Rajagopalan, Nandini, and Gretchen M. Spreitzer. 1996. "Toward a theory of strategic change: A multi-lens perspective and integrated framework." *Academy of Management Review* 22(1):48–79.

Ramos, Idalia. 2004. "Dual science career couples at the University of Puerto Rico at Humacao." Accessed April 27, 2011, from http://advance.uprh.edu/IdaliaRamos_DualScienceCareerCouples.pdf.

Roberson, Quinetta M. 2006. "Disentangling the meaning of diversity and inclusion in organizations." *Group and Organization Management* 31(2):212–236.

Rosser, Sue V. 1993. "Female-friendly science—including women in curricular content and pedagogy in science." *The Journal of General Education* 42(3):191–220.

———. 1999. "Different laboratory/work climates: Impacts on women in the workplace." *Annals of the New York Academy of Science* 869(1):95–101.

———. 2004. *The Science Glass Ceiling: Academic Women Scientists and the Struggle to Succeed.* New York: Routledge.

Rosser, Sue V., and Jean-Lou Chameau. 2006. "Institutionalization, sustainability, and repeatability of *ADVANCE* for institutional transformation." *Journal of Technology Transfer* 31:335–344.

Rosser, Sue V., and Jane Z. Daniels. 2004. "Widening paths to success, improving the environment, and moving toward lessons learned from the experiences of POWRE and CBL awardees." *Journal of Women and Minorities in Science and Engineering* 10:131–148.

Rosser, Sue V., and Eliesh O. Lane. 2002. "A history of funding for women's programs at the National Science Foundation." *Journal of Women and Minorities in Science and Engineering* 8:327–346.

Rosser, Sue V., and Mark Z. Taylor. 2009. "Why are we still worried about women in science?" *Academe* 95(3):7–10.

Rowley, Daniel J., and Herbert Sherman. 2003. "The special challenges of academic leadership." *Management Decision* 41(10):1058–1063.

Ryabov, Igor, and Ann Darnell. 2008. "Faculty work life survey comparison of 2003 and 2007 results". Accessed March 20, 2011, from http://academics.utep.edu/Portals/1224/Work%20Life%20Survey%20Evaluation%20Report%2008web.doc.

Sackett, Paul R., Cathy L. DuBois, and Ann W. Noe. 1991. "Tokenism in performance evaluation: The effects of work group representation on male-female and white-black differences in performance ratings." *Journal of Applied Psychology* 76:263–267.

Schein, Edgar H. 1992. *Organizational Culture and Leadership* (2nd ed.). San Francisco: Jossey-Bass.

Schiebinger, Londa, Andrea D. Henderson, and Shannon K. Gilmartin. 2008. "Dual-career academic couples: What universities need to know." Michelle R. Clayman Institute for Gender Research, Stanford University. Accessed October 15, 2010, from http://www.stanford.edu/group/gender/ResearchPrograms/DualCareer/DualCareerFinal.pdf.

Shaffer, Amanda. 2010. "In the loop: Keeping your colleagues informed." Presentation at the Midwest Regional *ADVANCE* meeting, Purdue University, West Lafayette, Indiana.

Shenkle, C. W., R. S. Snyder, and K. W. Bauer. 1998. "Measures of campus climate." In *Campus Climate: Understanding the Critical Components of Today's Colleges and Universities, New Directions for Institutional Research #98*, edited by Karen W. Bauer, 81–99. San Francisco: Jossey-Bass.

Sheridan, Jennifer, Christine Maidl Pribbenow, Eve Fine, Jo Handelsman, and Molly Carnes. 2007. "Climate change at the University of Wisconsin-Madison: What changed, and did *ADVANCE* have an impact?" *Women in Engineering Programs and Advocates Network (WEPAN) 2007 Conference Proceedings*, Paper #0045. Accessed January 6, 2011, from http://dpubs.libraries.psu.edu/DPubS?verb=Displayandversion=1.0andservice=UIandhandle=psu.wepan/1200322686andpage=record.

Silver, Barbara, Gloria Boudreaux-Bartels, Helen Mederer, Lynne C. Pasquerella, Joan Peckham, Mercedes Rivero-Hudec, and Karen Wishner. 2006. "A warmer climate for women in engineering at the University of Rhode Island." 2006 Annual Conference Proceedings Paper, American Society for Engineering Education. Accessed April 27, 2011, from http://www.uri.edu/advance/files/pdf/Papers%20and%20Presentations/ASEE_Final_Draft.pdf.

Smith, Janice W., Wanda J. Smith, and Steven E. Markham. 2000. "Diversity issues in mentoring academic faculty." *Journal of Career Development* 26(4):251–261.

Sollie, Donna L. 2009. "SEM transformation through 'small wins.' " Presentation at 2009 NSF *ADVANCE* PI Meeting, Washington, DC.

Spencer, Steven J., Claude M. Steele, and Diane M. Quinn. 1999. "Stereotype threat and women's math performance." *Journal of Experimental Social Psychology* 35(1):4–28.

Steele, Claude M., and Joshua Aronson. 1995. "Stereotype threat and the intellectual test performance of African Americans." *Journal of Personality and Social Psychology* 69(5):797–811.

Steinpreis, Rhea E., Katie A. Anders, and Dawn Ritzke. 1999. "The impact of gender on the review of curricula vitae of job applicants and tenure candidates: A national empirical study." *Sex Roles: A Journal of Research* 41(7–8):509–528.

Stepan-Norris, Judith. 2008. "Analysis of gender differences in 2006 faculty startup packages at UCI." Accessed October 15, 2010, from http://advance.uci.edu/media/Reports/Startup%20Packages%20Report%202006.pdf.

Stewart, Abigail J. 2009. "Making institutional transformation permanent: An interim report." Presentation at the 2009 NSF *ADVANCE* PI Meeting, Washington, DC. Accessed October 15, 2010, from http://www.advance.vt.edu/Advance_2009_PI_Mtg/PIMtg2009_Stewart_Institutionalization.pdf.

Stewart, Abigail J., Danielle LaVaque-Manty, and Janet E. Malley. 2004. "Recruiting women faculty in science and engineering: Preliminary evaluation of one intervention model." *Journal of Women and Minorities in Science and Engineering* 9(2): 169–181.

Stewart, Abigail J., Janet E. Malley, and Danielle LaVaque-Manty (Eds.). 2007. *Transforming Science and Engineering: Advancing Academic Women.* Ann Arbor: The University of Michigan Press.

Stuart, Rieky. 1999. "Organizational approaches to building gender equity." Paper presented at Made to Measure: Designing Research, Policy and Action Approaches to Eliminate Gender Inequity National Symposium. Halifax, Nova Scotia. Accessed April 27, 2011, from http://www.acewh.dal.ca/eng/reports/stuart.pdf.

Sturm, Susan. 2006. "The architecture of inclusion: Advancing workplace equity in higher education." Harvard Journal of Law and Gender 29:247–334.

———. 2007a. "Gender equity as institutional transformation: The pivotal role of organizational catalysts." In *Transforming Science and Engineering: Advancing Academic Women*, edited by Abigail J. Stewart, Janet E. Malley, and Danielle LaVaque-Manty, 262–280. Ann Arbor: University of Michigan Press.

———. 2007b. "The architecture of inclusion: The role of organizational catalysts." Talk presented at The Science of Diversity Conference, Columbia University, November 16, 2006. Version dated February 11, 2007. Accessed October 15, 2010, from http://www2.law.columbia.edu/ssturm/pdfs/2-23-07%20buffalo%20talk.pdf.

Suchman, Mark C. 1995. "Managing legitimacy: Strategic and institutional approaches." *Academy of Management Review* 20(3):571–610.

Thomas, David A., and Robin J. Ely. 1996. "Making differences matter: A new paradigm for managing diversity." *Harvard Business Review* 74(5):79–90.

Thompson, Mischa, and Denise Sekaquaptewa. 2002. "When being different is detrimental: Solo status and the performance of women and racial minorities." *Analyses of Social Issues and Public Policy* 2:183–203.

Trix, Frances, and Carolyn Psenka. 2003. "Exploring the color of glass: Letters of recommendation for female and male medical faculty." *Discourse and Society* 14(2):191–220.

Trower, Cathy A. 2008. "Competing on culture: Academia's new strategic imperative." Presentation at The New Norm of Faculty Flexibility: Transforming the Culture in Science and Engineering Conference, Iowa State University, Ames, Iowa. Accessed April 27, 2011, from http://www.advance.iastate.edu/conference/conferencepdf/2008_10–11trower_ppt.pdf.

Trower, Cathy A., and Richard P. Chait. 2002. "Faculty diversity: Too little for too long." *Harvard Magazine*, March-April. Accessed March 27, 2011, from http://harvardmagazine.com/2002/03/faculty-diversity.html.

United Nations Office of the Special Adviser on Gender Issues and Advancement of Women, Department of Economic and Social Affairs. Accessed April 27, 2011, from http://www.un.org/womenwatch/osagi/conceptsandefinitions.htm.

University of Alabama, Birmingham. 2008. "UAB *ADVANCE* Institutional Transformation 2008 Annual Report." Accessed October 15, 2010, from http://www.uab.edu/images/advimg/pdf/2008-Annual-Report5-27-08.pdf.

———. 2009. "UAB *ADVANCE* Institutional Transformation 2009 Annual Report." Accessed October 15, 2010, from http://main.uab.edu/Sites/faculty-development/images/72500.pdf.

University of California, Irvine. 2005. "Year 4 Report to NSF—9/30/05." Accessed October 15, 2010, from http://advance.uci.edu/ (Data and Reports).

———. 2006. "Year 5 Report to NSF—9/30/06." Accessed October 15, 2010, from http://advance.uci.edu/ (Data and Reports).

University of Maryland, Baltimore County. 2007. "NSF *ADVANCE* program at UMBC." Accessed April 20, 2011, from http://www.advance.vt.edu/IT_Program_Descriptions/U_Maryland_Baltimore_County_ADVANCE_2007.pdf.

———. 2008. "Looking back and moving forward." Poster at 2008 *ADVANCE* PI meeting, Washington, DC. Accessed April 20, 2011, from http://www.advance.vt.edu/Advance_2008_PI_Mtg/UMBC_Looking_Back_Moving_Forward_2008.pdf.

———. 2009. "*ADVANCE* 2009 Annual Report, *ADVANCE* at University of Maryland, Baltimore County." Unpublished document.

University of Michigan. 2006a. "Year end report for *ADVANCE* institutional transformation, year five: December 2006." Accessed October 15, 2010, from http://www.advance.rackham.umich.edu/PUBLIC_December_2006_Year_End_Report.pdf.

———. 2006b. "Final report *ADVANCE* departmental transformation grant faculty interviews 2006." Accessed October 15, 2010, from http://www.advance.rackham.umich.edu/DTG_FacultyInterviews_ADVANCE.pdf.

University of Puerto Rico, Humacao. 2007. "*ADVANCE* 2006–2007 annual report." Unpublished document.

———. 2009. "*ADVANCE* 2008–2009 annual report." Unpublished document.

University of Rhode Island. 2006. "*ADVANCE* 2005–2006 annual report." Accessed October 15, 2010, from http://www.uri.edu/advance/measuring_progress/NSF%20reports.html.

———. 2008. "*ADVANCE* 2007–08 annual report." Accessed October 15, 2010, from http://www.uri.edu/advance/measuring_progress/NSF%20reports.html.

University of Texas, El Paso. 2005. "NSF *ADVANCE* institutional transformation for faculty diversity, year end report: September 1, 2004 to August 31, 2005." Accessed October 15, 2010, from http://academics.utep.edu/Portals/1224/2004–05%20Annual%20Report.pdf.

———. 2008. "NSF *ADVANCE* Institutional transformation for faculty diversity, year end report: September 1, 2007 to August 31, 2008." Accessed October 15, 2010, from http://academics.utep.edu/Portals/1224/Final%20Version%202007–2008%20Website%20Report.pdf.

University of Washington. 2008. "*ADVANCE* final report 2001–2007, University of Washington." Accessed October 15, 2010, from http://www.engr.washington.edu/advance/resources/ADV%20Final%20report-2001–2007-FINAL%20with%20APPENDIX.pdf.

U.S. Chamber of Commerce. 2005. "Tapping America's potential: The Education for Innovation Initiative." Accessed April 27, 2011, from http://www.uschamber.com/reports/tapping-americas-potential-education-innovation-initiative.

U.S. Department of Labor. 2007. "The STEM workforce challenge: The role of the public workforce system in a national solution for a competitive science, technology, engineering, and mathematics (STEM) workforce." Washington, DC: Department of Labor. Accessed October 15, 2010, from http://www.doleta.gov/Youth_services/pdf/STEM_Report_4%2007.pdf.

Utah State University. 2004. "Year-end report for NSF *ADVANCE* project, year 1: July 2004." Accessed October 15, 2010, from http://advance.usu.edu/resources/1/Reports/Annual%20Report%2004.pdf.

———. 2006. "*ADVANCE* 2005–06 annual report." Accessed October 15, 2010, from http://advance.usu.edu/resources/1/Reports/Annual%20Report%2006.pdf.

———. 2007. "*ADVANCE* 2006–07 annual report." Accessed October 15, 2010, from http://advance.usu.edu/resources/1/Reports/06–07%20Annual%20Report.pdf.

———. 2008. "*ADVANCE* 2007–08 annual report." Accessed October 15, 2010, from http://advance.usu.edu/resources/1/more%20reports/Annual%20Report%2008%20%28year%205%29%20FINAL.pdf.

Valian, Virginia. 1999. *Why So Slow? The Advancement of Women.* Cambridge, MA: The MIT Press.

———. 2004. "Beyond gender schemas: Improving the advancement of women in academia." *National Women's Studies Association Journal* 16:207–220.

———. 2007. "Women at the top of science—and elsewhere." In *Why Aren't More Women in Science? Top Researchers Debate the Evidence*, edited by Stephen J. Ceci and Wendy M. Williams, 27–38. Washington, DC: American Psychological Association.

Valian, Virginia, Vita Rabinowitz, Shirley Raps, and Richard Pizer. 2004. "Advancing the careers of women scientists: Lessons learned from Hunter College's Gender Equity Project." Accessed April 27, 2011, from http://www.advance.cau.edu/pwrpt_rabinowitz.pdf.

van den Brink, Marieke. 2010. *Behind the Scenes of Science: Gender Practices in the Recruitment and Selection of Professors in the Netherlands.* Amsterdam: Pallas Publications–Amsterdam University Press.

van den Brink, Marieke, Yvonne Benschop, and Willy Jansen. 2010. "Transparency in academic recruitment: A problematic tool for gender equality?" *Organization Studies* 23(31):1459–1483.

van den Brink, Marieke, and Lineke Stobbe. 2009. "Doing gender in academic education: The paradox of visibility." *Gender, Work and Organization* 16(4):451–470.

Virginia Tech. 2008. "*AdvanceVT* annual report, year 5: September 2007–August 2008." Accessed October 15, 2010, from http://www.advance.vt.edu/Measuring_Progress/Annual_Reports/AdvanceVT_2008_Annual_Report_all.pdf.

———. 2009. "*AdvanceVT* annual report, year 6: September 2008–August 2009." Accessed October 15, 2010, from http://www.advance.vt.edu/Measuring_Progress/Annual_Reports/AdvanceVT_2009_Annual_Report.pdf.

Wasburn, Mara H. 2007. "Mentoring women faculty: An instrumental case study of strategic collaboration." *Mentoring and Tutoring* 15(1):57–72.

Weick, Karl E. 1984. "Small wins: Redefining the scale of social problems." *American Psychologist* 39(1):40–49.

Wenneras, Christine, and Agnes Wold. 1997. "Nepotism and sexism in peer-review." *Nature* 387:341–343.

West, Martha S., and John W. Curtis. 2006. "AAUP faculty gender equity indicators 2006." Accessed March 17, 2011, from http://www.aaup.org/AAUP/pubsres/research/geneq2006.

White, Judith S. 2005. "Pipeline to pathways: New directions for improving the status of women on campus." *Liberal Education* 91(1):22–27.

Whittaker, Robert J. 2008. "Journal review and gender equality: A critical comment on Budden et al." *Trends in Ecology and Evolution* 23(9):478–479.

Whitten, Barbara L., Shannon R. Dorato, Margaret L. Duncombe, Patricia E. Allen, Cynthia A. Blaha, Heather Z. Butler, Kimberly A. Shaw, Beverly A. P. Taylor, and Barbara A. Williams. 2007. "What works for women in undergraduate physics and what can we learn from women's colleges?" *Journal of Women and Minorities in Science and Engineering* 13(1):37–76.

Whitten, Barbara. L., Suzanne R. Foster, Margaret L. Duncombe, Patricia E. Allen, Paula Heron, Laura McCullough, Kimberly A. Shaw, Beverley A. P. Taylor, and Heather M. Zorn. 2003. "What works? Increasing the participation of women in undergraduate physics." *Journal of Women and Minorities in Science and Engineering* 9:239–258.

Williams, Joan C. 2000. "How the tenure track discriminates against women." *Chronicle of Higher Education* October 27. Accessed October 15, 2010, from http://chronicle.com/article/How-the-Tenure-Track/46312/.

———. 2005. "The glass ceiling and the maternal wall in academia." *New Directions for Higher Education* 130:91–105.

WISELI—Women in Science and Engineering Leadership Institute. 2007. "Final report of the *ADVANCE* program of University of Wisconsin-Madison, 2002–2007." Accessed October 15, 2010, from http://wiseli.engr.wisc.edu/docs/AnnReport_IT_2007FINAL.pdf.

Wylie, Alison, Janet R. Jakobsen, and Gisela Fosado. 2007. "Women, work, and the academy: Strategies for responding to 'post-civil rights era' gender discrimination." New York: Barnard Center for Research on Women. Accessed April 27, 2011, from http://faculty.washington.edu/aw26/WorkplaceEquity/BCRW-WomenWorkAcademy_08.pdf.

Xie, Yu, and Kimberlee A. Shauman. 1998. "Sex differences in research productivity: New evidence about an old puzzle." *American Sociological Review* 63:847–870.

———. 2003. *Women in Science: Career Processes and Outcomes*. Cambridge, MA: Harvard University Press.

Yen, Joyce W., and Christopher J. Loving. 2005. "The Cross-Department Cultural Change Program at the University of Washington." *Proceedings of the 2005 American Society for Engineering Education Annual Conference and Exposition*. Accessed April 27, 2011, from http://www.engr.washington.edu/advance/cultural_change/CDCCPASEEpaper_FINAL.pdf.

Yoder, Janice D. 1991. "Rethinking tokenism: Looking beyond the numbers." *Gender and Society* 5(2): 178–192.

Yoder, Janice D. 1994. "Looking beyond numbers: The effects of gender status, job prestige, and occupational gender-typing on tokenism processes." *Social Psychology Quarterly* 57:150–159.

Yoder, Janice D., and Laura M. Sinnett. 1985. "Is it all in the numbers? A case study of tokenism." *Psychology of Women Quarterly* 9:413–418.

Zelechowski, Deborah D., and Diana Bilimoria. 2003. "The experience of women corporate inside directors on the boards of Fortune 1000 firms." *Women in Management Review* 18(7):376–381.

Index